Shia'ism from Qur'an

Sayed Jawad Zaidi

Shia'ism from Qur'an

Copyrights 2016 by Sayed Jawad Zaidi

Yasin Publication

P.O. Box 338
8253-A Backlick Rd.
Newington, VA 22122

Web: http://www.yasinpublications.org/

Email: sjzaidi313@gmail.com

ISBN-13: 978-1500839352
ISBN-10: 1500839353

Library of Congress Control Number: 2017901176

بِسْمِ اللهِ الرَّحْمَنِ الرَّحِيمِ

In the name of Allah, the most Beneficent, the most Merciful.

وَالَّذِينَ اجْتَنَبُوا الطَّاغُوتَ أَن يَعْبُدُوهَا وَأَنَابُوا إِلَى اللهِ لَهُمُ الْبُشْرَى فَبَشِّرْ عِبَادِ ﴿١٧﴾

17 As for those who
stay clear of the worship of the Rebel
and turn penitently to Allah,
there is good news for them.
So give good news to My servants

الَّذِينَ يَسْتَمِعُونَ الْقَوْلَ فَيَتَّبِعُونَ أَحْسَنَهُ أُوْلَئِكَ الَّذِينَ هَدَاهُمُ اللهُ وَأُوْلَئِكَ هُمْ أُوْلُوا الْأَلْبَابِ ﴿١٨﴾

18 who listen to the word [of Allah
and follow the best [sense] of it.
They are the ones whom Allah has guided,
and it is they who possess intellect.

The Holy Quran, Surat al Zumar, 39:17-18

Dedication

I dedicate this book to my fifth Imam, Imam Muhammad bin Ali al-Baqir *peace be upon him* (Baqir al-Uloom; which means: the one who splits, scrutinizes and spreads knowledge).

Special Thanks to:

Almighty Allah (swt) for giving me the ability to compile this book, and giving me the guidance through Prophet Muhammad (pbuh) and his holy household (pbut).

Afterwards, I'd like to thank my parents for their love and support, my brother and sisters. Special thanks to my dear wife for the encouragement and the assistance; and to all my friends, who helped me with composing this book and encouraged me to complete this book.

Table of contents

Preface

In the name of Allah (swt) the All beneficent and the All merciful, the Lord of the worlds. All praises belong to Allah (swt), the Lord and the Creator of everything, the sender of the Prophets and Messengers. Honors, salutations and the best of Allah's (swt) blessings be upon the seal of the Prophets, Muhammad (pbuh), the best of Allah's (swt) Creation, and upon his Holy and pious Household, the divinely selected and made infallible for whom Allah (swt) sent down the *Ayate Tathir* (Quran 33:33).

By the grace of Allah (swt), the Holy Prophet (pbuh) and his Ahlul Bayt (pbut), I have compiled this book to enlighten the readers about "**Shi'a faith**" (the followers of the Holy Prophet (pbuh) and his *Ahlul Bayt* the people of his household (pbut)) from the Holy Qur'an.

The Purpose of this book?

The purpose of this book is to provide the verses of the Holy Qur'an with its interpretation in support of the beliefs, the practices, the core values and the principles of the followers of the Holy Prophet (pbuh) and his Ahlul Bayt (as), the Shi'ah faith of Islam. The purpose of this book is to inform and enlighten the readers about Shi'aism, and not to attack or differ with any other school of thought. Other than *Tawheed* (oneness of God) and the Prophethood; the Holy Qur'an is the "core" which holds ALL MUSLIMS together, all Muslims believe in the Qur'an as the sacred book, believe in its authenticity and do their best to understand and learn from it. My goal is to simply provide the Qur'anic verses, which provide a supportive argument regarding Shi'a beliefs.

What qualifies me to write this book?

Imam Jafar al Sadiq (as) said:

"Write and spread your knowledge among your brothers..." (Tabarsi)

Source: Hassan Ibn Fazl Ibn Hassan Tabarsi, *Mishkat ul Anwar Hadith # 736.* P. 120

Therefore, whatever I have learned so far in my life about the School of Ahlul Bayt (as), I put in together in the form of chapters in this book.

The reasons why I decided to write this book?

Following are the reasons why I decided to write this book:

1. To be able to answer to Allah (swt) on the Day of Judgment what I did with the capabilities and capacities given to me by Him (swt).
2. To spread Allah's (swt) words and the teachings of the Ahlul Bayt (as) (*as commanded by them*) to the people around me.
3. To provide verses of the Holy Qur'an in a 'reference book format' to support the beliefs of the Shi'ah faith of Islam.
4. Encourage the youth of America to read, learn and share the knowledge of Islam and the teachings of the Ahlul Bayt (as).
5. Describe the teachings of the Ahlul Bayt (as) in a simple, easy to understand, concise yet informative booklet.

Format used for references and in-text citation

I chose not to use APA, Chicago, or MLA etc. format for the in-text citations and references I used in this book. I have listed the reference of each source used in this book, directly below the referenced statement, so that the readers don't have to go back-and-forth and look for the source from the in-text citation.

Please Note: This book is not a translation or an extract of *'Shi'a fil Qur'an'* (Shi'a in the Qur'an) by Grand Scholar Ayatollah Sayed Sadiq Hussain Shirazi. In his book, the Grand Scholar discusses Qur'anic verses from *Surah al Fatiha* to *Surah al Naas* regarding the Shi'as of Imam Ali (as); whereas, I have chosen to compose this book in a form of 14 chapters regarding Shi'aism in the light of the Holy Qur'an and the narrations of the Holy Prophet (pbuh) from the books of *Ahle Sunnah Wal Jam'a* (Sunni School of Thought).

Introduction

There is no doubt that the Holy Qur'an is the word of God, as no man in the history of mankind has been able to come up with a single verse as majestic as the verses of the Holy Qur'an. It is beyond the comprehension of the entire mankind to understand and interpret the Holy Qur'an in its entirety; except for those, Allah (swt) vested with divine knowledge. For the most part, the Qur'an is meant for men and women of any level of intellect and from any social background, and "since the expounding of subtle knowledge is not without danger of misinterpretation, the Qur'an generally directs its teachings primarily at the level of the common man. The Qur'an reveals itself in a way suitable for different levels of comprehension so that each benefits, according to his own capacity." However, certain verses contain metaphors, which require divine gnosis far beyond the common man's understanding, but which nevertheless become comprehensible through their metaphorical form.

All Muslims MUST believe in the "Oneness of God," the Prophethood of all Prophets (pbut), and MUST believe in Muhammad (pbuh) as the last Prophet of God. Prophet Mohammad (pbuh) brought the Qur'an as an ULTIMATE miracle for the mankind. There are verses of the Qur'an, which are crystal clear, but others require us to know the context to understand the correct meaning (interpretation) of such verses.

Every story in the Qur'an contains a message, a lesson and guidance for mankind. The stories of the past are mentioned to warn mankind to not to repeat the same mistakes and they are made to make humans aware of the consequences of making such mistakes. These stories need interpretation from the guardians of the holy Qur'an. According to the followers of Ahlul Bayt (as), those guardians are the 12 holy Imams (as).

Different types of *tafaseer*

There are four different types of *Tafaseer* (exegesis, interpretation, explanation, commentary) of the holy Qur'an:

1. Using Qur'anic verses to explain other Qur'anic verses; for example, Al *Mezaan* by Allama Sayyid Muhammad Husain Tabatabai
2. Using Narrations of the Holy Prophet (pbuh) to explain the holy Qur'an.
3. Using the exegesis from the Imams of Ahlul Bayt (as) explains the holy Qur'an.
4. An expert using logic and historical events to explain the verses of the holy Qur'an.

In this book, I have used the Quranic exegesis by Ayatollah Agha Mahdi Puya, in his work ***Tafsir of Holy Qur'an***, available on: *http://www.islamicmobility.com/elibrary_14.htm*

And Ayatullah Sayyid Kamal Faqhih Imani's work: ***An Enlightening Commentary into the Light of the Holy Qur'an***, available on *http://www.islamicmobility.com/elibrary_20.htm*

And Ayatollah Nasir Mikarim Shirazi's work at: ***Qur'an, Translation and Commentary in Brief Available*** on *http://makarem.ir/compilation/?lid=1#*

Ayatollah Agha Mahdi Puya is a renowned Shi'a scholar from Iran, born in 1899. In his *Tafsir* work, he primarily relied on the narrations of the Imams of Ahlul Bayt (as) and he used the books of *Ahle Sunnah Wal Jam'a* as references to the specific events.

Ayatollah Sayyid Kamal Faqhih Imani is a renowned Shi'a scholar from Iran, and the founder of the Islamic Scientific Research Center in Tehran, Iran. He published his work on the *Tafsir* of the entire Qur'an in Persian language, which was later translated into English by Sayyid Abbas Sadr-Amili, it took the translator close to eight years to complete this work.

Ayatollah Nasir Mikarim Shirazi is one of the most prominent grand Marja (scholar of jurisprudence) of the school of Ahlul Bayt (as). He was born in Shiraz, Iran in the year 1924. He has written a number of books on the subject of jurisprudence, ethics and morals, analysis of the historic sermons of Ahlul Bayt (as), social and political issues, principles and practices of Islam, and the exegesis of the holy Qur'an.

Books for reference:

Introduction To The Science Of Tafseer Of The Quran by Ayatollah Jafar Subhani

Al-Mizan by Allama Sayyid Muhammad Hussain Tabatabai

Quranic Translation used in this book

All Qur'anic translations used in this book are from:

Qur'an: with a Phrase-by-Phrase English Translation by Ali Quili Qar'ie, 2004, ISBN 1-904063-20-9.

Criteria for authenticity of *ahadeeth/* narrations

According to the school of Ahlul Bayt (as) a *hadith/* narration is considered **authentic** on the bases on the following criteria:

- The contents of a narration and its chain of transmitters,
- Should not contradict the intellect; and should not contradict the holy Qur'an.
- Should not contradict the established facts.

Ahadeeth/ narration, books used in this book include:

All *Sahih Sitta* (six authentic) books of *Ahle Sunnah Wal Jam'a* (Sunni School of Thought).

1. *Sahih Bukhari* by Muhammad Ibn Ismail al-Bukhari
2. *Sahih Muslim* by Muslim Ibn al-Hajjaj

3. *Sunan Abu Dawood* by Abu Dawood Sulayman Ibn al-Ash'ath
4. *Jami al-Tirmidhi* by Muhammad Ibn Isa at-Tirmidhi
5. *Sunan Ibn Majah* by Abu Abdulllah Muhammad Ibn Yazid Ibn Majah
6. *Sunan al-Sughra* by Ahmad Ibn Shuayb al-Nasai

All six of these books are available online at *http://sunnah.com/*

I have also used *ahadeeth/* narrations from:

1. *Al-Kafi* by Sheikh Muhammad Ibn Yaqub Ibn Ishaq al-Kulayni
2. *Bihar ul Anwar* by Allama Muhammad Baqir Majlisi

Please Note: Not all *Ahadeeth/* narrations are deemed authentic in these books, according to the school of Ahlul Bayt. Each and every narration must be carefully examined with the aforementioned criteria to determine its authenticity. All *Ahadeeth/* narrations used in this book (in support) are considered to be authentic by the experts of *Ahadeeth/* narrations.

Other Resources: All other books used/ referenced in this book, and the books recommended at the end of each chapter are available for free online at the following websites:

http://www.al-islam.org/library/quran-hadith

http://islamiclib.wordpress.com/

http://hubeali.com/

http://shiasunni.info/books

http://www.shiamultimedia.com/englishbooks.html

http://www.shiasearch.com/

https://www.facebook.com/groups/shiabooks4free/

https://www.facebook.com/groups/230663520379545/

http://www.maaref-foundation.com/english/index.htm

http://www.alhassanain.com/english/book.php

http://www.ghaemiyeh.com/en/

http://shiaislamiclibrary.com/

I hope you find this book helpful in expanding your knowledge about the followers of Prophet Muhammad (pbuh) and his holy household (pbut).

Abbreviations used in this book:

(swt) = *Subhanahu wa taala*: the most glorified

(pbuh) = peace be upon him and his progeny

(pbut) = peace be upon them

(S) = *Salalahu alihe waa'Aalehi wasalam* Pbuh = peace be upon him and his progeny

(as) = Allah's blessings be upon him (them)

(sa) = Allah's blessings be upon her

(ra) = May Allah be pleased with him/her

(atf) = ajalahu wa ta'ala faraj: May Allah hasten Imam Mahdi's reappearance

Chapter 1

The Attributes of Allah (swt) according to Qur'an

There is misconception amongst Muslims about the attributes of Allah (swt) and that is because of the following reasons:

1. Misinterpretation of the verses of the holy Qur'an.
2. Fabricated hadith (narrations) about the attributes of Allah (swt).
3. Influences of Judeo-Christianity ideologies about God in Islam from early reverts.

But all three of these reasons are intertwined. When former Jews and Christians converted to Islam during or after Prophet's (pbuh) life, they brought the concept of God from their religion into Islam and there were also those for their personal gains during the Ummayad and Abbasid dynasties, fabricated narrations attributing them to the Prophet Muhammad (pbuh) regarding the attributes of Allah (swt); such narrations were later used in misinterpreting the Holy Qur'an.

Some of the examples of such fabricated narrations from the prominent non-Shi'a Muslim books are as follows:

1. Narrated in *Sahih Bukhari* Vol. 6, Book 60, Hadith 105. *http://sunnah.com/urn/42600*

By Abu Sa'id Al-Khudri:

During the lifetime of the Prophet (pbuh) some people said: O Allah's Messenger (pbuh)! Shall we see our Lord on the Day of Resurrection?" The Prophet (pbuh) said, "Yes; do you have any difficulty in seeing the sun at midday when it is bright and there is no cloud in the sky?"

They replied, "No." He said, "Do you have any difficulty in seeing the moon on a full moon night when it is bright and there is no cloud in the sky?" They replied, "No." The Prophet (pbuh) said, "(Similarly) you will have no difficulty in seeing Allah (swt) on the Day of Resurrection as you have no difficulty in seeing either of them.... (The narration continues with further elaborations, and discusses that Allah (swt) will expose his 'Shin' to the people so they may believe).

2. Similar narration is mentioned by Abed al-Rahman Ibn Sakhr Al-Azdi *AKA Abu* Huraira in **Sunan Abu Dawood** (English) Book 41, Hadith 4712. *http://sunnah.com/abuDawood/42/135*

3. Narrated in **Sahih Bukhari** Book 97, Hadith 62
   http://sunnah.com/bukhari/97/62

   By Jarir bin Abdullah:

   The Prophet (pbuh) said, *"You will definitely see your Lord with your own eyes."*

4. Narrated in **Sahih Bukhari, Book** 79, Hadith 1
   http://sunnah.com/bukhari/79/1

   By Abu Huraira:
   The Prophet (pbuh) said, "Allah created Adam in His picture, sixty cubits (about 30 meters) in height. When He created him, He said (to him), "Go and greet that group of angels sitting there, and listen what they will say in reply to you, for that will be your greeting and the greeting of your offspring."(Narration continues…)

5. Narrated in **Sahih Bukhari** Vol. 6, Book 60, Hadith 372
   http://sunnah.com/urn/45270

   By Abu Huraira:

   "The Prophet (pbuh) said: *"It will be said to the Hell, 'Are you filled?' It will say, 'Are there any more (to come)?' On that Allah will put His Foot on it, and it will say 'Qati! Qati! (Enough! Enough!).*

From the aforementioned narrations it may appear that Allah (swt) consists of a physical "**human-like body**" and human beings will be able to see Allah (swt) in the hereafter.

The followers of Ahlul Bayt (as), the Shi'a school of thought **negates** such notions. Our holy Imams (as) have clearly stated to us that Allah (swt) does NOT possess a physical body, and a human will NEVER be able to see Allah (swt) with his or her own EYES. Humans will not be able to visualize Allah (swt), in this world or the hereafter, nor in any circumstances whatsoever.

Imam Ali (as) said:

> *"(O Allah!) I testify that he who likens You with the separateness of the limbs or with the joining of the extremities of his body did not acquaint his inner self with knowledge about You and his heart did not secure conviction to the effect that there is no partner for You. It is as though he has not heard the (wrongful) followers declaiming their false gods by saying, "By Allah! We are certainly in manifest error when equaled you with the master of the worlds" (Holy Quran, 26: 97-98).*

> *They are wrong who liken You to their idols and outfit You with the apparel of the creatures by their imagination, attribute to You parts of the body by their own thinking and consider You after the creatures of various types, through the working of their intelligence. I testify that whoever equated with anything out of Your creation took a match for You and whoever takes a match for You is an unbeliever, according to what is stated in the unambiguous verses and indicated by the testimony of Your clear arguments. (I also testify that) You agree that Allah Who cannot be confined in (the fetters of) intelligence so as to admit a change of condition by entering its imagination nor in the shackles of mind so as to become limited and an object of alterations.*

Source: *Nahjul Balagha* (The Peak of Eloquence) by Imam Ali Ibn Abu Talib (as) With Commentary By Martyr Ayatollah Murtada Mutahhari (2009) 7th Edition, Tahrike Tarsile Qur'an, Inc. NY. Sermon 90, P. 449

The human vision and mind is limited. Humans can only process a **limited** amount of information; whereas, Allah (swt) is **beyond any limits and indefinite.** Allah (swt) is **NOT** bound to any set: time, space or matter.

The above excerpt further confirms that a human being will **NEVER** be able to physically see Allah (swt).

The concept of humans unable to visualize Allah (swt) is stated in the plain language of the holy Qur'an:

Surah Al-An'am 6:103

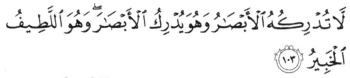

The sights do not apprehend Him,
Yet He apprehends the sights,
and He is the All-attentive, the All-aware.

The above verse is easy to comprehend because in its plain language it states "the sights do not apprehend him." This indicates, that it is beyond human apprehension to see God. However, controversy still exists within the Muslim *Ummah* (nation) regarding the ability to visualize Allah (swt). It is crucial to know how Muslims should interpret, understand, and learn the meaning of the verses of the holy Qur'an. Particularly, the meaning of the verses that discuss *Allah's hands, spirit, chair, thrones, house, and looking at Allah (swt) or the like.*

The way to interpret, understand, or learn the meaning of the verses in the Qur'an is through the teaching of the Ahlul Bayt (as). The Ahlul Bayt (as), the twelve Imams, have explained the verses in relation to the ability to visualize Allah (swt) in details. The explanations of the Ahlul Bayt have been written in one of the oldest works in Shi'a literature, by one of the great scholars of all time

Sheikh Abu Jafar Muhammad bin Ali bin Hussain bin Musa Ibn Babawayhi al-Qummi, *AKA* Sheikh Sudooq in his work called

'A Shia Creed' (English Translation). Below is the explanation of such Qur'anic verses:

1. Allah's open hands
Surah al-Ma'idah (5:64)

وَقَالَتِ ٱلۡيَهُودُ يَدُ ٱللَّهِ مَغۡلُولَةٌ غُلَّتۡ أَيۡدِيهِمۡ وَلُعِنُواْ بِمَا قَالُواْ بَلۡ يَدَاهُ

مَبۡسُوطَتَانِ يُنفِقُ كَيۡفَ يَشَآءُ وَلَيَزِيدَنَّ كَثِيرًا مِّنۡهُم مَّآ أُنزِلَ إِلَيۡكَ مِن

رَّبِّكَ طُغۡيَٰنًا وَكُفۡرًا وَأَلۡقَيۡنَا بَيۡنَهُمُ ٱلۡعَدَٰوَةَ وَٱلۡبَغۡضَآءَ إِلَىٰ يَوۡمِ ٱلۡقِيَٰمَةِ كُلَّمَآ

أَوۡقَدُواْ نَارًا لِّلۡحَرۡبِ أَطۡفَأَهَا ٱللَّهُ وَيَسۡعَوۡنَ فِي ٱلۡأَرۡضِ فَسَادًا وَٱللَّهُ لَا

يُحِبُّ ٱلۡمُفۡسِدِينَ ﴿٦٤﴾

The Jews say, 'Allah's hand is tied up.'
Tied up be their hands,
And cursed be they for what they say!
Rather, His hands are wide open:
He bestows as He wishes.
Surely many of them will be increased
By what has been sent to you from your Lord
in rebellion and unfaith,
And We have cast enmity and hatred amongst them
Until the Day of Resurrection.
Every time they ignite the flames of war,
Allah puts them out.
They seek to cause corruption on the earth,
And Allah does not like the agents of corruption.

Meaning of Hands wide open: Allah (swt), the Almighty, has been the most generous. He spends according to His infinite wisdom and universal plans.

Source: Ayatollah Agha Mahdi Puya, *Tafsir of Holy Qur'an, Surah* 5, verse 64, P. 460.

http://www.islamicmobility.com/elibrary_14.htm

2. Hand, right hand of Allah

The word *ayd, yadhay* is used by Allah (swt) in the holy Qur'an at a few places, which are as follows:

Surah al-Dhariyat (51:47)

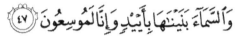

We have built the sky with might,
And indeed it is We who are its expanders.

Surat Sad (38:75)

قَالَ يَـٰٓإِبْلِيسُ مَا مَنَعَكَ أَن تَسْجُدَ لِمَا خَلَقْتُ بِيَدَىَّ أَسْتَكْبَرْتَ أَمْ كُنتَ مِنَ ٱلْعَالِينَ ﴿٧٥﴾

And
He said, 'O Iblis!
What keeps you from prostrating
Before that which I have created
*With Me [own] two **hands**?*
Are you arrogant,
Or are you [one] of the exalted ones?'

Now **ayd (hand)** means **"strength"** (*A Shi'a Creed*, P. 29) similar to:

Surat Sad (38:17)

أَصْبِرْ عَلَىٰ مَا يَقُولُونَ وَٱذْكُرْ عَبْدَنَا دَاوُۥدَ ذَا ٱلْأَيْدِ إِنَّهُۥٓ أَوَّابٌ ﴿١٧﴾

Be patient over what they say,

And remember Our servant, David,
[The man] of strength.
Indeed, he was a penitent [soul].

Verse discusses 'right hand' of Allah (swt)

Surat Al-Zumar (39:67)

وَمَا قَدَرُوا ٱللَّهَ حَقَّ قَدْرِهِ وَٱلْأَرْضُ جَمِيعًا قَبْضَتُهُۥ يَوْمَ ٱلْقِيَـٰمَةِ وَٱلسَّمَـٰوَٰتُ مَطْوِيَّـٰتٌۢ بِيَمِينِهِۦ سُبْحَـٰنَهُۥ وَتَعَـٰلَىٰ عَمَّا يُشْرِكُونَ ٦٧

They do not regard Allah
With the regard due to Him,
Yet the entire earth will be in His fist
on the Day of Resurrection,
*And the heavens, scrolled, in His **right hand**.*
Immaculate is He
And exalted
Above [having] any partners that they ascribe [to Him].

The meaning of 'right hand is Allah's 'power' (*A Shi'a Creed*, P. 29).

The heavens with their vast expanse are more than a rolled up scroll in His (Allah's) right hand (power), the hand of power and will. This is figurative. Allah (swt) is not a creature of flesh and blood, with hands and fingers.

Source: Ayatollah Agha Mahdi Puya, *Tafsir of Holy Qur'an, Surah* 39, verse 67, P. 66.
   http://www.islamicmobility.com/elibrary_14.htm

3. Spirit of Allah (RoohAllah)

Surat al-Hijr (15:29)

فَإِذَا سَوَّيْتُهُ وَنَفَخْتُ فِيهِ مِن رُّوحِي فَقَعُوا لَهُ سَاجِدِينَ ﴿٢٩﴾

So when I have proportioned him
And breathed into him of My spirit,
Then fall down in prostration before him.

In this verse, the spirit (*Ruh*) was created by Allah (swt), and Allah had breathed it into Prophet Adam (as) and also Prophet Jesus (as). "My Spirit" refers to a prior creation of Allah (swt), similarly Allah (swt) has used the terms "my house" in Surat al Hajj (22:26), and "my Earth" in Surat al Ankabut (29:56), and "my paradise" in Surah al Fajr (89:30). Therefore, the word "my" is associated with creating the entities and ownership to Allah (swt) **only**. (*A Shi'a Creed*, P. 29).

4. The Chair

Surah al Baqirah (2:255)

اللَّهُ لَا إِلَهَ إِلَّا هُوَ الْحَيُّ الْقَيُّومُ لَا تَأْخُذُهُ سِنَةٌ وَلَا نَوْمٌ لَهُ مَا فِي

السَّمَوَاتِ وَمَا فِي الْأَرْضِ مَن ذَا الَّذِي يَشْفَعُ عِندَهُ إِلَّا بِإِذْنِهِ يَعْلَمُ

مَا بَيْنَ أَيْدِيهِمْ وَمَا خَلْفَهُمْ وَلَا يُحِيطُونَ بِشَيْءٍ مِّنْ عِلْمِهِ إِلَّا بِمَا

شَاءَ وَسِعَ كُرْسِيُّهُ السَّمَوَاتِ وَالْأَرْضَ وَلَا يَئُودُهُ حِفْظُهُمَا وَهُوَ

الْعَلِيُّ الْعَظِيمُ ﴿٢٥٥﴾

Allah—there is no god except Him—
Is the Living One, the All-Sustainer.
Neither drowsiness befalls Him nor sleep.
To Him belongs whatever is in the heavens
And whatever is on the earth.
Who is it that may intercede with Him
Except with His permission?
He knows that which is before them
And that which is behind them,

And they do not comprehend
Anything of His knowledge
Accept what He wishes.
His seat embraces the heavens and the earth,
And He is not wearied by their preservation,
And He is the All-exalted, the All-supreme.

The chair or seat refers to Allah's knowledge of the heavens and the earth. (*A Shi'a Creed*, P. 44).

5. The Throne

Surat Taha (20:5)

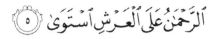

The All-beneficent, settled on the **Throne**.

The Throne refers to the authority and the decree of Allah (swt). (*A Shi'a Creed*, P. 44).

6. Allah's House

Surah al Hajj (22:26)

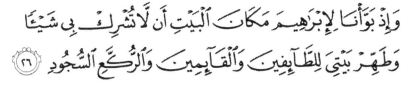

When We settled for Abraham the site of the House
[Saying], Do not ascribe any partners to Me,
And purify My House for those who go around it,
And those who stand [in it for prayer,
And those who bow and prostrate.

'My House' refers to the Holy Kaaba in Makkah. The Kaaba is a sanctuary for all mankind and a place to worship towards. The Kaaba was first built by Prophet Adam (as) by the command of Allah (swt), and then later rebuilt by Prophet Ibrahim (as) and his son Prophet Ismail (as), as a sign of Allah (swt) on Earth.

7. Seeing Allah (swt) on the day of Judgment
Surat al Qiyamah (75:22-23)

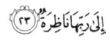

Some faces will be fresh on that day,

وُجُوهٌ يَوْمَئِذٍ نَّاضِرَةٌ ﴿٢٢﴾

إِلَى رَبِّهَا نَاظِرَةٌ ﴿٢٣﴾

Looking at their Lord,

'Looking at their Lord' refers to looking at their lord's reward. (*A Shi'a Creed*, P. 30).

Shi'a view of the attributes of Allah (swt)

According to the School of Ahlul Bayt (as) and the holy Qur'an, Shi'a believe in Allah (swt) is as follows:

Allah is One (Wahid), Alone (Ahad), Peerless (laysa kamithlihu shay'), Eternal (Qadim), Without Beginning or End; Allah is the First and the Last (al-Awwal WA al-akhir). Allah is the All-knowing (al-alim),the Wise (al-hakim), the Just (al-adil), the Living (al-hayy), the Omnipotent (al-qadir), Independent of all things (al-ghaniy), the All Hearing (as-sami), the All-Seeing (al-Basir), is not bound to time, space or matter. Allah is limitless, nothing is equal to Him, nor has He any opposite. He has no wife, no child, and no partner and there is none comparable to Him. Vision does not perceive Him, yet He perceives everything. Allah cannot be comprehended (in entirely). Allah is above all deficiencies. Yet everything we imagine will be a creature like ourselves.

Imam Baqir (as) said:

> *"Allah (swt) is far greater than the explanation of the wise, and far beyond the research of discriminative knowledge."*

(Summary of Doctrine of Belief in Allah)

Source: Ayatollah Muhammad Rida Al-Muzaffar, *The Faith of Shi'a Islam*. Chapter: Tawhid, Doctrine of Belief in Allah. P. 6

Qur'anic verses about the attributes of Allah (swt)

Surat al Ikhlas 112:1-4

In the Name of Allah,
The All-beneficent, the All-merciful

قُلْ هُوَ ٱللَّهُ أَحَدٌ ﴿١﴾

Say, 'He is Allah, the One.

ٱللَّهُ ٱلصَّمَدُ ﴿٢﴾

Allah is the All-embracing.

لَمْ يَلِدْ وَلَمْ يُولَدْ ﴿٣﴾

He neither begat, nor was begotten,

وَلَمْ يَكُن لَّهُ كُفُوًا أَحَدٌ ﴿٤﴾

Nor has He any equal.'

Surat Ibrahim 14:10

۞ قَالَتْ رُسُلُهُمْ أَفِى ٱللَّهِ شَكٌّ فَاطِرِ ٱلسَّمَٰوَٰتِ وَٱلْأَرْضِ يَدْعُوكُمْ لِيَغْفِرَ لَكُم مِّن ذُنُوبِكُمْ وَيُؤَخِّرَكُمْ إِلَىٰٓ أَجَلٍ مُّسَمًّى قَالُوٓا۟ إِنْ أَنتُمْ إِلَّا بَشَرٌ مِّثْلُنَا تُرِيدُونَ أَن تَصُدُّونَا عَمَّا كَانَ يَعْبُدُ ءَابَآؤُنَا فَأْتُونَا بِسُلْطَٰنٍ مُّبِينٍ ﴿١٠﴾

Their apostles said, 'Is there any doubt about Allah,
The originator of the heavens and the earth?!
He calls you to forgive you a part of your sins,
And grants you respite until a specified time.'
They said, 'You are nothing but humans like us
Who desire to bore us
From what our fathers used to worship.
So bring us a manifest authority.'

Surat An'am, 6:103

$$\text{لَّا تُدۡرِكُهُ ٱلۡأَبۡصَـٰرُ وَهُوَ يُدۡرِكُ ٱلۡأَبۡصَـٰرَ وَهُوَ ٱللَّطِيفُ ٱلۡخَبِيرُ ﴿١٠٣﴾}$$

The sights do not apprehend Him,
Yet He apprehends the sights,
and He is the All-attentive, the All-aware.

Surat al Anbiya 21:22

$$\text{لَوۡ كَانَ فِيهِمَآ ءَالِهَةٌ إِلَّا ٱللَّهُ لَفَسَدَتَاۚ فَسُبۡحَـٰنَ ٱللَّهِ رَبِّ ٱلۡعَرۡشِ عَمَّا يَصِفُونَ ﴿٢٢﴾}$$

Had there been gods in them other than Allah,
They would surely have fallen apart.
Clear is Allah, the Lord of the Throne,
Of what they allege [concerning Him].

Surat An'am 6:133

$$\text{وَرَبُّكَ ٱلۡغَنِيُّ ذُو ٱلرَّحۡمَةِۚ إِن يَشَأۡ يُذۡهِبۡكُمۡ وَيَسۡتَخۡلِفۡ مِنۢ بَعۡدِكُم مَّا يَشَآءُ كَمَآ أَنشَأَكُم مِّن ذُرِّيَّةِ قَوۡمٍ ءَاخَرِينَ ﴿١٣٣﴾}$$

Your Lord is the All-sufficient
Dispenser of mercy.
If He wishes, He will take you away,
And make whomever He wishes to succeed you,
Just as He produced you
From the descendants of other people.
Surat Taha 20:8

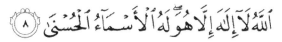

Allah - there is no god except Him to Him belong the Best Names.

Surat al Rum 30:40

اللَّهُ الَّذِى خَلَقَكُمْ ثُمَّ رَزَقَكُمْ ثُمَّ يُمِيتُكُمْ ثُمَّ يُحْيِيكُمْ هَلْ
مِن شُرَكَآئِكُم مَّن يَفْعَلُ مِن ذَلِكُم مِّن شَىْءٍ سُبْحَنَهُ وَتَعَالَى عَمَّا
يُشْرِكُونَ ﴿٤٠﴾

It is Allah who created you and then He provided for you, then He makes you die, then He will bring you to life. Is there anyone among your partners who does anything of that kind? Immaculate is He and exalted above [having] any partners that they ascribe [to Him]!

Surat an An'am, 6:133

وَرَبُّكَ الْغَنِىُّ ذُو الرَّحْمَةِ إِن يَشَأْ يُذْهِبْكُمْ وَيَسْتَخْلِفْ
مِنْ بَعْدِكُم مَّا يَشَاءُ كَمَا أَنشَأَكُم مِّن ذُرِّيَةِ قَوْمٍ
ءَاخَرِينَ ﴿١٣٣﴾

Your Lord is the All-sufficient
dispenser of mercy.

Justice of Allah (swt)

Surat al Nisa 4:40

$$إِنَّ ٱللَّهَ لَا يَظْلِمُ مِثْقَالَ ذَرَّةٍ وَإِن تَكُ حَسَنَةً يُضَـٰعِفْهَا وَيُؤْتِ مِن لَّدُنْهُ أَجْرًا عَظِيمًا ﴿٤٠﴾$$

Indeed Allah does not wrong [anyone]
[even to the extent of] an atom's weight,
and if it be a good deed
He doubles it [s reward],
and gives from
Himself a great reward.

Surat al Maidah 5:42

$$إِنَّ ٱللَّهَ يُحِبُّ ٱلْمُقْسِطِينَ ﴿٤٢﴾$$

...Indeed Allah loves the just.

Surat al Anfal 8:49

$$إِذْ يَقُولُ ٱلْمُنَـٰفِقُونَ وَٱلَّذِينَ فِى قُلُوبِهِم مَّرَضٌ غَرَّ هَـٰٓؤُلَآءِ دِينُهُمْ وَمَن يَتَوَكَّلْ عَلَى ٱللَّهِ فَإِنَّ ٱللَّهَ عَزِيزٌ حَكِيمٌ ﴿٤٩﴾$$

When the hypocrites said,
and [also] those in whose
hearts is a sickness,
'Their religion has deceived them.
'But whoever puts his trust in Allah,
then Allah is indeed all-mighty,
all-wise.

Surat Ghafir, 40:31

مِثْلَ دَأْبِ قَوْمِ نُوحٍ وَعَادٍ وَثَمُودَ وَالَّذِينَ مِنْ بَعْدِهِمْ وَمَا اللَّهُ يُرِيدُ ظُلْمًا لِّلْعِبَادِ ﴿٣١﴾

Like the case of the people of Noah,
 of Ad and Thamud,
and those who were after them,
 and Allah does not desire any wrong for [His] servants.

Surat al Nisa 4:79

مَّا أَصَابَكَ مِنْ حَسَنَةٍ فَمِنَ اللَّهِ وَمَا أَصَابَكَ مِن سَيِّئَةٍ فَمِن نَّفْسِكَ وَأَرْسَلْنَاكَ لِلنَّاسِ رَسُولًا وَكَفَىٰ بِاللَّهِ شَهِيدًا ﴿٧٩﴾

Whatever good befalls you is from Allah;
 and whatever ill befalls you is from yourself.
We sent you as an apostle to mankind,
and Allah suffices as a witness.

Surat an An'am 6:131

ذَٰلِكَ أَن لَّمْ يَكُن رَّبُّكَ مُهْلِكَ الْقُرَىٰ بِظُلْمٍ وَأَهْلُهَا غَافِلُونَ ﴿١٣١﴾

This is because your Lord would never destroy the towns unjustly while their people were unaware.

Surat al A'raf 7:29

قُلْ أَمَرَ رَبِّي بِالْقِسْطِ وَأَقِيمُوا وُجُوهَكُمْ عِندَ كُلِّ مَسْجِدٍ وَادْعُوهُ مُخْلِصِينَ لَهُ الدِّينَ كَمَا بَدَأَكُمْ تَعُودُونَ ﴿٢٩﴾

Say, 'My Lord has enjoined justice,'
and [He has enjoined,] 'Set your heart [on Him]

at every occasion of prayer,
and invoke Him,
putting your exclusive faith in Him.
Even as He brought you forth in the beginning,
so will you return.'

Surat Yunus 10:4

إِلَيْهِ مَرْجِعُكُمْ جَمِيعًا وَعْدَ اللَّهِ حَقًّا إِنَّهُ يَبْدَؤُاْ الْخَلْقَ ثُمَّ يُعِيدُهُ

لِيَجْزِيَ الَّذِينَ ءَامَنُواْ وَعَمِلُواْ الصَّلِحَتِ بِالْقِسْطِ وَالَّذِينَ كَفَرُواْ

لَهُمْ شَرَابٌ مِّنْ حَمِيمٍ وَعَذَابٌ أَلِيمٌ بِمَا كَانُواْ يَكْفُرُونَ ٤

To Him will be the return of you all [that is] Allah's true promise.
Indeed He originates the creation, then He will bring it back that He
may reward those who have faith and do righteous deeds with justice.

Surat Yunus 10:54

وَلَوْ أَنَّ لِكُلِّ نَفْسٍ ظَلَمَتْ مَا فِي الْأَرْضِ لَافْتَدَتْ بِهِ وَأَسَرُّواْ

النَّدَامَةَ لَمَّا رَأَوُاْ الْعَذَابَ وَقُضِيَ بَيْنَهُم بِالْقِسْطِ وَهُمْ لَا

يُظْلَمُونَ ٥٤

Were any soul that has done wrong to possess whatever there is on
the earth, it would surely offer it for ransom. They will hide their
remorse when they sight the punishment; and judgement will be made
between them with justice and they will not be wronged.

End of Chapter notes:

Imam Ali (as) sermons # 49 and 64 from *Nahjul Balagha* (*The Peak of Eloquence*)

Sermon 49: *About Allah's Greatness and Sublimity*

Praise be to Allah Who lies inside all hidden things and towards Whom all open things are guided. He cannot be seen by the eye of an onlooker, but the eye which does not see Him cannot deny Him while the mind that proves His existence cannot perceive Him. He is so high in sublimity that nothing can be more sublime than He, while in nearness, He is so near that no one can be nearer than He. But his sublimity does not put Him at a distance from anything of His creation, nor does His nearness bring them on an equal level to Him. He has not informed (human) with about the limits of His qualities. Nevertheless, He has not prevented it from securing some essential knowledge of Him. He is such that all signs of existence testify for Him till the denying mind also believes in Him. Allah is sublime beyond what is described by those who liken Him to things or those who deny Him.

Source: *Nahjul Balagha* (The Peak of Eloquence) by Imam Ali Ibn Abu Talib (as) With Commentary By Martyr Ayatollah Murtada Mutahhari (2009) 7th Edition, Tahrike Tarsile Qur'an, Inc. NY. P. 403

Sermon 64: *About Allah's attributes*

Praise be to Allah for Whom one condition does not proceed another, so that He may be the First before being the Last or He may be Manifest before being Hidden. Everyone called one (alone) save He is by virtue of being small (in number), and everyone enjoying honor other than Him is humble. Every powerful person other than Him is weak. Every master (owner) other than Him is a slave (owned).

Every knower other than Him is a seeker of knowledge. Every controller other than Him is sometimes imbued with control and sometimes with disabilities. Every listener other than Him is deaf to light voices while loud voices make him deaf and distant voices also leave him. Every onlooker other than Him is blind to hidden colors and delicate bodies. Every manifest thing other than Him is hidden, but every hidden thing other than Him is incapable of becoming manifest.

He did not create what He created to fortify His authority nor for fear of the consequences of time, nor to seek help against the attack of an equal or a boastful partner or a hateful opponent. On the other hand all the creatures are reared by him and are His humbled slaves. He is not conditioned on anything so that it be said that He exists therein, nor is He separated from anything so as to be said that He is away from it. The creation of what He initiated or the administration of what He controls did not fatigue Him. No disability overtook Him against what He created. No misgiving ever occurred to Him in what He ordained and resolved it. But His verdict is certain, His knowledge is definite, His governance is Overwhelming. He is wished for at times of distress and He is feared evening's bounty.

Source: *Nahjul Balagha* (The Peak of Eloquence) by Imam Ali Ibn Abu Talib (as) With Commentary By Martyr Ayatollah Murtada Mutahhari (2009) 7th Edition, Tahrike Tarsile Qur'an, Inc. NY. P. 415

Books on this topic

A Commentary on Theistic Arguments by al-Shaykh Abdollah Jawadi Amuli

Allah: The Concept of God in Islam by Yasin T. Al-Jibouri

A Discussion of the Kursi by al-Syed Muhammad Hussain Tabatabai

Al-Tawhid and its Social Implications by Ayatollah Ali Khamenei

At-Tawhid or Monotheism by al-Shaykh Muhammad Taqi Mesbah Yazdi

Arsh of Allah by al-Syed Muhammad Hussain Tabatabai

Arsh – the Throne of Allah by al-Shaykh Muhammad Saeed Bahmanpour

Basic Teachings of Islam by al-Syed Muhammad Beheshti

Cognizance of Unitarianism by al-Shaykh Mushtaq Hussain Shahidi

Divine Purpose by al-Syed Nadeem Jafri

Divine Revelation – An Islamic Perspective on Divine Guidance and Human Understanding by al-Shaykh Mohammad Ali Shomali

Does God Have a Mind? By Dr. Muhammad Legenhausen

Essence of Tawhid: Denial of Servitude but to God by Ayatollah Ali Khamenei

Essence of Thoughts by al-Shaykh Yousef Saanei

Excerpt from the Causes Responsible for Materialist Tendencies in the West by Ayatollah Murtadha Mutahhari

Fundamentals of Knowing God by Reza Berenjkar

God of Islam by AyatollahSayyid Saeed Akhtar Rizvi

God and his Attributes by Sayyid Mujtaba Musavi Lari

God in Islamic Traditions: a Glance at al-Tawhid by Shaykh as-Saduq by Dr. Karim Aghili

God in the Quran by al-Syed Muhammad Beheshti

Identity of Allah by al-Syed Nadeem Jafri

Image of God in the Quran by al-Shaykh Mohammad Ali Shomali

Inner Secrets of the Path by al-Syed Haydar al-Amuli

Inner Voice by al-Syed Saeed Akhtar Rizvi

Islamic Teachings in Brief by Allamah Muhammad Hussain Tabatabai

Knowing Allah by al-Shaykh Muhammad Javad Bahonar

Let's Learn about God by Ayatollah Nasir Makarem Shirazi

Monotheism for Young Adults by Nayerreh Tavassoli

One, Followed with Indefinite Zeros by Dr. Ali Shariati

Our Belief by Ayatollah Nasir Makarem Shirazi

Seeing Allah by Dr. V. J. Majd

Tawheed by Al-Balagh Foundation

Tawhid in Ten Lessons by Ayatollah Nasir Makarem Shirazi

Tawhid by al-Shaykh Muhammad Taqi Misbah Yazdi

The Concept of God in Islam by Yasin T. Al-Jibouri

The Nature of Understanding Allah (swt) by al-Shaykh Hussain Madhahiri

The Purpose and Aim of Creating the Human by al-Syed Kamal al-Haydari

Understanding God's Mercy by al-Shaykh Mohammad Ali Shomali

Wisdom of the Unseen by al-Syed Amir Raza

Chapter 2

The infallibility of the Prophets (pbut) from Qur'an

Shi'a, the followers, of the Ahlul Bayt (as) believe that all 124,000 prophets of Allah (swt) were infallible. Infallibility means that even though they could have committed sins, they chose not to because of their ability to understand the greatness of Allah (swt). Also because they had divine knowledge about the consequences of committing any sin. After the demise of the last of Allah's (swt) Prophets, Allah (swt) blessed the mankind with 13 more infallibles for guidance. These thirteen infallibles served to protect the religion of Islam and to preserve Islam in its true essence. *Shi'as* believe that Allah (swt) sent in total 124,013 messengers and/or guides to be examples for the rest of mankind to follow.

Qur'anic verses about the infallibility of the Prophets and Imams of Ahlul Bayt (as)

Surat al Nisa 4:64:

وَمَآ أَرْسَلْنَا مِن رَّسُولٍ إِلَّا لِيُطَاعَ بِإِذْنِ اللَّهِ ۚ وَلَوْ أَنَّهُمْ إِذ ظَّلَمُوٓاْ أَنفُسَهُمْ جَآءُوكَ فَٱسْتَغْفَرُواْ ٱللَّهَ وَٱسْتَغْفَرَ لَهُمُ ٱلرَّسُولُ لَوَجَدُواْ ٱللَّهَ تَوَّابًا رَّحِيمًا ٦٤

We did not send any apostle
but to be obeyed by
Allah's leave. Had they,
when they wronged themselves,
come to you and pleaded to

Allah for forgiveness,
and the Apostle had pleaded for
forgiveness for them,
they would have surely found Allah
all-Clement, all-Merciful.

This verse proves that ALL apostles (messengers) of God do not perform any acts without Allah's (swt) permission. Would Allah (swt) allow them to commit a sin?

Surat al Nisa 4:59

يَٰٓأَيُّهَا ٱلَّذِينَ ءَامَنُوٓاْ أَطِيعُواْ ٱللَّهَ وَأَطِيعُواْ ٱلرَّسُولَ وَأُوْلِى ٱلْأَمْرِ مِنكُمْ ۖ فَإِن تَنَٰزَعْتُمْ فِى شَىْءٍ فَرُدُّوهُ إِلَى ٱللَّهِ وَٱلرَّسُولِ إِن كُنتُمْ تُؤْمِنُونَ بِٱللَّهِ وَٱلْيَوْمِ ٱلْأَخِرِ ۚ ذَٰلِكَ خَيْرٌ وَأَحْسَنُ تَأْوِيلًا ﴿٥٩﴾

O you who have faith!
Obey Allah and obey the Apostle
and those vested with
authority among you...

And

Surat al Nisa 4:80

مَّن يُطِعِ ٱلرَّسُولَ فَقَدْ أَطَاعَ ٱللَّهَ ۖ وَمَن تَوَلَّىٰ فَمَآ أَرْسَلْنَٰكَ عَلَيْهِمْ حَفِيظًا ﴿٨٠﴾

Whoever obeys the Apostle certainly obeys Allah;
and as for those who turn their backs [on you],
We have not sent you to keep watch over them.

In the abovementioned verses Allah (swt) commands people of the faith to obey Allah (swt), His apostle (Prophet Muhammad pbuh) and 'those vested with authority among you.' The three mentioned in the verse are to be obeyed because obeying any one is the same as obeying Allah (swt). Allah (swt) sent Prophet Mohammad pbuh with his divine message and he also commanded to follow 'those vested with authority.' If 'those vested with authority,' were not pure or sinned, then Allah's order to obey them would be an **injustice.** It would be difficult for humans to follow the actions of guides who themselves could not tell the difference between right and wrong and indulged in sinful behavior. But Allah (swt) is all-just and all-knowing. Due to this, Allah (swt) wouldn't command humans to follow a sinner. Therefore "those vested with authority" are as sinless and pure as all of the Prophets of Allah (pbut).

Note: 'Those vested with authority' refers to the 12 Holy Imams of the Ahlul Bayt (as) and this topic is discussed in detail in <u>Chapter 7</u> of this book. The holy Qur'an places 'obedience to those vested with authority' as same as obeying the Prophet (pbuh), and this statement is NOT a conditional statement, which is a proof that after Holy Prophet (phuh), the 12 Holy Imams (as) are to be followed in a similar manner.

Question: Did Allah (swt) tell us, whom not to obey?

Allah (swt) has provided humans with a list of attributes that should not be associated with a religious leader. The following verses of the holy Qur'an give these 'attributes' and if 'one' of these attributes is to be found in a person who claims to be a religious leader or a religious guide, then it is incumbent upon a believer (a Muslim) to disassociate from the leadership from that individual. .

Surat al Qalam 68:8-14

So do not obey the deniers,

وَدُّوا لَوْ تُدْهِنُ فَيُدْهِنُونَ ﴿٩﴾

who are eager that you should be pliable [towards you].

وَلَا تُطِعْ كُلَّ حَلَّافٍ مَهِينٍ ﴿١٠﴾

And Do not obey any vile swearer,

هَمَّازٍ مَشَّاءٍ بِنَمِيمٍ ﴿١١﴾

Scandalmonger, talebearer,

مَنَّاعٍ لِلْخَيْرِ مُعْتَدٍ أَثِيمٍ ﴿١٢﴾

Hinderer of all good, sinful transgressor,

عُتُلٍّ بَعْدَ ذَٰلِكَ زَنِيمٍ ﴿١٣﴾

Callous and, on top of that, baseborn,

أَن كَانَ ذَا مَالٍ وَبَنِينَ ﴿١٤﴾

[only] because he has wealth and children.

And

Surat al Insan 76:24

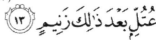

فَاصْبِرْ لِحُكْمِ رَبِّكَ وَلَا تُطِعْ مِنْهُمْ ءَاثِمًا أَوْ كَفُورًا ﴿٢٤﴾

So submit patiently to
the judgement of your Lord,
and <u>do not</u> obey any
sinner or ingrate among them,

If a Caliph, a governor or a leader of the Muslim nation in the past or present, has/have/had one of these 'attributes' associated with him/ her/ them; then it is obligatory for a Muslim to not only to **NOT** obey that individual, but also NOT to put a *"veil of righteousness"* by using *Razi-Allah anho* (may Allah swt be pleased with him) with their names.

Prophet of Allah's (swt) command to obey him
Surat al Shu'ara 26:150-152

$$\text{فَٱتَّقُوا۟ ٱللَّهَ وَأَطِيعُونِ ۝}$$

So be wary of Allah and obey me [Prophet Salih AS]

$$\text{وَلَا تُطِيعُوٓا۟ أَمْرَ ٱلْمُسْرِفِينَ ۝}$$

and do not obey the dictates of the profligate,

$$\text{ٱلَّذِينَ يُفْسِدُونَ فِى ٱلْأَرْضِ وَلَا يُصْلِحُونَ ۝}$$

who cause corruption in the land and do not bring about reform.

These verses (150-152) of Surat Al-Shu'ara are from the conversation of Prophet Salih (as) with the people of Thamud. In these verses it is illustrated that Prophet Salih (as) asked the people to obey Allah (swt) and obey him (*if he wasn't infallible, a perfect guide for the people of his time, then he wouldn't order people to obey him*). Therefore, this concludes the following:

1. The prophets are to be obeyed unconditionally.
2. The sinners and wrongdoers are not to be obeyed.
3. The only logical conclusion is that the prophets are not in the categories of the sinners or the wrongdoers, thus are infallible human beings.

End of Chapter notes:

Ba'set-e-Rasool (27th Rajab) The Declaration of the Prophethood according to the School of Ahlul Bayt (as)

The majority of Muslims believe that Prophet Muhammad (pbuh) became a Prophet at the age of 40. In contrary, Shi'as believe that Prophet Muhammad (pbuh) was a Prophet of Allah (swt) his entire life. Further, his Prophethood extends beyond his life on earth to even before the creation of Prophet Adam (as), as reported in a hadith of Prophet Muhammad (pbuh):

> *"I was a Prophet when Adam (as) was between soul and body (i.e. When Adam's creation was in its preliminary stages"*

Source: Abu al-Qasim Sulaiman Ibn Ahmad Ibn Al-Tabarani, *Al-Mu'jjam al-Kabir; Al Khasa'is al-Kubra,* V.1, P.4

And

> *"When Allah intended to create the creatures, He first created the 'Noor (Light) of Muhammad."*

Source: Shihab al-Din Abu al-Abbas Ahmad Ibn Muhammad Ibn Abu Bakr AKA Al-Qastalani, *Al Mawahibu'l-Ladunniyah,* vol. 1, pp. 5, 9, 10

And in **Surat al Maidah 5:15,** where Allah (swt) refers to Prophet Muhammad (pbuh) as "Noor" or "light":

$$قَد جَاءَكُم مِنَ اللَّهِ نورٌ وَكِتابٌ مُبينٌ$$

...Certainly there has come to you a light from Allah,

and a manifest Book.

Imam Hasan Askari (as) narrates:

When the Prophet reached to the age of forty years the Almighty Allah (swt) made him absolutely humble and sincere and found him to be most obedient to Him. So He created a light in his eyes and when He issued the command, the doors of the heavens were opened up.

Angels arrived in groups to the earth to see the Prophet and the Almighty Allah joined His mercy from the leg of the Arsh to His (pbuh) Eminence. Archangel Jibraeel (Gabriel) came down encompassing the earth and the sky and holding the arm of the Prophet said: "O Muhammad, read." He asked: **"What should I read?"**

(**Note:** *Prophet (pbuh) said: **"What should I read?"** Not I* ***don't know how to read!!*** *As the majority of the Muslims are told to believe in, this is a clear difference between man-made Imams and the Imams of Ahlul Bayt (as) whom Allah (swt) appointed as guides*).

Surat al Alaq 96:1

Read in the Name of your Lord who created;

Then Archangel Jibraeel accompanied by many angels conveyed the rest of the divine revelation to him. When the angels returned to the heaven, the Prophet (pbuh) descended from Mount Hira, and such glory beamed from him that no one could endure the light. Every tree and herb and stone he passed, bowed down before His Eminence, and saluted him with the epithet of the Messenger of Allah (pbuh), saying in fluent language: Peace be upon you, O Prophet of Allah. Peace be upon you, O Messenger of Allah (pbuh).

On entering, his house was illuminated by his effulgence and Khadija (as) asked, *"What light is this?"* He (pbuh) replied, *"This is the effulgence of prophecy*: Say, ***"There is no god but Allah; Muhammad is the Messenger of Allah"*** Khadija (as) replied, *"I have known for years that you were a Prophet."* She then repeated the creed and professed the faith. He (pbuh) then said to her, *"I am cold, cover me with another garment,"* and laying down he received a divine communication:

Surah al Muddaththir 74:1-3

يَـٰٓأَيُّهَا ٱلْمُدَّثِّرُ ۝١

O you who are clothed!

قُمْ فَأَنذِرْ ۝٢

Arise and warn,

وَرَبَّكَ فَكَبِّرْ ۝٣

and your Lord do magnify."

The Holy Prophet (pbuh) arose and raising his hands to his ears, said: Allah is the greatest (*Allahu Akbar*). Whoever heard the voice attested to his veracity. It is mentioned in *Nahjul Balagha* that at that time, except for the house of the Prophet (pbuh), Islam had not entered any other house. Imam Ali (as) and Lady Khadija (as) used to witness the effulgence of divine revelation and Prophethood and smell the fragrance of Prophethood.

Note: *The verse regarding the **witness of the Prophethood** refers to Imam Ali (as) since he was there in-person witnessing the revelation of the Quran and Prophet Muhammad (pbuh) declaring his Prophethood*

Surat Ar Ra'ad 13:43

وَيَقُولُ ٱلَّذِينَ كَفَرُوا۟ لَسْتَ مُرْسَلًا قُلْ كَفَىٰ بِٱللَّهِ شَهِيدًۢا بَيْنِى وَبَيْنَكُمْ وَمَنْ عِندَهُۥ عِلْمُ ٱلْكِتَٰبِ ۝٤٣

The faithless say,
'You have not been sent [by Allah].'
Say, 'Allah suffices as a witness between me
and you,
*and **he who possesses the knowledge of the Book.'***

** He refers to Imam Ali (as), and the criteria for one to be called a 'witness' specifies that a person must have observed the event in person.

In *Nahjul Balagha,* the Imam (as) continues…and we (*Imam Ali (as) and Lady Khadija (as)*) heard the wails of Satan when revelation descended on the Prophet (pbuh). I asked: *"What wail is it?"* He (pbuh) replied: *"It is Satan and he had despaired that people will ever worship him now. O Ali, I also hear whatever you hear and see what you see, but you are not a prophet, you are my legatee and you shall have a good end."*

Tabarsi etc. have narrated that during the time a terrible famine struck Mecca and Abu Talib had many children. The Holy Prophet (pbuh) told Abbas: *"Your brother, Abu Talib is having many issues and the times are very hard. Let us distribute his burden."* The Holy Prophet (pbuh) took Imam Ali (as) under his care and he always accompanied the Prophet (pbuh). So much so that he declared his Prophethood and the first to profess faith in him was Imam Ali (as).

Through many authentic chains, it is narrated that Holy Prophet (pbuh) said: I was a trader and I reached Mina during the Hajj season and came to Abbas to sell some goods to him. Suddenly I saw a person emerge from the tent and he began to look at the sky. Seeing that the sun has begun its decline from the peak, he stood up to pray.

Then a boy came out and stood beside him. Then a lady came and stood behind them and they all prayed the ritual prayer. I asked Abbas what religion these people were following, and that I have seen nothing like it. He said: "This is Muhammad bin Abdullah, and he claims that the Almighty Allah has invested him with Prophethood and he says that the treasures of Kaiser and Kisra will be obtained by him in booty."

And that lady is his wife, Khadija (as) and that boy is the son of his uncle who has professed faith in him. Except these, no one else has professed faith in him. Afif used to regret that he didn't profess faith that day. In another report, it is mentioned that Lady Khadija (as) asked Waraqa bin Naufal, her cousin who followed the Christian religion and was well versed in heavenly scriptures, and was a very old man who had lost his vision: *"Who is Jibraeel?"* Waraqa replied: *"Quddus, Quddus…How did you learn about him in a town where God is not worshipped?"* Khadija (as) said: *"Muhammad bin Abdullah (pbuh) says that Jibraeel came to him."* Waraqa replied:

"He is right, I have read about his distinctive qualities in divine books. Jibraeel is the great angel of God who came to Prophet Musa and Prophet Isa (as)."

Waraqa continued: *"I have read in the Taurat and Injeel that the Almighty God will send a Prophet who would be an orphan. God will afford refuge to him. That he would be poor, but the Almighty God will make him needless of the people. He would walk on water and speak to the dead and stones and trees will salute him and testify to his Prophethood."*

Then Waraqa added: *"I have dreamed for three consecutive nights that Almighty God has sent a prophet towards Mecca. I don't find anyone else more deserving of the office of Prophethood."* Then Khadija (as) went to a Jewish monk named Adas. He was so old that his eyebrows hung upon his eyes. Khadija (as) said: *"Tell me about Jibraeel."* Adas immediately fell down in prostration exclaiming: *"Quddus Quddus... How did you hear the name of Jibraeel in a town where people do not worship God?"* Khadija (as) adjured him not to disclose this to anyone and told him that Muhammad claims that Jibraeel visits him. Adas said: *"Jibraeel is that great angel of God who came to Prophet Musa and Prophet Isa (as). Sometimes Satan also comes in the form of an angel. Take this amulet of mine to him. If it is Satan or Jinn it will leave him alone and if this is really a divine matter, no harm will come to him."* Lady Khadija (as) returned from there to find the Holy Prophet (pbuh) seated and Jibraeel was reciting the following verses to him:

Surah al Qalam 68:1-3

$$\text{نٓ ۚ وَٱلْقَلَمِ وَمَا يَسْطُرُونَ ﴿١﴾}$$

Nun.
By the Pen and what they write:

$$\text{مَآ أَنتَ بِنِعْمَةِ رَبِّكَ بِمَجْنُونٍ ﴿٢﴾}$$

you are not, by your Lord's blessing, crazy,

$$\text{وَإِنَّ لَكَ لَأَجْرًا غَيْرَ مَمْنُونٍ ﴿٣﴾}$$

and yours indeed will be an everlasting reward,

Khadija (as) was pleased to hear these verses. Then Adas came to the Prophet (pbuh) and witnessed the signs he had read in the books. He said: *"Please show me the seal of Prophethood."* When he saw the seal of Prophethood, he fell down in prostration exclaiming: *"Quddus, Quddus! By Allah, you are the prophet whose glad tidings Prophet Musa and Isa (as) gave."*

Then he said to Lady Khadija (as): *"The great affair and profound news will be seen from him."* And he asked the Prophet if he had also been commanded Jihad to which the Prophet replied in negative. Adas said: *"You will be driven out of this town. You will be commanded Jihad, and if I survive till that time, I will fight with the infidels."*

Source:

Allama Muhammad Baqir Al-Majlisi, *Hayat al Qulub,* Vol 2: The
   Holy Prophet (S) assumes the prophetical office. *http://www.al-
   islam.org/hayat-al-qulub-vol-2-allamah-muhammad-baqir-al-
   majlisi/holy-prophet-s-assumes-prophetical-office*

Books on this topic

Background of the Birth of Islam by al-Syed Muhammad Beheshti

Beacons of Light by Abu Ali at-Tabrisi

Hayatul Qulub – Vol. 1 – Stories of the Prophets by Muhammad Baqir al-Majlisi

Infallibility by Allama Sayid Murtaza Askari

Justice, Peace and Prophet Muhammad by al-Syed Muhammad Rizvi

Life of the Prophet Mohammad before Starting the Mission by Dr. Ahmad Rahnamaei

Man and Universe by Ayatollah Murtadha Mutahhari

Meraj and the Prophet of Islam by Ayatollah Nasir Makarim Shirazi

Muhammad (S.A.W.A) is The Last Prophet by Ayatollah Sayyid Saeed Akhtar Rizvi

Muhammad in the Bible by Abdul Ahad Dawood

Muhammad [s] in the Mirror of Islam by al-Syed Muhammad Hussain Tabatabai

Muhammad and His God before the Revelation by Dr. Hatem Abu Shahba

Muhammad, Prophet of Islam by Yasin T. al-Jibouri

Muhammad, the Messenger of God by al-Syed Muhammad Rizvi

Passing Away of the Prophet by Mohammad Reza Hakimi

Pearls of Wisdom by Hussain Naghavi

Prayers of the Final Prophet by al-Syed Muhammad Hussain Tabatabai

Prophethood by Ayatollah Sayyid Saeed Akhtar Rizvi

Prophecies about the Holy Prophet of Islam in Hindu, Christian, Jewish and Parsi Scriptures by al-Syed Saeed Akhtar Rizvi

Prophet Muhammad (saws) – The Last Messenger in the Bible by Kais al-Kalby

Seal of the Prophets and His Message: Lessons on Islamic Doctrine by Sayyid Mujtaba Musavi Lari

Stories of the Prophets by Sayyed Abul Hasan Ali Nadwi

Sunan al-Nabi (saws) by al-Syed Muhammad Hussain Tatabata'i

The Character of the Holy Prophet of Islam by Ayatollah Ruhollah Khomeini

The Character of the Noble Prophet by Ayatollah Murtadha Mutahhari

The Infallibility of The Prophets In The Qur'an by Ayatollah Sayyid Saeed Akhtar Rizvi

The Influence of the Character of Prophet Muhammad (s) on the Spread of Islam during the Meccan Period by Asghar Muntazir Qaim

The Life of Muhammad – The Greatest Liberator, the Holiest Prophet by Allama Baqir Shareef al-Qurashi

The Life of Muhammad the Prophet by Ayatollah Saeed Akhtar Rizvi

The Message by Ayatollah Jafar Subhani

The Prophet Muhammad (PBUH) by Ayatollah Sayed Muhammad Shirazi

The Prophet of Islam by Ayatollah Sayed Sadiq Hussain Shirazi

The Prophets of Islam by Sayed Muhammad Hussain Shamsi

The Revealer, the Messenger, the Message by Ayatollah Sayed Baqir As-Sadr

The Unschooled Prophet (saws) by Ayatollah Murtadha Mutahhari

Who is Muhammad? by Jafar Subhani

Chapter 3

Qur'an and Ahlul Bayt (People of the Household of the Holy Prophet PBUH)

The best way to introduce the Ahlul Bayt to the world is to recall what the Holy Quran say about them. Several verses of the Holy Quran refer specifically to the virtues of the Ahlul Bayt and their outstanding position in Islam. Whenever the Holy Quran refers to the Ahlul Bayt, it refers to a specific group of people who were related to the Holy Prophet (pbuh) not only by blood, but more importantly by faith. The term Ahlul Bayt does not refer to all of the Holy Prophet's (pbuh) blood relatives. It also does not refer to his friends or his wives.

Verse of Purification

Surat al-Ahzab 33: 33

وَقَرْنَ فِي بُيُوتِكُنَّ وَلَا تَبَرَّجْنَ تَبَرُّجَ الْجَاهِلِيَّةِ الْأُولَى ۖ وَأَقِمْنَ الصَّلَاةَ وَآتِينَ الزَّكَاةَ وَأَطِعْنَ اللَّهَ وَرَسُولَهُ ۚ إِنَّمَا يُرِيدُ اللَّهُ لِيُذْهِبَ عَنكُمُ الرِّجْسَ أَهْلَ الْبَيْتِ وَيُطَهِّرَكُمْ تَطْهِيرًا

Stay in your houses
and do not display your finery
with the display of the former
[days of] ignorance.
Maintain the prayer and
pay the zakat,
and obey Allah and His Apostle.
Indeed Allah desires to repel all impurity from you,
O People of the Household,
and purify you with a thorough purification.

Note Arabic grammar in this verse:

In the Arabic language every subject, object, and particular to this verse a group of people (in this verse) is categorized by gender. In Arabic the subject or object is either 'masculine' or 'feminine'. However, when a Qur'anic verse is translated into English or other languages the Arabic sentence loses its 'specifications of gender' of the subject. For example, a 'group of people' in the English language cannot be recognized to a certain gender unless it is otherwise specified in the sentence or with a preceding sentence.

The verse 33:33 is using '2nd person feminine plural possessive pronoun' (*highlighted and underlined*) to address the wives of the Holy Prophet (pbuh). The passage continues to use a feminine plural until the last three verses where it changes the subject to the '3rd person masculine singular imperfect verb, subjunctive mood' (**Bold and Underlined**). In the last three verses it uses a 3rd person masculine which indicates that the subject of discussion in the *purification of the members of Household of the Holy Prophet (pbuh)* include male in the household; therefore, according to this verse (33:33) the "household" of the Holy Prophet (pbuh) refers to individuals other than the wives of the Holy Prophet (pbuh).

Source: The Quranic Arabic Corpus, linguistic resource http://corpus.quran.com/wordbyword.jsp?chapter=33andverse=33

In *Kutub al-Sittah* (Six Authentic Books of Ahl Sunnah:

Jami at-Tirmidhi:

Narrated by Umar bin Abi Salamah - the step-son of the Holy Prophet (pbuh):

> "When these Ayat (verse 33:33) were revealed to the Prophet (pbuh): Allah (swt) only wishes to remove the Rijs (impurities) from you, O members of the family, and to purify you with a thorough purification (33:33) in the home of Umm Salamah, the Holy Prophet (pbuh) called for Fatimah, Hassan, Husain, and wrapped him in the cloak, and Ali was behind him (pbuh), so he

wrapped him in the cloak, then he (pbuh) said: 'O Allah! These are the people of my house, so remove the Rijs (impurities) from them, and purify them with a thorough purification. So Umm Salamah said: 'and am I with them O Messenger of Allah? He said: 'You are in your place, and you are more virtuous to me."

Source: Jami at-Tirmidhi, (English version) Chapters on Tafsir, Vol. 1, Book 44, Hadith 3205. http://sunnah.com/urn/642360

Commentary by Ayatollah Agha Mahdi Puya on this verse (33:33)

When this verse was revealed, the Holy Prophet (pbuh) was under a blanket (cloak) along with Ali, Fatimah, Hassan and Hussain, and he declared that his family consisted of only these persons. Um Salamah, his wife, within whose quarters the revelation came, asked permission to be included in the group under the blanket, but she was politely refused permission. The group has been known ever since with the epithet "*panjatan pak*" or "the holy group of five". These are the persons who were compared by the Holy Prophet (pbuh) with the ark of Noah (as), wherein those who embarked were saved, while those who sought shelter elsewhere were drowned…

Abu Dawood and Malik relate from Anas that for six months after the revelation of this verse every morning, while going for Fajr Salat, the Holy Prophet (pbuh) used to recite this verse at the door of Fatimah's (sa) house.

Source: Ayatollah Agha Mahdi Puya, *Tafsir of Holy Qur'an* Surat 33, verse 33, P. 30.
http://www.islamicmobility.com/elibrary_14.htm

Hadith al-Thaqalayn *(Narration of two weighty things)*

Hadith al-Thaqalayn holds a prominent place in the School of Ahlul Bayt (as), as this hadith was narrated by the Holy Prophet (pbuh) at four prominent places:

1. At Arafat
2. At Ghadir Khumm

3. In the Mosque of Madina
4. In the Prophet's Chamber During His Last Illness

Prophet Muhammad (pbuh) said:

> *"I am leaving among you two weighty things: the one being the Book of Allah in which there is right guidance and light, so hold fast to the Book of Allah and adhere to it. He exhorted (us) (to hold fast) to the Book of Allah and then said: The second are the members of my household, I remind you (of your duties) to the members of my family."*

Source: *Sahih Muslim* (English) Book 31, Hadith 5920.
http://sunnah.com/muslim/44

Another variation:

Prophet Muhammad (pbuh) Said:

> *"I am leaving behind me two weighty things. One of them is the Book of Allah; that is the strong rope of Allah. Whosoever holds firmly to it, will be the guided, and whosoever leaves it goes astray."*

Source: *Riyadh as-Salihin,* Book 1, Hadith 346
http://sunnah.com/riyadussaliheen/1/346

Note about Hadith al-Thaqalayn: This hadith has been narrated by eight Companions of the Holy Prophet (pbuh) and eight disciples of the companions, by sixty well-known scholars and more than ninety authors from Ahle Sunnah (Sunni School of thought) including: Al-Bukhari, Al-Nasai, Ahmad Ibn Hanbal, Abu Dawood, and many others, with a total of more than **378 different sources** for this hadith; and yet no one has been able to bring up a single narration for any wives of the Holy Prophet (pbuh) that they were amongst 'Ahlul Bayt'. For the exact list of sources, please visit:

http://www.al-islam.org/hadith-al-thaqalayn-a-study-of-its-tawatur

The Verse of Malediction (Mubahilah)

Surat Ale Imran 3:61

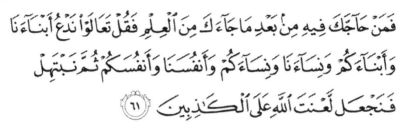

Should anyone argue
with you concerning him,
after the knowledge that
has come to you, say,
'Come! Let us call our sons
and your sons,
our women and your women,
our souls and your souls,
then let us pray earnestly and
call down Allah's curse upon the liars.'

Commentary by Ayatollah Agha Mahdi Puya on this verse

This verse refers to the well-known event of *mubahilah* mentioned in every book of history, traditions and commentary written by Muslim scholars.

The Holy Prophet (pbuh) was sending invitations to all to accept the true religion of Allah (swt). Tribes after tribes, regions after regions were coming into the fold of Islam. One such invitation was sent to the Christians of Najran, a town in Yemen, in the 9th year of Hijra. A deputation of 60 scholars came to discuss the matter with the Holy Prophet (pbuh). Abdul Masih, the chief monk, asked him as to who was the father of Jesus (as), thinking that the Holy Prophet (pbuh) would accept God as the father of Jesus (as). Verse 59 (below) of this Chapter was revealed and presented to the Christians as a reply, but they did not listen to reason.

Surat Aly Imran 3:59

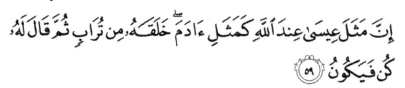

Indeed the case of Jesus
with Allah is like
the case of Adam:
He created him from dust,
then said to him,
'Be,' and he was.

Then this verse (3:61) was revealed to call them to a 'spiritual contest by invoking the curse of Allah (swt) on the liars' (*or Mubahilah in Arabic*). The Christians agreed to this contest.

Early next morning, the 24th of the month of *Dhil Hijjah*, the Holy Prophet (pbuh) sent Salman (ra) to the selected site, outside the city area, to set up a shelter for those whom he would take with him, as his sons, his women and selves.

A large number of companions assembled in the masjid, making themselves available for the selection. On the opposite side of the field, selected for the contest, the Christians, with their selected men, women and children appeared on the scene.

At the appointed hour, a huge crowd, standing in wait, saw the Holy Prophet (pbuh) coming in with Imam Hussain (as) in his arms, Imam Hassan (as) holding his index finger (*brought them as his sons*), walking beside him, Bibi Fatimah Zahra (sa) close to his heels (*brought her to represent women*), and Imam Ali (as) just behind her (*brought him to represent himself, his nafs*). It should be noted that although there was provision for "women" and "selves" [plural] the Holy Prophet (pbuh) selected one "woman" (Fatimah) and one "self" (Ali), because there were no woman and no man amongst his followers at that time who could be brought into the contest of spreading the truth and exposing the liars. They alone were the truthful ones.

The Holy Prophet (pbuh) raised his hands to the heaven and said: *"O my Lord! These are the people of my house"*. The chief Christian monk looked up and down at the faces of the Pure Five (*Panjatan Pak*), from whom emanated a radiant and brilliant glow; and this sight filled him with awe and anguish. He cried out aloud:

> *"By Jesus! I see the faces that if they turn upward to the heavens and pray, the mountains shall move. Believers in Jesus of Nazareth, I tell you the truth. Should you fail to come to some agreement with Muhammad, he, along with the Godly souls with him, shall wipe out your existence forever, should they invoke the curse of God on you."*

The Christians saw the wisdom of their chief and readily agreed to arrive at a settlement. As *'there is no compulsion in religion'* (2:256), the Holy Prophet (pbuh) gave them complete freedom to practice their faith. He also agreed to protect their lives and possessions; and for this service the Christians consented to pay a nominal fee (*Jizya*) to the Holy Prophet (pbuh). It was an extraordinary manifestation of the glory of Islam; therefore, the followers of Muhammad (pbuh) and the progeny of Muhammad (pbut) celebrate this unique blessing of Allah (bestowed on the Ahlul Bayt as) as a "Thanksgiving" occasion of great joy and comfort.

Many Muslim scholars, commentators and traditionalists whom the 'Ummah' acclaim with one voice, have given the details of this event with following conclusions:

1. The seriousness of the occasion demanded absolute purity, physical as well as spiritual, to take part in the fateful event.

2. Only the best of Allah's creations (the Ahlul Bayt as) were selected by the Holy Prophet (pbuh) under Allah's guidance.

3. This event and verse beyond all doubts, established the **purity**, the **truthfulness** and the sublime **holiness** of the Ahlul Bayt (as).

4. This event also unquestionably confirmed as to who were *the members of the family* of the Holy Prophet (pbuh).

A very large number of Muslims (and also non-Muslims) witnessed the contest and came to know that Ali, Fatimah, Hassan and Hussain (as) were the "Ahlul Bayt" mentioned in verse 33 of al Ahzab Chap 33, known as '*ayat al tathir*' or the verse of purification.

In this verse (3:61), the divine command allows the Holy Prophet (pbuh) to take with him "sons", "women" and "selves"; therefore, had there been "women" and "selves" worthy to be selected for this symbolic contest, among his companions, he would certainly have selected them. However, only Fatimah (sa) and Ali (as) (and their two sons) were chosen. It is worthwhile to ponder about why the awaiting companions (among whom were the three caliphs (Abu Bakr, Umar and Uthman) and the wives (including Ayesha and Hafsa) of the Holy Prophet pbuh) were not selected to represent him during *Mubahilah.* According to the Prophet (pbuh) there were none as **truthful** or as **purified** as to deserve selection for representing Allah's (swt) message as the Ahlul Bayt.

The word '*anfus*' is the plural of '*nafs*' which means soul or self. When used in relation to an individual, it implies another being of the same identity with complete unity in equality. Therefore, one is the true reflection of the other in thought, action and status, to the extent that at any occasion or for any purpose, any one of them can represent the other. Even if the word *nafs* is interpreted as "the people", it is clear that Ali alone is "the people" of the Holy Prophet (pbuh).

After the departure of the Holy Prophet (pbuh), within a year, the symbolic event of *Mubahilah* was ignored by some of his followers. The house of Fatimah (sa) was set on fire. Umar bin Khatab kicked the door of her house, which fell on her. The injury caused by the falling door led to her death. In view of the following saying of the Holy Prophet (pbuh) her killer stands condemned forever:

> "*Fatima is my flesh and blood, anyone who causes suffering to her, in fact causes suffering to me. He who has pained me, in fact, has pained Allah (swt); and, indeed, he is a disbeliever*", said the Holy Prophet in the light of verse 57 of al Ahzab.

Source: *Sahih Bukhari*, Book 62, Hadith 114.
http://sunnah.com/bukhari/62/114

The assault of the Prophet's daughter happened when a large crowd under the leadership of the second Caliph came to arrest Imam Ali (as), the '*nafs*' of the Holy Prophet (pbuh). Imam Ali (as) was deprived of his rightful position to represent Islam and spread the truthful message of Allah (swt.) After the death of Holy Prophet (pbuh), his absence in the world enabled some to distort and corrupt the true religion of Allah (swt) and misuse the name of Islam to enforce tyranny, injustice and ignorance that existed in the pre-Islamic age. .

The assault of Fatima (sa) was just one of the tragedies that came over the household of the Prophet (pbuh). After the Prophet had passed away, the enemies of Islam used his absence as an excuse to oppress the one's he kept protected under his cloak. Ali (as) was killed in the mosque of Kufa while he was praying before Fajr Salat. Imam Hassan (as) was killed by a deadly poison. This poison was given to him by a woman hired by Muawiyah bin Abu Sufyan. Imam Hussain (as), along with his family, friends and relatives, were killed in the desert of Karbala. The martyrdom of Husain (as) and his relatives and friends was by the army of Yazid (son of) Muawiyah. Yazid and his army held the women and children of the household of the Holy Prophet (pbuh) as captives. The Ahlul Bayt (as) were taken from town to town, tortured and harassed. The body of the martyred Imam (as) was left unburied for several days. The perpetrators of this tyranny and injustice were those who had seen with their own eyes Imam Hassan (as) and Imam Hussain (as) going to the contest with the Holy Prophet (pbuh) as his sons on the day of *Mubahilah*.

As indicated through the event of *Mubahilah*, the Ahlul Bayt (as) are representatives of the path of truth, and their enemies are the upholders of falsehood. The enemies of Islam did not only assault and martyr the Ahlul Bayt alone. But their mission was and is to destroy any follower of the true message of Islam. In present day, those who follow the true representatives of Islam as the Prophet declared *at* Mubahilah are labeled as dissenters by extremists. On this basis many *Shi'a* have been harassed, persecuted and killed by those who denied and ignored not only the *ayah al Mubahilah* and *ayah al Tathir* but also many such verses of the Qur'an and clear traditions of the Holy Prophet (pbuh). The followers of the Ahlul Bayt (as) have been suffering, death and destruction on account of their adherence to the true path, at the hands of the enemies of the Holy Prophet (pbuh) and his holy household (pbut). However, they never gave up their faith because they do not long for worldly possessions or fear death. Their main desire is to follow the true message of Allah (swt) as was sent by Allah (swt), given to the Prophet (pbuh) and represented by the Ahlul Bayt (as).

Source: Ayatollah Agha Mahdi Puya, _Tafsir of Holy Qur'an_ Surat 3, verse 61, P. 283-289.

_http://www.islamicmobility.com/elibrary_14.htm_

Love Prophet Muhammad's (pbuh) Relatives

Surat al Shura 42:23

ذَٰلِكَ ٱلَّذِى يُبَشِّرُ ٱللَّهُ عِبَادَهُ ٱلَّذِينَ ءَامَنُوا۟ وَعَمِلُوا۟ ٱلصَّٰلِحَٰتِ قُل لَّآ أَسْـَٔلُكُمْ عَلَيْهِ أَجْرًا إِلَّا ٱلْمَوَدَّةَ فِى ٱلْقُرْبَىٰ وَمَن يَقْتَرِفْ حَسَنَةً نَّزِدْ لَهُۥ فِيهَا حُسْنًا إِنَّ ٱللَّهَ غَفُورٌ شَكُورٌ ﴿٢٣﴾

That is the good news
Allah gives to His servants
who have faith
and do righteous deeds!
Say, 'I do not ask you any
reward for it except love of [my] relatives.'
Whoever performs a good deed,
We shall enhance for
him its goodness.
Indeed Allah is all-forgiving, all-appreciative.

Commentary by Ayatollah Agha Mahdi Puya on this verse:

This verse commands the Muslims to love the Ahlul Bayt if they want to repay the Holy Prophet (pbuh) for his service of Prophethood, so that they should follow the Ahlul Bayt in word and action, because they have been thoroughly purified by Allah (swt) Himself, they are the truth, they are the custodians of the word of Allah (swt), they alone know the true interpretation of the holy Qur'an.

From the beginning to the end of their lives, every member of the Ahlul Bayt (as) had presented an ideal Islamic pattern of life, not equaled by any among the followers of the Holy Prophet, therefore love and devotion to them was ordained to provide the highest form of guidance to mankind. Unless one loves and follows the Ahlul Bayt (as), one cannot sincerely avail of the guidance offered by the Holy Prophet (pbuh).   Love implies sincere attachment, which must manifest in every thought and deed.

Imam Jafar as Sadiq (as) said:

> *"He who obeys Allah's commands is our devotee; and he who disobeys His commands is our enemy."*

'*Qurba*' means nearness, whereas '*Fil qurba*' means for the sake of nearness. The unanimous traditions of utmost authenticity assert that nearness to the Holy Prophet (pbuh) means love for his relatives, who were nearest to him in excellence and accomplishments. So, when he (pbuh) was asked to point out his relatives, he pronounced the names of Ali (as), Fatimah (sa), Hassan (as) and Hussain (as) and their children. There is not a single tradition of the Holy Prophet (pbuh) that referees '*qurba*' to the relatives of the Quraysh, or the relationship of the Holy Prophet (pbuh) with the Quraysh or the relatives of the believers, or being Arabs, etc. as concocted by the anti-Ahlul Bayt (as) commentators. The structure of the verse proves that the Holy Prophet (pbuh) has been commanded to demand recompense, as an exception, not from everyone, but from those '*believers*' "*who take the way to their Lord*" mentioned in:

Surat al Furqan 25:57

قُل مَّا أَسْتَلُكُمْ عَلَيْهِ مِنْ أَجْرٍ إِلَّا مَن شَآءَ أَن يَتَّخِذَ إِلَىٰ رَبِّهِ
سَبِيلًا ﴿٥٧﴾

*Say, 'I do not ask you any reward for it, except that anyone who wishes should **take the way to his Lord.***

The recompense is in the interest of the believers themselves, not in any way profitable to the Holy Prophet (pbuh) in his personal life. Instead of *'arham'* (the blood relatives), *'Fil qurba'* (for the sake of nearness) has been used to show that not only relationship, but also nearness in character and accomplishment is taken into consideration as the most important quality. So, on the basis of this verse, love of the Ahlul Bayt (as) has become an obligatory function of the faith, a fundamental condition without which no amount of devotion to Allah (swt) and good deeds will be of any use.

Source: Ayatollah Agha Mahdi Puya, *Tafsir of Holy Qur'an* Surat 42, verse 23, P. 17-18.
   http://www.islamicmobility.com/elibrary_14.htm

It has been narrated that the Abbasid caliph Harun al-Rashid asked the seventh Imam of the school of Ahlul Bayt (as), Imam Musa Ibn Jafar (as) how he could attribute himself to the Holy Prophet (pbuh) while he was the descendent of Ali (as) and Lady Fatima (sa); how could he be related to the Holy Prophet? The Imam then cited to him in verses 84-85 of Surat al An'am that refers to the descendants of Prophet Ibrahim (as) as follows:

Surat al An'am, 6:84-85

وَوَهَبْنَا لَهُ إِسْحَٰقَ وَيَعْقُوبَ كُلًّا هَدَيْنَا وَنُوحًا هَدَيْنَا
مِن قَبْلُ وَمِن ذُرِّيَّتِهِ دَاوُدَ وَسُلَيْمَٰنَ وَأَيُّوبَ وَيُوسُفَ
وَمُوسَىٰ وَهَٰرُونَ وَكَذَٰلِكَ نَجْزِى ٱلْمُحْسِنِينَ ﴿٨٤﴾

84 And We gave him Isaac and Jacob and guided each of them.

And Noah We had guided before, and from his offspring, David and

Solomon, Job, Joseph, Moses and Aaron thus do We reward the virtuous

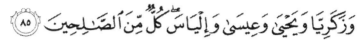

85 and Zechariah, John, Jesus and Ilyas, each of them among the righteous.

The Imam (as) then asked the caliph who is the father of Isa (Jesus)? Harun answered that he was fatherless. The Imam (as) replied, *"Then you can see that Allah (swt) linked him to Ibrahim (as) through his mother, Mariam (as) and Allah did the same for us, linking us to Prophet Muhammad (pbuh) through our mother Lady Fatima al-Zahra (sa)."*

In many instances, the Holy Prophet (pbuh) refers to Lady Fatima (sa) with intense love and affection, such as when he says, *"Fatima is a part of me. Her happiness is my happiness, and her pain is my pain."* The Holy Prophet (pbuh) would also point towards the children of Fatima (sa), Hassan and Hussain (as) and say on many occasions, *"These are my sons,"* and *"This is my son."* That is why the community of the companions in Medina would refer to both Hassan (as) and Hussain (as), as the 'sons of Prophet Mohammad (pbuh)'.

Source: Sayed Moustafa al-Qazwini (2005), *Inquiries About Shi'a Islam* (Second Edition) P. 42

The verses about feeding the poor, the orphan, and the prisoner

Surat Al-Insan 76:5-13

إِنَّ ٱلْأَبْرَارَ يَشْرَبُونَ مِن كَأْسٍ كَانَ مِزَاجُهَا كَافُورًا ﴿٥﴾

5 Indeed the pious will drink from a cup seasoned with Ka'fur

عَيْنَا يَشْرَبُ بِهَا عِبَادُ اللَّهِ يُفَجِّرُونَهَا تَفْجِيرًا ﴿٦﴾

6 a spring where the servants of Allah drink, which they make to gush forth as they please.

يُوفُونَ بِالنَّذْرِ وَيَخَافُونَ يَوْمًا كَانَ شَرُّهُ مُسْتَطِيرًا ﴿٧﴾

7 They fulfill their vows and fear a day whose ill will be widespread.

وَيُطْعِمُونَ الطَّعَامَ عَلَى حُبِّهِ مِسْكِينًا وَيَتِيمًا وَأَسِيرًا ﴿٨﴾

8 They give food, for the love of Him, to the needy, the orphan and the prisoner,

إِنَّمَا نُطْعِمُكُمْ لِوَجْهِ اللَّهِ لَا نُرِيدُ مِنكُمْ جَزَاءً وَلَا شُكُورًا ﴿٩﴾

9 [saying,] 'We feed you only for the sake of Allah. We do not want any reward from you nor any thanks.

إِنَّا نَخَافُ مِن رَّبِّنَا يَوْمًا عَبُوسًا قَمْطَرِيرًا ﴿١٠﴾

10 Indeed we fear from our Lord a day, frowning and fateful.'

فَوَقَاهُمُ اللَّهُ شَرَّ ذَٰلِكَ الْيَوْمِ وَلَقَّاهُمْ نَضْرَةً وَسُرُورًا ﴿١١﴾

11 So Allah saved them from the ills of that day, and granted them freshness and joy.

وَجَزَاهُم بِمَا صَبَرُوا جَنَّةً وَحَرِيرًا ﴿١٢﴾

12 And He rewarded them for their patience with a garden and [garments of] silk,

مُّتَّكِئِينَ فِيهَا عَلَى الْأَرَائِكِ لَا يَرَوْنَ فِيهَا شَمْسًا وَلَا زَمْهَرِيرًا ﴿١٣﴾

13 reclining therein on couches. They will find in it neither any [scorching] sun, nor any [biting] cold.

This Chapter 76, Surat Al-Insan in the Holy Quran descended to honor a sacred gesture performed by the Ahlul Bayt (as). Allah (swt) entitled this chapter, Mankind to draw attention of the people to the beauty of mankind's deeds on earth, and to tell them that they should not be selfish or greedy. Rather, they should be caring and thoughtful people who spend their time thinking of other human beings around them. The chapter begins:

$$ هَلْ أَتَى عَلَى ٱلْإِنسَنِ حِينٌ مِّنَ ٱلدَّهْرِ لَمْ يَكُن شَيْئًا مَّذْكُورًا ﴿١﴾ $$

1 Has there been for man a period of time
when he was not anything worthy of mention?

$$ إِنَّا خَلَقْنَا ٱلْإِنسَنَ مِن نُّطْفَةٍ أَمْشَاجٍ نَّبْتَلِيهِ فَجَعَلْنَهُ سَمِيعًا بَصِيرًا ﴿٢﴾ $$

2 Indeed We created man
from the drop of a mixed fluid so that We may test him.
So We made him endowed with hearing and sight.

$$ إِنَّا هَدَيْنَهُ ٱلسَّبِيلَ إِمَّا شَاكِرًا وَإِمَّا كَفُورًا ﴿٣﴾ $$

3 Indeed We have guided him to the way,
be he grateful or ungrateful.

This introduction prepares our minds for the sacrifice of the Family of the Holy Prophet (pbuh).

One morning Fatimah Zahra (sa) found out that both her sons (Imam Hassan and Imam Hussain) were ill. Then the Holy Prophet (pbuh) came to see them and advised Ali (as) and Fatimah (sa) to make a covenant (*Nazr*) to Allah (swt) that they would observe fasts for three consecutive days if their sons got well. Soon they returned to normal health; so Ali (as), Fatimah (as), Hassan (as), Hussain (as) and Fizza (ra) fasted for three successive days. Each day a different person came at about the time of breaking the fast and knocked at the door. The first day a person came and said:

"O Ahlul Bayt of the messenger (pbuh) of Allah (swt), I am a poor man. I am hungry Give me something to eat."

All that was there to eat was given away to him. All of them used water to break their fasts and went to sleep without food.

The second day a person came and said:

"O Ahlul Bayt of the messenger (pbuh) of Allah (swt), my parents are dead. I am a destitute. Will you satisfy my hunger?"

All that was there to eat was given away to him. All of them used water to break their fasts and went to sleep without food.

The third day a person came and said:

"O Ahlul Bayt of the messenger (pbuh) of Allah (swt), I am a just-now-freed slave. Give me some food."

All that was there to eat was given away to him. All of them used water to break their fasts and went to sleep without food.

After completion of three fasts, Lady Fatimah (sa) offered prayers of thankfulness to Allah (swt); and then the Holy Prophet (pbuh) informed her that Jibrail had brought the above mentioned verses in their praise.

Source:

Sayed Moustafa al-Qazwini (2005), *Inquiries About Shi'a Islam* (Second Edition) P. 49

Ayatollah Agha Mahdi Puya, *Tafsir of Holy Qur'an* Surat 76, verse 5-13, P. 29-30. http://www.islamicmobility.com/elibrary_14.htm

End of Chapter notes

Fourteen narrations of the Fourteen infallibles

From *'Fascinating discourses of Fourteen Infallibles (as)'* by Muhammad Muhammadi Eshtehardi

Sayings of Prophet Muhammad (pbuh):

1. The worst of all men is the one who sells his hereafter (dooms day) for his world (life), and worse than him is the one who sells (bargains) his resurrection day for the world (benefits) of the others.

2. Indeed, there are ten signs of the pious. 1. He makes friend for the sake of Allah (pleasure). 2. He makes enemy for the Almighty Allah. 3. He enters companionship for Allah. 4. He gets separated for Allah. 5. He becomes angry for the sake of Allah. 6. He gets happy for Allah. 7. He acts for the sake of lord. 8. He asks Allah for the fulfillment of his need. 9. He shows humility and humbleness for Allah, whereas, he possesses the virtues of fear from Almighty and has sincerity modesty, vigilance and carefulness. 10. He performs good deeds for Allah.

3. One who starts a morning in a condition that he does not make effort about the affairs of the Muslims is not one of the Muslims. And a person who hears the voice of a man who calls the Muslims to his help but he does not respond him, is not a Muslim.

4. The Prophet of Islam (pbuh) sent a group of Muslims to the battle front against the enemies. When they returned to the court of Apostle of Allah he said to them, 'Well done, bravo, the group who performed the small jihad (holy war) and the big jihad has (yet) to be performed by them.' They said 'oh Prophet of Allah what is the great jihad?'
    The Prophet replied, 'jihad and war against the passions. (Of ego).'

5. When the innovations and heretical practices become evident in my ummah it is necessary for the scholar to make his knowledge manifested and open (with regards to making the innovations public) so, curse of Allah be upon the scholar who does not do it.

6. There is a good deed above each good deed, to the extent that a man is slain on the way of Allah. So when he is slain on the way of Allah then there is no good deed above (better than) it.

7. Cursed is the one who puts the load of his life responsibilities upon the shoulders of the people.

8. A time will come upon my ummah so that people will not recognize the scholar but those wearing beautiful dress, and will not recognize the Quran but when recited in a melodious tone and will not serve Allah except in the month of Ramadan. So when the condition of people will become such, Allah will appoint and set a ruler over them who shall not have knowledge, forbearance and mercy.

9. Oh community of Muslims! Definitely avoid committing adultery because it has six peculiarities three (will emerge) in this world and three in the hereafter. Moreover, those three which appear in this world (consist of): 1.This becomes the cause of getting dishonored. 2. Causes to bring poverty. 3. Causes the shortening of age.
    And those which take place in the hereafter are: 1. It causes the anger of Allah. 2. It causes the severances and graveness of accounting. 3. It causes the eternity and perpetuity (of man) in the hell fire.

10. The example of my house hold (Hazrat Zahra (sa)) and the twelve Imams (as)) is like that of Noah's (as) ship. Who so ever boards it will get rescued (salvation) and the one who opposes the boarding of it, gets drowned.

11. Oh Abu Dhar! Do value and esteem five things before five others (to happen). 1. Your youth before your old age. 2. Your health before your ailment. 3. Your wealth before your poverty.4. Your leisure time before getting busy. 5. Your life before your death.

12. Drinker is similar to the idolater. Oh Ali Allah does not accept the service of the drinker (up to) forty days. And if he dies with in forty days, he has died as an infidel.

13. I am the city of knowledge and Ali is its gate so who so ever intends to acquire knowledge must come through the gate.

14. Oh people! I have left among you something which if you get (hold of) it, you will not go astray: The book of Allah (Quran) and my progeny, household.

Sayings of Imam Ali Ibn Abi Talib (as):

1. The one who recognized himself (self-cognition) has recognized his Allah.

2. Indeed, Allah raised Muhammad (pbuh) upon the righteousness so that he may move His servants out of the (state of) adoration of servants towards His own adoration, and from the commitment of His slaves towards His own commitment and from the obedience of His slaves towards His own obedience and from the guardian ship of his servants to His own guardian ship.

3. The worth of all the men is in the good deeds that they perform.

4. The one who is pleased and satisfied with the deed of a nation (group) is like the one who has shared that with it. And for all those entering into a falsehood there are two sins; the sin of practice and the sin of being pleased with it.

5. Ali (as) was questioned about faith. So he replied: Faith rests upon four pillars.
   1. Patience 2. Certitude 3. Justice 4. Jihad (holy war). And patience out of those, has four branches. (i) Keenness and eagerness (ii) fear (iii) Piety (iv) wait.
   The one who is keen and eager for Heaven steps aside the passionate temptations and the one who has the fear of hell fire abstains and refrains from the forbidden deeds and the one who has asceticism in the world takes the calamities and anguishes (of life) easy and the person who is looking forward to and waiting for death makes haste and hurry towards the good deeds.

And Jihad (holy war) is based upon four branches.
  1. The ordering of good deeds.
  2. Stopping from the bad deeds.
  3. Truthfulness on the battle front of struggle and combat.
  4. The enmity with transgressors.
The one who orders the good deeds strengthens the backs of faithful. And the one who stops people from bad deeds has rubbed the noses of the infidels upon dust (belittled and weakened them). And the one who truth fully stands up in the battle field has discharged an obligatory practice. And the one who gets enraged and furious with the transgressors and gets angry for Allah, Allah too becomes enraged and angry for his sake and will please him on the resurrection day.

6. So indeed, Jihad (holy war) is a door out of the doors of Heaven. Allah has opened it upon His special friends (saints). And that (Jihad) is the dress of piety and the firm and securing armored Jacket of Allah and His dependable shield and the one who abandons it because of being uninclined to it, Allah makes him put on the dress of humility.

7. Indeed, the erupting of sedition and iniquity is due to the following of lustful desires and the artificial laws and rules, those orders and laws which are against the book of Allah. And a group of men stands up to defend those as against the religion and constitution of Allah. If falsehood had completely segregated from the righteousness, it would not have remained concealed and hidden from those who are in the search of truth. And if the righteousness had been purified from the falsehood the tongues of the enemies and rivals would have shortened from it. But they fetch a piece of right and a piece and part of falsehood and mix them up. This is where Satan overwhelms his friends. And only those who are the object of the beneficence of Allah get salvation.

8. Indeed the religion of Allah is not identified through persons; instead, it is recognized by the sign of Rights. Therefore, do identify the right so as to identify people of the right.

9. Do not be the slave of another person, since; Allah has made you a free person.

10. Verily, ordering the good deed and stopping from the evil doings do neither draw the death closer nor diminishes and decreases the sustenance. Instead these increase the reward and turn it into a great one.

And the superior of the two is uttering the word of justice before the tyrant and oppressive ruler.

11. An ardent (honorable) one never at all commits adultery.

12. The world's example is that of a snake which is soft to touch but it has a perilous poison in its body cavity. The ignorant one forms an attachment with it but the sage and sane person guards himself from it.

13. I recommend you five things for obtaining which if you have to move around on the camel backs in the deserts even then it is worthwhile and befitting.
    I.   Do not have hope in anyone except Allah.
    II.   Do not be afraid of anything except your sins.
    III.   If one of you is questioned about something which he does not know. He must not be shy and must say I do not know.
    IV.   When one of you does not know a thing he must not feel shame and shy in learning it.
    V.   Exercise patience and forbearance in every work, since, the patience does not have any example with regards to faith except that of body with the head. The body without head does not have any good and beneficence, (similarly) faith without patience does not have any beneficence in it.

14. What has the son of Adam (as) got to do with pride (since) he begins as a semen and ends as a corpse? (Both being unclean dirt and contamination).

Sayings of Lady Fatimah al Zahra (sa)

1. Praise and Eulogy Is for Allah for the blessing and bounties, which He has bestowed. And thanks to Him upon what He revealed (to His servants) And Praise Is for Him upon the common boons and blessings which He bestowed upon His servants without their request and upon the comprehensive and complete blessings which He granted to all and sundry and gave It to us, consecutively. Those graces and favors, which are uncountable.

   And are Irredeemable and not compensable due to their plentiful-ness of number. And the Imagination of their end is out of the reach of human mind. He invited the servant to thankfulness for the sake of the consecutive and continuous enhancement of blessings. And opened the door of eulogy and Praise (of Allah) upon them so that He may make his favors and beneficences great and plentiful for them.

2. 'Oh Allah! Belittle me in my eyes and glorify and magnify your station to me. And inspire me (about) Your obedience and the practice which may cause Your pleasure and the shunning and evading from things (matters) which are the cause of Your wrath, oh the most merciful of all!'

3. I testify that there is no Deity (Lord) except the sole and matchless Allah. And testify of the singleness of Allah is a word that Allah has declared sincerity (as) its reality, and made the hearts the center of its contact and union. And has made the specifications and research of the oneness of Allah's station obvious and evident in the light of meditation. The Allah Who cannot be seen by the eyes and tongues are unable and baffled to describe His virtues and attributes. And the intelligence and apprehension of man is helpless and destitute from the imagination of his lowness.

4. Allah made all the beings without previous matter, sample, shape and pattern; and made them wear the dress of life by His main and might, and created them according to His divine will and intention, short of it that He might have needed their creation, or have wished any benefit for Himself from their shaping and sketching, except this that he wanted to give a proof of His wisdom and make the people (creations) aware about His obedience and submission, and Invited them to his servitude and worship and make His Invitation grand and ostentatious.

5. Allah fixed the reward for His obedience and torment for His Insubordination and disobedience, so that He may restrain His servants from His wrath and fury and lead them to His paradise.

6. And I testify that my father Muhammad (pbuh) is the apostle and the servant of Allah. And Allah' selected and chose him before appointing him at the post of Prophethood. And He named him before choosing and selecting him. And chose him before everything and delegating him. Then all the creations were hidden and covered in the covers of unseen and were hidden amid the screen and curtain of fear and fright and stayed near the last and final border of non-entity (nothingness), for, Allah was aware of and knew the end of matters and because of His encompassing the incidents of times and ages, and His knowledge of the predestinates.

Allah appointed him (as apostle) so that he may complete all His matter and Implement His order and materialize His decrees and predestinates.

7. Allah saw nations and groups had various different sects in their religion and scattered and staying on the verge of the fires of differences, busy with their idol worshipping. They denied God with all the signs and symbols of him. (Irfan) So Allah illuminated the darkness's through my father Muhammad (pbuh) and removed the darkness's from their hearts, removed (cured) the blindness of the eyes.

8. My father Muhammad (pbuh) stood up with (his) guidance among the people. And saved them from perversion and aberration, and turned their blindness into enlightenment and guided them towards the firm religion. And called (invited) them to the straight way.

9. You the servants of Allah, are the ones to maintain His injunctions and prohibitions, and the carriers of His religion, and His revelation, and the trustees of Allah upon your souls, and the propagators of His religion among the other nations.

10. Oh the servants of Allah! (Beware) the real leader from Allah, is present among you and the commitment has previously been made to you and the remaining and left over of the prophet hood has been appointed for your guidance. That is the speaking book of Allah the truthful Quran, and a beaming and gleaming light, in which all the secrets and facts about the completion of man and his prosperity have been exhibited and illuminated. It guides from darkness towards light of guidance. Its followers are the subject of envoy of others.

11. The book of Allah is the guide of its followers towards the pleasure of Allah. Listening (carefully) to it leads to the salvation. The enlightened and conspicuous evidences and proofs of Allah can be obtained through it. And (also the knowledge) of His interpreted intentions and fear invoking constraining prohibitions and His sufficing testimonies and conspicuous arguments, and desired virtues and allowed endowments and gifts and obligatory divine laws. (Can be obtained from it).

12. And (Allah made) the kindness to parents as a protection (shield) to His wrath and displeasure.

13. And (Allah rendered) prohibition from drinking wine the cause of taking

distance from contaminations, (evils).

14. And Allah prohibited polytheism for the sake of (bringing about) sincerity in (His) adoration and worship.

Sayings of Imam Hassan Ibn Ali (as)

1. Praise and Eulogy is for Allah who hears the conversation of who so ever talks and if he remains silent (then) He knows whatever is there in his interior (soul). And who ever lives, his sustenance is upon Allah and who so ever dies his resurrection is with Allah.

2. Oh my son! Do not become the companion of anyone (and don't befriend) but when you come to know about the places he comes and goes to (visits). And after you have minutely observed (his character) and got pleased with his association and social conduct then acquire his company, on the basis of forgiving the faults and (extending) consolation during the hardships.

3. The most sighting eye is the one which penetrates (views) into the blessings and beneficences, and the most auditory ear is the one which takes in (comprehends and retains) admonition, and gets benefitted by it. The healthiest of hearts is the heart which is pure from doubts.

4. A person asked him "what is fear?' He said, 'to have courage upon friend and recoiling from the enemy.

5. Do not make haste in punishing the sinner for his sin and let a way (passage) between the two (fault and punishment) excuse and apology.

6. All the beneficences of both the worlds come to the hand and are achieved by the mind (wits).

7. There is no poverty like the ignorance.

8. Teach others your knowledge and learn the knowledge of others so you will bring your knowledge to perfection and learn something, which you do not know.

9. A person asked him, 'What is generosity and magnanimity' He replied, 'To secure and protect the religion, and respecting one's soul, (self-respect) and softness of conduct (gentleness in behavior) and permanency of favor and kindness and the discharging of rights

10. Nice conduct and behavior with people is the height of intelligence and wits.

11. There is a distance of four fingers between the rights and false hood (eyes and ears). What you saw with your eyes that is right. And you have heard plenty number of false and untrue things through your ears.

12. Ignorant is the one who is foolish about his wealth. (Regarding spending it). Who is slack and negligent about his honor, when he is abused and reviled, he does not respond.

13. The annihilation of people lies in three things Arrogance, and greed and jealousy.

14. And know it that indeed whoever fears Allah (adopts piety) Allah paves his way of salvation out of the inequities. And makes him firm in his matter. And provides him (the path of) guidance. And makes his proof and arguments successful and enlightens his face and grants him what he desires. He is with those upon whom Allah has bestowed His beneficences and boons from among the Prophets and the truthful and the martyrs and pious ones.

Saying of Imam Hussain Ibn Ali (as)

1. Blind be the eye which does not see you (O Allah swt) (Whereas) you are observing him.

2. None is in peace on the resurrection day except the one who fears Allah in the world.

3. Allah, firstly mentioned, 'command for good and forbid to do evil' as one of His obligatory services, since, He knew that if these two obligatory are performed and established, all the obligatory services out of easy and hard will get performed and established. Because, 'command for good and forbid to do evil' invites to Islam, along with giving out the right of those having right and opposing of the tyrants and oppressors.

4. I do not see (consider) death except prosperity and do not consider life along with oppressors and tyrants except affliction and anguish.

5. If you do not have religion and you are not afraid of the resurrection day then be free in your world.

6. A group worships Allah for the avidity (reward of paradise) this is the service of traders and a group worships Allah due to fear (from hell and the torment of Allah) this is the service of slaves (who obey their masters being afraid of them). And a group worships Allah as thanksgiving, so this is the service of free men and is the superior most service.

7. I have not stood up upon the incentive and provocation of self-conceit and arrogance and not as a chaos creator and oppressor and indeed I have come out (stood up) wishing the rectification of my grandfather Mohammed (S) ummah. I want to order the good deed and forbid the evil and put into practice the character and morale of my grandfather Muhammad (S) and father Ali Ibn Abi Talib (as)

8. The intellect does not achieve completion except by observance and following of the right.

9. Weeping for the fear of Allah is (causes) salvation from the fire (Hell).

10. Take care, not to do anything for which you have to apologize. Because the faithful does not commit wrong (sin) and does not apologize and the hypocrite commits sin all the days and (then) extends apologies.

11. It is from the signs of ignorance to enter into dispute with those not having thought and meditation.

12. Emulate and compete each other in achieving the human values and rush and hasten to get the spiritual treasures.

13. Most generous of the people is the one who grants to the person who does not have any expectation from him

14. One who removes an anguish and sorrow of a faithful, Allah grants him the deliverance from the sorrows and dejections of world and the hereafter.

Saying of Imam Ali Ibn Hussain Zain al Abideen (as)

1. Indeed, the inner knowledge and gnosis and the zenith of the religion of a Muslim is abandoning such talk which is meaningless and futile, and the scarcity of his dispute and argument, and his forbearance and his patience and fortitude and his politeness and good conduct.

2. (Oh people) contemplate, meditate, and practice for the (place, thing) that you have been created for, Allah did not at all create you in vain and useless.

3. There is no drop which is dearer to Allah more than two drops: The drop of blood (which drips out) on the course of Allah (Jihad) and the drop of tear in the darkness of night by which a servant does not want anything except (pleasing and loving) Allah.

4. There are three (things), which are refuges and shelters for a faithful; to refrain his tongue from the people and their back biting, and keeping himself busy with things (matters) which are beneficial for his futurity, here after and the world; protracted and lengthy weeping upon his sin.

5. The assemblies of the pious men are the invitations to righteousness and piety

6. If people knew what (brilliant result) lies in seeking knowledge they would have definitely sought it even by shedding the blood of their hearts and plunging into the depth of oceans.

7. Guard against lies, both small of it and big, in all conditions, both in seriousness and joke.

8. And the sins which are the cause of rejection of prayers are: (1) Bad intention and (2) the wickedness of interior and (3) hypocrisy with the (religious) brothers and (4) disbelieving in the prayers being granted and

(5) delaying the obligatory services till their time is passed. and (6) abandoning the achievement of proximity of Allah through favor (to people) and alm giving and (7) using obscene language and abusing during conversation.

9.   There is nothing dearer and lovelier to Allah, following His cognition, than the modesty and purity of belly and the private parts (of human body).

10. The person whose soul is worthy and respectable in his eyes, the world is humble and despised in his view.

11. The best keys to the matters is truth and the best termination and finalization of the matters is faithfulness, loyalty and fidelity.

12. Be careful, about committing sin along with joy (avoid it) since the felicity of committing sin is itself a bigger sin (than the actual sin).

13. The sins and transgressions which become the reason and cause for the changing and termination of benediction and beneficence's are:
     (1) Oppression and wrongs to the people (2) Abandoning the piety and ordering the good deed (3) and ingratitude for beneficence and favor and (4) discontinuing thank giving.

14. The one who has the fear of (Hell) fire hastens and rushes away from sin with repentance towards Allah, and reverts back and refrains from (committing) forbidden acts.

Saying of Imam Muhammad Ibn Ali al Baqir (as)

1.   Islam is founded and based upon five things the maintaining of services and the giving out of alms and the Hajj of the House of Allah (kaabah) and the fasting of Ramadan month and the guardian ship of us the Ahle bait (Household of the Prophet (S)) So in four of those there exists excuse (leave and permission) But in (accepting and believing) guardianship no room for excuse or allowance has been given. And for the person who does not possess wealth, there exists no Zakat (alms giving) and the one who is devoid of wealth, does not have to perform Hajj.

And the one who is ill offers his prayers sitting and may not observe fast. Nonetheless, the guardianships is binding and obligatory while he is healthy or ill or whether he is rich and wealthy or possessing no wealth.

2. The obedience of Imam following His recognition is the loftiest apex and peak and the most worthy of stations and the key to the religion, and gate way and door to the affairs and pleasure of the merciful (Allah). Moreover, if a man keeps standing whole night for prayers and keeps on fasting during the day and gives out all his wealth as alms and perform Hajj all the years of his life and does not recognize the guardianship of the saint of Allah so as to love him and perform all his practices under his guidance and leadership, he does not have any right out of His rewards and he is not from among the faithfuls.

3. The person who loves for the sake of Allah and detests and despises for the sake of Allah and gives for the sake of Allah is among those whose faith has achieved completion.

4. Indeed faithful is the one who when pleased and glad his pleasure does not make him enter into sin and falsehood (He does not commit any sin while happy). And when unhappy and angry his anger does not oust him from the word of righteousness. (He does not abandon the right course) And when he gains power his power does not make him commit excess and oppression and make him go for a thing upon which he does not have any right.

5. Indeed, when a man earns the wealth from Haram (prohibited) sources, no Hajj and no umrah and no strengthening of his blood kinship is never at all accepted and approved. (By Almighty God).

6. The completion, entire completion of a man lies in understanding and appreciating the religion (the necessary laws of and principles of jurisprudence), the patience and forbearance upon the occurrence of incidents and the appraisement and assessment of (his) economy.

7. There are three things out of the completions and worth's and values of the world and thereafter: 1. forgiving the one who has committed excess and aggression against you. 2. Joining the one who cuts off relations and ties with you. 3. Forbearance and tolerance for the one who committed a folly and showed insane behavior and conduct towards you.

8. Allah dislikes and hates the importunately soliciting and urging of men to the other men for some problems (needs, wants, desires) and He approves and loves it for Himself.

9. I recommend you to have five virtues. 1. If you have undergone oppression and tyranny, you do not oppress. 2. If a dishonesty has been committed with you, do not commit dishonesty. 3. If you have been falsified and contradicted do not get annoyed and vexed. 4. If you have been praised do not get pleased and glad. 5. And if you are vilified and disparaged do not be impatient and apprehensive.
    And do contemplate and ponder about what is said about you. So if you observe and come to know about something which exists in you (vice) then do know that to lose your honor and falling down in Allah's view for a right and just thing is much more of a greater and graver calamity than losing respect in the eyes of people. And if your condition is contrary to what has been said about you, then you have earned a reward and recompense short of any physical strain.

10. Certainly, Allah grants this material world to the one whom he loves and the one whom he despises. And he does not bestow his religion to anyone except whom He loves.

11. Beware! Caution! Do not acquire enmity because it rotten and turns the heart evil and causes to develop hypocrisy.

12. Indeed, the most terrifically sorry of all the people on the resurrection day will be the servant who defines and shows the way of justice to the people and himself opposes it.

13. The ugliest and most evil of the earnings is the gaining of interest.

14. If people come to know what (evil) lies in begging, No one will beg from the other and if the one who is begged from knows the evil of rejecting the one who begs, nobody will turn down anyone's request.

Saying of Imam Jafar Ibn Muhammad al Sadiq (as)

1. Nothing follows a person after his death except three virtues and qualities.

(1) The alms and charity that he may have executed by the grace of Allah in his life and which continues on after his death. (i.e.) (Like schools, hospitals, social welfare institutions, books, wells, bridges, roads etc.) (2) And a decent and good tradition (left over by him) which is put into practice (after his death). (3) A pious son who prays for him.

2. Some of the rights of a Muslim upon his Muslim brother are that he salutes him when he meets him. And visits him when he becomes ill, and when he is absent he wishes him his benevolence and beneficence i.e., defends him in his absence). and prays for him when he seeks, saying God take pity on you and accepts his invitation when he invites him and escorts his funeral when he dies.'

3. The Muslims' right upon (another) Muslim is that he must not be full and satiated and his brother remains hungry. And he must not get his thirst quenched and his brother remains thirsty. And he must not dress himself up when his brother is naked. So how great and exuberant is the right of a Muslim upon his Muslim brother. And he (as) said do wish for your Muslim brother the same which you want for yourself.

4. The most beloved of the brothers to me is the one who presents and indicates to me my faults and short comings.

5. Be kind and affectionate to your fathers (ancestors) your sons will treat you kindly and nicely and exhibit (be) modest to the women of other (people) they will treat your woman with modesty and chastity.

6. The one who is pious in the world, Allah places wisdom in his heart and makes his tongue reproduce it (He utters the words of wisdom). And makes him aware and knowledgeable about the faults and short comings of the world and its diseases and ailments and their cures. And transfers him out of the world in a pure and perfect condition toward the house of peace (i.e. the next world).

7. The smallest thing which turns a man out of faith (renders him faithless) is that he keeps counting the faults and lapse missteps of his brother in faith so that one day he may reprimand him.

8. It is from the disposition and manners of the ignorant that he answers before listening, and quarrels before understanding and gives judgment upon what he is unaware of.

9. Indeed when the sin is committed by a servant secretly, it does not harm but the one who commits it. Whereas, if it is committed openly and conspicuously and a restraints is not put upon it then it harms the general public.

10. A man does not become proud hearted and arrogant but for the self-abjection which he finds in his soul.

11. Two units of service offered by a married person is superior to seventy cycles of service offered by an unmarried one.

12. Toiling and laboring hard for one's family (wife and children and dependent) is like becoming the warrior of a holy war on the course of Allah.

13. Our intercession and mediation will not be won and attained by that person who depreciates and undervalues the Salat (namaz/daily prayers).

14. It is required for the faithful to have eight qualities in him.
    (1) being gracious during the hardship and calamities. (2) Being patient in wake of affliction. (3). being thankful at the time of comfort and abundance. (4) Being contented with sustenance granted by Allah. (5) Not committing excess and aggression upon enemies. (6) Not loading his own load (responsibilities) upon the shoulders of his friends. (7) His body remains troubled by him (due to services), and (8) The people remain comfortable and at ease from him. (He does not bother and trouble others).

Saying of Imam Musa Ibn Jafar al Kadhim (as)

1. I found the knowledge of people in four (things) firstly, that you know your lord (recognition of Allah) and secondly that you know it as to what factors He made use of in creating you, and thirdly that you know as to what does he want and intend from you and fourthly that you learn what is it that will expel you from your religion.

2. Indeed, there are two arguments and proofs from Allah for the people.
    I. The conspicuous and apparent arguments.
    II. The esoteric and intrinsic argument (proof) Nonetheless, apparent authorities are the Prophets, apostles and messengers and the Imams (as) However, the esoteric (ones) are the (human) intellects (minds).

3. Comprehend and understand the religion of Allah, for jurisprudence is the key to vision and the completion of worship and the cause of reaching the lofty grades and magnanimous stations in the world and here after.
    And the superiority and magnanimity of jurisprudent over the adorer and worshiper is like that of the superiority of sun to the stars. And Allah does not get pleased with (accept) any practice of that person who does not achieve the comprehension and understanding of his religion.

4. Put in endeavor and exercise effort that your time is scheduled into four hours (parts). An hour (part of it) for the supplication to Allah and an hour (another part) of it for the affairs of economy and livelihood and still another hour (part of it) for social contacts with the brothers and the persons of confidence who may let you learn your short comings and faults and they have a sincere interior (heart) for you.
    And a part of it in which you enjoy the unforbidden and lawful entertainments. And with this part of time you get the strength and vigor for the (rest of) three other (parts of) times.

5. Indeed, the greatest and biggest of all the people in worth and value is the person who does not consider the world a station and abode for himself moreover, there is no price and worth of your bodies except the paradise, so, do not sell them without (achieving) it.

6. Bad is the person who has two faces and two tongues (double cross and hypocrite). He praises and commends his brother (in faith) in his presence and when he is absent he back bites and slanders him. If he achieves (something) he gets jealous of him and if he is afflicted, he leaves and abandons him.

7. Indeed, the intelligent and wit-full one does not converse with the person who, he is afraid, would contradict and falsify him. And does not ask anything from a person who, he is afraid, would refuse him And he does not promise anyone a thing which he does not have the strength for, and does not desire and wish and hope for a thing over which he may be reprimanded and rebuked. And does not take steps towards anything about which he may be afraid that he would fail and become feeble, from achieving it.

8. O, Hisham! Indeed, cultivation and growth takes shape in a soft, even land and not in a rocky (barren) land. So similarly, wisdom grows and develops in a humble heart and does not grow in a proud, vain and arrogant heart.

9. The one who restrains his anger from reaching people Allah stops chastisement from getting him on the dooms day.

10. And so combat and fight a holy war against your ego so as to move it away from its lust and passions. Because indeed it is obligatory for you like waging holy war against your enemy.

11. Allah has prohibited heaven for all the users of abusive and obscene language. The shameless person, who does neither care about what he says and nor what is said about him.

12. The one who squanders, wastes and spends lavishly, the beneficence's and blessings are abated, terminated and cease to exist with him.

13. The worst of the servants of Allah are those whose company is undesirable due to their obscene and filthy language (false, futile and dirty conversation).

14. Beware of not spending in (the course of) Allah's obedience otherwise, you spend twice on the way of Allah's disobedience (sin, transgression).

Saying of Imam Ali Ibn Musa al Reza (as)

1. He who compares and likens Allah to his creations is a polytheist and the one who attributes something which has been forbidden for him is an infidel.

2. Faith has four pillars: (1) trusting and relying upon Allah, (2) contentment and pleasure with the divine will, and (3) submit to ordinance of Allah, (4) delegation and turning over (the affairs) to Allah. i.e. (Total submission and reassignment to Allah).

3. Indeed Imamate is the rein of religion and the system of Muslims and the righteousness and welfare of the world and the honor and glory of faithful's. Verily, Imamate is the growing and ongoing root of Islam and its elevated and sublime branch. Services, alms, fasting, Hajj and Jihad (the holy war) attain completion and perfection and the booty (tributes) and alms gets plentiful and abundant, and the Allah's bounds, sanctions, and ordinances get executed, and the frontiers and boundaries (of Islamic lands) get safe and secure, through Imam.

4. The intellect of a Muslim man does not mature and complete till he has ten qualities: (1) Benevolence and benefaction be expected and hoped from him. (2) And people be secure and peaceful from his evil doing. (3) He considers the small amount of benefaction from others as abundant and plentiful. (4) And takes plenty of his own benevolence and goodness to be a meagre amount of it. (5) He does not get tired and exhausted by the demands and requirement asked to be fulfilled. (6) He does not get fatigued and restless from seeking knowledge for all the length of his life. (7) He loves poverty more than the plentiful and affluence, on the course of Allah. (8) He loves disgrace and abjectness on the way of Allah more than the honor on the course of His enemy. (9) Anonymity is more liked by him than fame. (10) He does not see a person but that he says 'He is better and more pious than myself.

5. Had Allah not frightened people by paradise and hell even then it would have been obligatory for them to obey Him and not commit His disobedience because of His favors and kindnesses upon them. And His granting them the beneficence's to start with, without any of their rights.

6. Be careful of greed and jealousy, since, these (vices) have perished the previous nations. And beware of stinginess because it is a calamity which will not be found in a free man and a faithful.
    This (vice) is against and controversial to faith.

7. Allah dislikes futile (useless) talk and squandering the wealth and much begging (asking things).

8. Do not acquire and adopt the company of drinker and do not salute him.

9. The one who repents upon the sins is like the one who does not have a sin.

10. Cleanliness is from the morality and character of Prophets.

11. The best wealth is the one by which the honor of man is protected.

12. The one who happens to meet a poor Muslim and salutes him against the way he salutes a wealthy person shall meet Allah on the resurrection day in a way that He will be angry with him.

13. Allah forbade the drinking of wine, since, it causes corruption, disturbance, and intoxication of the minds of its drinker and this becomes the cause of his refusing and denying of Allah and uttering obnoxious language about HIM and His Prophets. And becomes the cause of all the sins including murdering and accusing falsely chaste woman of adultery and committing adultery and lessening of abstinence and refraining from forbidden deeds (sins). So this is the reason of it that all the drinks which intoxicate are prohibited and forbidden. Since these drinks too have the same negative results which the wine has got.

14. Give alms although with a small amount of a thing because indeed all that is intended for the sake of Allah; although those may be meagre and small yet becomes great, and magnanimous by virtue of the righteousness and purity of intention.

Saying of Imam Muhammad Ibn Ali al Jawad al Taqi (as)

1. Delaying repentance is a deception and prolonging the period before making repentance is an amazingly wandering. And adducing pretexts and making excuses before Allah is an annihilation. And insisting upon sin is being (considering oneself) safe from the scheme of Allah. And no one ever thinks himself safe from the scheme of Allah except the community of losers.

2. If the ignorant keeps silent, people would not differ.

3. It is sufficient for a man's being dishonest that he becomes the trustee of dishonest ones.

4. Four qualities assist one upon practicing, health and wealth and knowledge and divine grace.

5. The one who lends ear to a speaker he has worshiped him. So if the speaker is from Allah's side (speaks the word of Allah) then he has adorned Allah and if the speaker is speaking from the tongue of Satan then he has worshiped Satan.

6. Do know that you are not away from the sight of Allah, So see to it that in what condition you are living (sinfulness or piety).

7. The one who commits aggression and tyranny and the one who helps him upon it and the one who is pleased over it, are all party and participants in it.

8. The honor of faithful lies in his needless from the people.

9. The one who obeys his lustful desire and passions has helped his enemy reach (achieve) his wish.

10. The people of good deeds are needier towards practicing them then those who have the need of them. Because they (good doers) have the reward, pride and memories of those deeds for themselves and to their credit. So the man who performs a good deed first of all its benefit reaches his own self.

11. Good state and sound health is the best providence and grant of Allah.

12. Modesty is the decoration of poverty and thanksgiving is the decoration of ambience and wealth. And patience and endurance is the ornament and decoration of calamity and distress. And humility is the decoration of lineage. And eloquence is the decoration of speech; and committing to memory is the decoration of tradition. And bowing the shoulders is the decoration of knowledge. And the decency and good morale is the decoration of mind. And smiling face is the decoration of munificence and generosity. And not boasting of doing favor is the decoration of good deed. And humility is the decoration of service. And spending less is the decoration of contentment. And abandoning the meaningless and unnecessary things is the decoration of abstention and fear of Allah.

13. And do know that indeed Allah is the All clement and All-knowing and His wrath is upon the one who does not accept His pleasure. And verily the one who does not accept His grant is refused that. And the one who does not accept his guidance goes astray.

14. There are three (acts, which make the servants reach the good pleasure and approval of Allah
    1. Plentiful of repentance.
    2. Soft natured and forbearance.
    3. Abundance of alms giving.
    And there are three acts the doer of which does not repent.
    1. Not making hurry.
    2. Taking advice.
    3. Trusting Allah while making decision.

Saying of Imam Ali Ibn Muhammad al Hadi al Naqi (as)

1. There is no security from the evil of the one who is disregarded and humiliated in his own eyes.

2. The world is a market, a community reaps benefit in it and there is another one which faces loss.

3. The one who is pleased with himself: (his own state and condition) those displeased and angry with him shall get abundant in number.

4. Poverty and adversity is the cause of getting the soul's rebelion and revolt and the gravity of dismay.

5. The one who thinks he is obliged to commit sin has attributed the responsibility of his sin towards Allah and has accused Him of cruelty and excess upon His servants.

6. Allah cannot be defined and described except with what He has defined himself. And how can that one (Allah) be defined? intellects are unable from the perception of who He is, and the imaginations are short of finding Him. And the memories of mind are unable to encompass Him, and the eyes and vision is unable to sight and summon Him. And the eyes are short of strength and weak for seeing and bounding Him.

7. Jealousy is the cause of erosion of good deeds and the attracter of chastisement.

8. Compensate and remind yourself of regrets and envoys of dissipations by giving priority and preference to fore sighted ness, resolution and sound judgment.

9. Whenever a time comes that the justice overwhelms and over comes cruelty it is prohibited to form negative bad conjecture and opinion about anyone except when one knows it about him. And whenever a time comes that the cruelty and oppression over whelms the (quantum of) justice then one must not have good opinion about the beneficence of a person till such time he knows it (for sure).

10. Sustain and prolong the beneficences and benevolences by decent neighborhood with them. And keep seeking the benevolences by thank giving, over those.

11. The torturing and teasing of parents is followed by shortage (of sustenance) and being driven towards belittlement. and humiliation.

12. Talking nonsense and futile things is the enjoyment and pleasure of foolish and insane ones, and the activity of ignorant ones.

13. Allah has made the world a place of calamities and the resurrection day the spot of rewards. And He has made the anguishes and calamities of life a way to the rewards of justice day. And made the reward of resurrection day the replacement and compensation for the troubles and anguishes of world (life).

14. Beware of Jealousy for its effect will appear upon you and it shall not affect your enemy.

Saying of Imam Hassan Ibn Ali al Askari (as)

1. The love of the pious ones for the pious ones is a reward and recompense for those pious. And the love of debauch (libertine) for the pious ones is a sublimity and superiority for the pious ones. And the grudge of the debauch for the pious ones is the decoration for the pious ones. And the grudge and enmity of pious ones against the debauch and libertine is a humility for the debauch (sybarite).

2. An age will approach when the people's faces would be laughing (exalting) and their hearts would be dark, bleak and dirty. The Sunnah to them would be innovation and heresy and innovation would be (considered) Sunnah among them. The faithful would be belittled and debased among them, and the transgressor would be honorable and respectful among them. Their lords and chiefs would be ignorant and aggressive ones. And the religious scholar's would be on the threshold of the aggressors and tyrants.

3. The best of your brothers is the one who forgets your sin and remember and mentions your favor done to him.

4. Rage and anger is the key to all evils.

5. Humbleness is a boon and beneficence which does not get subjected to the jealousy of people.

6. Observing the middle way in economy has a quantity when it exceeds that then it is stinginess and avarice. And there is a limit to bravery and gallantry and when it exceeds that then it is rashness and impetuousness.

7. This very politeness, courtesy and civility is sufficient for you that you refrain from doing what you dislike in others. (The bad deeds and evils).

8. Allah has made the fasting obligatory so that those rich and wealthy taste and realize the touch (agony of) hunger and consequently become kind to the poor.

9. Refrain and avoid fame seeking and striving for power, as these two invite man towards annihilation.

10. Indeed, generosity and charity has a quantity so when it exceeds that it becomes spending lavishly (squandering). And so does foresightedness and caution has a limit and when it exceeds that then it is cowardice.

11. Be afraid of Allah and become a decoration and do not become a (source of) a disgusting and miserable object (for us).

12. The sustenance which has become guaranteed (by Allah) must not refrain and make you so busy so that you do not perform the obligatory practices.

13. A greedy one does not get more than what has been destined for him.

14. You are leading shortening lives and limited durations and death suddenly approaches. Who so ever sows benevolence and beneficence reaps joy and pleasure and the one who sows evil reaps repentance and shame. Everybody reaps, what he sows.

Saying of Imam Muhammad Ibn Hassan al Mahdi (atf)

1. I am the Mahdi (the rightly guided one) I am the upholder and upkeeper of the age. I am the one who fills it (the earth) with justice just as it is filled up with aggression and cruelty. The earth does not remain empty of the Proof and authority of Allah.

2. I am the remnant (the remainings of the Allah's affair) upon His earth and the avenger and vengeance taker from His enemies.

3. Indeed, the divine destinies will never be over whelmed and overcome and the divine will does never get rejected and nothing can supersede the divine grace.

4. Indeed, we have thorough knowledge which encompasses your news (incidents and affairs of life). And nothing out of your news remain hidden from us.

5. And the person who eats anything from our wealth money (like khomas) indeed, he eats up fire (putting fire into his belly) and soon he will enter the hell fire.

6. Allah raised *Mohammed (S)* as beneficence for the worlds and completed His favors with him and ended the (series of) Apostles by him. And sent him toward all the people (for their guidance).

7. And when the incidents occur and take shape then turn to those who describe our Hadiths since they are my proof and authority over you and I am the authority of Allah upon them.

8. Our hearts are the utensils of the Divine will so when Allah wishes something, we too wish the same.

9. So know it that the right of Imamate is with us and among us. And who so ever says (believes) it to be with others than us, he is a blamer, liar. And nobody except us claims it but the gone astray and deviated one.

10. Those who fix a time (regarding the advent of Imam Mahdi (as)) are liars.

11. And the how-ness of benefiting from me in my occultation is like the benefiting from the sun when it disappears from the eyes behind the clouds.

12. And as for the reason of the incidence of occultation so Allah says ', Oh those who believe! Do not question about the things which if get apparent and disclosed to you would feel bad about those.'

13. And pray much for the quickness of deliverance for that is your (own) deliverance.

14. And indeed I am the safety and security for the people of the earth.
Oh the light of light, oh the administrator of the affairs, oh the raiser of those who are in the graves!
Shower your benediction upon Muhammad and his household.
And free me and my shias out of the (state of) anguish to have joy and deliverance and exodus out of the sorrow and grief. And broaden the way of your kindness for us. And send us something from yourself which may make us comfortable and in (the state of) deliverance. And treat us in a way that you are fit and worthy for it. Oh the kind one, oh the merciful of all the merciful.

Source: Muhammad Muhammadi Eshtehardi, *Fascinating discourses of Fourteen Infallibles (as)* 3rd edition, Publisher: Ansariyan Publications, Qum, Iran

Books on this topic

50 Life Lessons from the Ahl al-Bayt by Ayatollah Naser Makarem Shirazi

Ahlul Bayt: Ethical Role Models by Sayid Mahdi as-Sadr

Ahlul-Bait (a.s.) in the Qur'an and Sunnah by al-Balagh Foundation

Analysis of the History of Aale Muhammad by Qadi Bohlool Bahjat Afandi

Anecdotes from the Lives of the 14 Ma'sumeen by al-Balagh Foundation

Anecdotes of the Ahlul-Bayt by Ayatollah Murtadha Mutahhari

Brief History of the Fourteen Infallibles by World Organization for Islamic Services

Fascinating Discourses of Fourteen Infallibles by Muhammad Muhammadi Eshtehardi

Hayatul Qulub – Vol. 3 Succession to Muhammad (saws) by Muhammad Baqir al-Majlisi

The Suffering of the Ahlul Bayt by Mateen J. Charbonneau

The Fourteen Infallibles: A Compilation of Speeches and Lectures by Dr. Sayed Ammar Nakshawani

The Fourteen Innocents (as) by Dr. Ainur Raza

The Position of Lady Fatima al-Zahra (s) in the Verse of Mubahala from a Sunni Perspective by Muhammad Yaqub Bashvi

The Lantern on the Path to Allah Almighty by Shaikh Hussain Ibn Ali Ibn Sadiq al-Bahran

Tragedy of Fatima Daughter of Prophet Muhammed: Doubts Cast and Rebuttals by Yasin T. Al-Jibouri

Chapter 4

Qur'an on Imam'mat

Edward W. Lane in <u>An Arabic-English Lexicon</u> (Vol 1, P. 91) defines the word *"Imam"* as" *"a learned man, whose examples are followed"*

Other Qur'anic Arabic dictionaries define the word "Imam" as:

> *A leader, ruler, guardian, vicegerent, master, guide, or someone to be followed.*

Source: Abdul Mannan Omar, (2004), *Dictionary of the Holy Qur'an*, P 32. ISBN: 09632067-8-8. Publisher: Noor Foundation-International Inc.

Shi'as believe that after the demise of the Holy Prophet (pbuh), an Imam must be appointed by Allah (swt) to act as a custodian and guardian of the commandments of Islam. Further, such appointee was needed to rightfully lead the people onto the right path. First and foremost, only Allah (swt) can appoint an Imam/ Leader/ Caliph/ Viceregent/ Viceroy as clearly stated in the following verses of the Holy Qur'an:

Surat al-Baqirah 2:30

وَإِذْ قَالَ رَبُّكَ لِلْمَلَـٰٓئِكَةِ إِنِّي جَاعِلٌ فِي ٱلْأَرْضِ خَلِيفَةً قَالُوٓا۟ أَتَجْعَلُ فِيهَا مَن يُفْسِدُ فِيهَا وَيَسْفِكُ ٱلدِّمَآءَ وَنَحْنُ نُسَبِّحُ بِحَمْدِكَ وَنُقَدِّسُ لَكَ قَالَ إِنِّيٓ أَعْلَمُ مَا لَا تَعْلَمُونَ ﴿٣٠﴾

When your Lord said to the angels, 'Indeed I am going to set a vicegerent on the earth,' they said, 'Will You set in it someone who will cause corruption in it, and shed blood, while we celebrate Your praise and proclaim Your sanctity?' He said, 'Indeed I know what you do not know.'

Also in:

Surat al-Baqirah 2:124

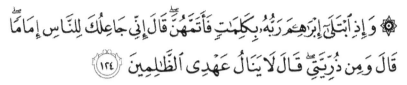

*And when his Lord tested Abraham with certain words, and he fulfilled them, He said, 'I am making you the **Imams** of mankind.' Said he, 'And from among my descendants?' He said, 'My pledge does not extend to the **unjust**.'*

The above verses indicate that the Imammat, caliphate or divinely appointed leadership can only be ordained by Allah (swt). In addition, it also shows that an **unjust** person cannot be an Imam or a divinely appointed leader. Therefore, not just anyone is entitled to assume the 'office of Islamic leadership.' The only ones to fill the position of Islamic leadership are the ones whom Allah examines and who fulfills Allah's test.

Furthermore, in Qur'an, Allah (swt) mentions to summon every group of people with their imams or leaders in:

Surat Al-Isra (17:71-72)

يَوْمَ نَدْعُواْ كُلَّ أُنَاسٍ بِإِمَٰمِهِمْ فَمَنْ أُوتِىَ كِتَٰبَهُۥ بِيَمِينِهِۦ فَأُو۟لَٰٓئِكَ يَقْرَءُونَ كِتَٰبَهُمْ وَلَا يُظْلَمُونَ فَتِيلًا ﴿٧١﴾

The day We shall summon every group of people with their imam, then whoever is given his book in his right hand – they will read it, and they will not be wronged so much as a single date-thread.

وَمَن كَانَ فِى هَٰذِهِۦٓ أَعْمَىٰ فَهُوَ فِى ٱلْءَاخِرَةِ أَعْمَىٰ وَأَضَلُّ سَبِيلًا ﴿٧٢﴾

(17:72) But whoever has been blind in this (world), will be blind in the Hereafter, and (even) more astray from the (right) way.

Many people misinterpret the meaning behind the word 'imam' in the aforementioned verses. They try to interpret it as 'a book of deeds', but they fail to address "why are a group of people (plural) being raised with an imam (singular entity)?" Also, "why is 'book' being mentioned as '*Kitab*' again in the next sentence?" Indeed, the 'Imam' in this verse refers to their leader (a human being) not a book of their deeds, and this concept is further explored in the following verse:

Surat al-Qasas 28:41

$$\text{وَجَعَلْنَٰهُمْ أَئِمَّةً يَدْعُونَ إِلَى ٱلنَّارِ وَيَوْمَ ٱلْقِيَٰمَةِ لَا يُنصَرُونَ ﴿٤١﴾}$$

*We made them **Imams** who invite to the Fire, and on the Day of Resurrection they will not receive any help.*

There are two types of Imams in this world. The first type are self-appointed or elected by the common people. These are the types who will lead people to Hell fire. The second type are Imam's that are appointed through the divine decision of Allah (swt) and given their positions through the divine Abrahamic progeny. These are the rightfully appointed who were selected by Allah (swt) to guide mankind *(those who are willing to be guided)*, this can be observed in the following verse:

Surat al-Anbiya 21:73

$$\text{وَجَعَلْنَٰهُمْ أَئِمَّةً يَهْدُونَ بِأَمْرِنَا وَأَوْحَيْنَآ إِلَيْهِمْ فِعْلَ ٱلْخَيْرَٰتِ وَإِقَامَ ٱلصَّلَوٰةِ وَإِيتَآءَ ٱلزَّكَوٰةِ ۖ وَكَانُوا۟ لَنَا عَٰبِدِينَ ﴿٧٣﴾}$$

*We made them **imams**, guiding by Our command, and We revealed to them the performance of good deeds, the maintenance of prayers, and the giving of zakat, and they used to worship Us.*

And in:

Surat al-Sajdah 32:24

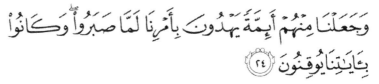

*And amongst them We appointed **imams** to guide [the people] by Our command, when they had been patient and had conviction in Our signs.*

The question that arises here is: Who are the "Imams" that "Guide" people by "Allah's command?"

The key point to note here is by "Allah's command." While national and tribal leadership can be through an electoral process, leadership of a monotheistic religion cannot be through the same process. In order to be in the position of being a religious guide, an *Imam,* one has to be appointed by Allah (swt). Further, all of the messengers and guides in the Abrahamic faiths have been appointed by Allah (swt) from the same divine progeny.

End of Chapter Notes

The Identity of the Imams appointed by Allah (swt)

Jabir Ibn Abdullah Ansari (ra) narrates:

Prophet (pbuh): *"There are Twelve Imams"* Then he mentioned their names one by one and told Jabir: *"You will meet the fifth Imam; Say my Salam (greetings) to him."*

Sources:

1. Sheikh Muhammad bin Muhammad bin Nu'man al-Harithi Al-Mufid, *Kitab al-Irshad* (Arabic)
2. Muhammad Ibn Jarir al-Tabari. *The History of al Tabari,* Vol. 13, P. 96
3. bn Hajar al-Haytami, *Al-Sawa'iq al-Muhriqah* (Arabic) P. 80

In another narration, Salman al-Muhamadi (ra) narrates:

Imam Hussain (as) was sitting on Prophet Muhammad's (pbuh) lap, he (pbuh) was kissing his eyes and mouth and saying: *"You are a leader and son of a leader, you are an Imam and the son of an Imam and the father of Imams. You are a proof of Allah (swt) and the son of His proof and the father of proofs. They will be nine in number and they will be from your progeny, and the ninth of them will be the Qa'im (the one who will rise)."*

Source: Abu Jafar Muhammad Ibn Ali Ibn Babawaih al-Qummi Shaykh Sudooq, *Kamal al-Din*, Vol 1, P. 262

Imam Sadiq (as): *"Thus Allah continued to choose them (the Imams) for His creatures, from the progeny of al-Hussain,, from the offspring of every Imam. Whenever an Imam would pass away from among them, He (Allah swt) would appoint for His creatures an Imam, and a guiding authority from his (i.e. the deceased Imam's) offspring."*

Source: Sheikh Muhammad Ibn Ya'qub Ibn Ishaq al-Kulayni, *Al-Kafi*, Vol 1 P. 203

Imam Ali Ibn Hussain al-Sajjad, Zain al Abideen's (as) Announcement of his Imammat

Right after the tragedy of Karbala, Muhammad al-Hanafiyah (son of Imam Ali through Khawlah bint Ja'far al-Hanafiyah) claimed that he was the Imam after his brother, Imam Hussain (as) had become an Imam after the eldest brother, Imam Hassan (as). Imam Zain al Abideen (as) said that his uncle's claim was wrong; that he (Imam Zain al Abideen as) was the Imam after his father, by "**Divine Appointment.**"

This family "feud" apparently could not be resolved; and ultimately Imam Zain al Abideen (as) suggested that the "Black Stone" (*al-Hajar'ul-aswad*) of Ka'bah be approached for its judgment. Muhammad al Hanafiyah readily agreed and both parties went to Mecca during the Hajj season, when thousands of pilgrims had assembled for the pilgrimage.

The news must have spread like wildfire that Ali bin Hussain (as) and Muhammad al-Hanafiyah wanted the Black Stone to judge between them (regarding the claim of Imammat). Everyone must have wondered how a stone could judge between two people. They must have eagerly waited to see the outcome when the two parties would approach the Stone. What would they say when the Stone, being a stone, would not respond to their arguments?

This must have been the feeling of the crowd when the uncle and the nephew slowly advanced towards the Black Stone. First, Muhammad al-Hanafiyah talked to the Stone; there was no response. Imam Zain al Abideen (as) said: *"Had you, O Uncle, been the Wasi (possesses knowledge from God) and Imam, it would certainly have answered you."*

Muhammad al-Hanafiyah said: "Now, O Nephew, you pray and ask it." Imam Zain al Abideen (as) prayed to Allah and then asked the Black Stone to declare who is the *'Wasi'* and the Imam after al-Hussain son of Ali (as).

There was a tremor in the Stone and then Allah (swt) made it speak in Arabic: *"O Allah, verily Wisayah and Imamah, after al-Hussain Ibn Ali is for Ali Ibn al-Hussain, the son of Ali bin Abi Talib and Fatimah bint Rasulillah."* Muhammad al-Hanafiyah was astonished by this verdict, accepted the verdict and declared his allegiance for Imam Zain al Abideen (as) right away.

This 'dispute' was the beginning of the end of the *Kaisaniyah movement*, which wanted to accept Muhammad al-Hanafiyah as Imam. The schism in the Shi'a rank was arrested; and as it was only a 'family feud', Yazid could not object to it in any way, but the miraculous nature of the episode and the timing served its purpose. The pilgrims on returning to their homes must have felt compelled to narrate this strange story; and thus the Shi'as throughout the Muslim world came to know, without any formal proclamation, that Imam Zain al Abideen (as) was their divinely appointed Leader and the Guide.

Source: Ayatollah Sayyid Saeed Akhtar Rizvi. *The Illustrious Period of the Imammat of Imam Zayn al-Abidin*: **Announcement of His Imamat.** Vol. 5, No. 3 and 4 - 1979. Publisher Muhammadi Trust of Great Britain and Northern Ireland

http://www.al-islam.org/al-serat/vol-5-no-3-4-1979/illustrious-period-imamate-imam-zayn-al-abidin-sayyid-saeed-akhtar-rizv-0#announcement-his-imamat

Imam Muhammad Ibn Ali al Jawad, al Taqi (as) proving his Imammat using jurisprudential knowledge

Imam Muhammad Ibn Ali Al Taqi, Al Jawad (as) was only six-years old when his father Imam Ali Ibn Musa Ar Reza (as) was martyred, and he (Imam al Jawad as) assumed the role of Imammat (Divine Leadership). The Shi'as became extremely confused and started to disagree with one and another about the Imammat, because they thought that a six-year old child could not be an Imam and the Imammat should be entrusted to an older man. A group of the Shi'a gathered in one of their houses, among them were ar-Rayyan bin as-Salt, Yonus, Safwan bin Yahya, Muhammad bin Hakeem and Abdurrahman bin al-Hajjaj. They discussed the matter of the Imammat and began to cry. Yonus said to them, *"Stop your crying and wait until this child (Imam al Jawad) grows up."* Ar-Rayyan bin as-Salt said, *"If it is decreed by Allah the Almighty, then a two day old child can be like a hundred years old man, but if it is not decreed by Allah swt, then even if one lives for five thousand years, he will not be able to do what the masters can do or even a part of it. This is worth pondering over."*

This was the decisive answer that revealed the shining reality which the *Twelver Shi'a* believe in: childhood or adulthood have nothing to do with the position of Imammat, which is like the position of Prophethood in most of its specifications, for both Imammat and Prophethood are in the decree of Allah (swt), Who entrusts with them whomsoever He chooses from amongst His people.

Delegations of jurisprudence and scholars

A significant number of scholars and jurisprudents, whom were selected by the Shi'a delegates in Baghdad and other countries, came to Medina following the martyrdom of Imam Reza (as) in order to ascertain the new Imam. They were about eighty men, as historians have mentioned in their books. When they arrived in Medina, they went to the house of Abdullah the son of Imam Musa al Kadhim (as), who came to them and sat at the head of their meeting. He claimed himself to be the imam after Imam Reza (as) and the religious authority of the *Umma* (Muslim nation). A man stood up and called out to the scholars, *"This is the son of the messenger of Allah. Whoever has a question, let him ask."* One of the scholars stood up and asked him, *"What do you think about the man who says to his wife: I divorce you as many times as there are stars in the sky?"*

Abdullah the son of Imam Musa al Kadhim answered against the jurisprudence of the Ahlul Bayt (as) saying, *"She is divorced thrice before the Gemini."*

The scholars and the jurisprudence were astonished at this answer, which was different from the answer of the infallible Imams (as). The infallible Imams had determined that the divorce could only be achieved once. Also, they couldn't determine why Abdullah singled out the Gemini from all the stars and planets.

Another one of the jurisprudents asked him, *"What is your opinion regarding a man who has sexual intercourse with an animal?"*

Again he answered contrary to the law of Allah (swt). He said, *"His hand should be cut off and he should be whipped a hundred times."*

The attendees were astonished. Some of them began to cry because of these rulings that contradicted the verdicts of Allah (swt). They became very confused. While they were in this state, a door near the front of the meeting was opened out of which emerged Muwaffaq the servant, and then Imam Muhammad al Jawad (as) appeared with such a loftiness that made all heads bow to him submissively. The scholars and the jurisprudence stood up out of respect. A man introduced him to the attendees as the Imam (as) after his father and as the great authority for Muslims.

The man who had asked the first question came to the Imam (as) and asked him, *"What do you think about the man who says to his wife: I divorce you as many times as there are stars in the sky?"*

Imam al Jawad (as) said, *"O man, read in the Book of Allah: (Divorce may be (pronounced) twice, then keep (them) in good fellowship or let (them) go with kindness) and then it is at the third (that divorce becomes irrevocable)..."* (From Surat al-Baqira 2:226-232)

The attendants were amazed at the intelligence of the Imam (as) and were certain that they had reached the aim, which they had sought. The asker told Imam al Jawad (as) of the ruling of his uncle Abdullah the son of Imam al Kadhim concerning the same matter. Imam al Jawad (as) turned to his uncle and said: *"O uncle, fear Allah and do not give any ruling when there exists in the society one who is more aware than you."*

Abdullah bowed his head to the earth and did not know what to say. The man with the second question came to Imam al Jawad (as) and asked him, *"What is your opinion regarding a man who has sexual intercourse with an animal?"*

Imam al Jawad (as) said: *"He should be subjected to a*

discretionary punishment, and the animal should be marked with a lasting mark on its back and taken out of the country so that the shame of it does not remain with the man."

The asker informed Imam al Jawad (as) of the fatwa of his uncle. Imam al Jawad (as) strongly rejected that ruling and, turning to his uncle, angrily said, *"There is no god but Allah swt! O Abdullah, it is so great a matter to Allah that when tomorrow you will stop before Him, He will ask you: why did you give a ruling to my people about that which you did not know, whereas there was someone in the society who was more aware than you?"* Abdullah began making excuses and justifying his answer by saying, *"I have seen my brother Ar-Reza (as) answer this question with this same answer."*

Imam al Jawad (as) denied this and shouted at him, *"Imam Reza (as) was asked about a gravedigger who had dug out a dead woman, had sex with her and takes her clothes. He (Imam Reza as) ordered to cut his hand off for stealing, to whip him for committing adultery and to exile him for maiming the dead."*

The scholars and the jurisprudence, then asked Imam al Jawad (as) many questions regarding different matters of jurisprudence. Historians say that there were about thirty thousand questions (asked in different meetings) during the visit of the scholars and the jurisprudents, until they became satisfied of his Imammat and returned to their countries spreading the news that the next Imam was Muhammad Ibn Ali al Jawad (as). They related to the Muslims what they had witnessed of his abundant knowledge and said that he (as) was a great miracle of Islam for though he was so young in age, he possessed such a high level of knowledge of the religion that could neither be defined nor described.

Source: Baqir Shareefal-Qurashi, (2005)   *The Life of Imam Muhammad Al-Jawad (as). The confusion of the Shi'a.* P. 64-69. Publisher: Ansariyan Publications, Qum, Iran.

Books on this topic:

A Concise Treatise on the Twelve Imams by Ayatollah Jawad al-Tabrizi

A Short Account of the Lives of the Fourteen Infallibles by Mehdi Rahimi

A Survey into the Lives of the Infallible Imams by Ayatollah Murtadha Mutahhari

Ahl al-Bayt and Caliphate by Ayatollah Murtadha Mutahhari

Biographies of Leaders of Islam by Ali Naqi Naqawi

Imammat: The Vicegerency of the Prophet by Ayatollah Sayyid Saeed Akhtar Rizvi

Imamat by Ayatollah Sayyid Saeed Akhtar Rizvi

Imammat and Leadership by Mujtaba Musavi Lari

Imamate and Malukiyat by Syed Hasan Zafar Naqvi

Lets Learn About Imamate by Ayatollah Nasir Makarim Shirazi

Life Sketches of the Fourteen Infallibles by Allama Zeeshan Haider Jawadi

Shi'ism - Imamate And Wilayat by Sayid Muhammad Rizvi

The Message of Islam Contininues by Dr. Syed Haider Hussain Shamsi

The Role of Holy Imams in the Revival of Religion Vol 1, 2 by Allama Sayed Murteza Askari

The Scholarly Jihad of the Imams by al-Syed Saeed Akhtar Rizvi

Wilayah by Ayatollah Murtadha Mutahhari

There is a great series of books on the **biographies of all 12 Imams** by **Allama Baqir Shareef Al-Qurashi,** available for free on:
http://www.maaref-foundation.com/english/index.htm
And
http://islamiclib.wordpress.com/2013/08/12/ahlul-bayt-as-the-holy-household-of-prophet-muhammad-saws-imamate/

Also

Life Sketch of all 12 Imams by **Allama Zeeshan Haider Jawadi,** also available for free on:
http://islamiclib.wordpress.com/2013/08/12/ahlul-bayt-as-the-holy-household-of-prophet-muhammad-saws-imamate/

Chapter 5

The significance of the 'Twelve Imams' from Qur'an

The Holy Qur'an mentions the word "Imam" in both its singular and plural forms at **twelve** places, which are as follows:

1. **Surat al-Baqirah** 2:124

﴿ وَإِذِ ٱبْتَلَىٰٓ إِبْرَٰهِـۧمَ رَبُّهُۥ بِكَلِمَٰتٍ فَأَتَمَّهُنَّ قَالَ إِنِّي جَاعِلُكَ لِلنَّاسِ إِمَامًا قَالَ وَمِن ذُرِّيَّتِي قَالَ لَا يَنَالُ عَهْدِى ٱلظَّٰلِمِينَ ﴿١٢٤﴾

2. **Surat al-Tawbah** 9:12

وَإِن نَّكَثُوٓاْ أَيْمَٰنَهُم مِّنۢ بَعْدِ عَهْدِهِمْ وَطَعَنُواْ فِي دِينِكُمْ فَقَٰتِلُوٓاْ أَئِمَّةَ ٱلْكُفْرِ إِنَّهُمْ لَآ أَيْمَٰنَ لَهُمْ لَعَلَّهُمْ يَنتَهُونَ ﴿١٢﴾

3. **Surat Hud** 11:17

أَفَمَن كَانَ عَلَىٰ بَيِّنَةٍ مِّن رَّبِّهِۦ وَيَتْلُوهُ شَاهِدٌ مِّنْهُ وَمِن قَبْلِهِۦ كِتَٰبُ مُوسَىٰٓ إِمَامًا وَرَحْمَةً أُوْلَٰٓئِكَ يُؤْمِنُونَ بِهِۦ وَمَن يَكْفُرْ بِهِۦ مِنَ ٱلْأَحْزَابِ فَٱلنَّارُ مَوْعِدُهُۥ فَلَا تَكُ فِي مِرْيَةٍ مِّنْهُ إِنَّهُ ٱلْحَقُّ مِن رَّبِّكَ وَلَٰكِنَّ أَكْثَرَ ٱلنَّاسِ لَا يُؤْمِنُونَ ﴿١٧﴾

4. **Surat al-Hijr** 15:79

فَٱنتَقَمۡنَا مِنۡهُمۡ وَإِنَّهُمَا لَبِإِمَامٍ مُّبِينٍ ﴿٧٩﴾

5. **Surat al-Isra** 17:71

يَوۡمَ نَدۡعُواْ كُلَّ أُنَاسٍ بِإِمَٰمِهِمۡ فَمَنۡ أُوتِيَ كِتَٰبَهُۥ بِيَمِينِهِۦ

فَأُوْلَٰٓئِكَ يَقۡرَءُونَ كِتَٰبَهُمۡ وَلَا يُظۡلَمُونَ فَتِيلًا ﴿٧١﴾

6. **Surat al-Anbiya** 21:73

وَجَعَلۡنَٰهُمۡ أَئِمَّةً يَهۡدُونَ بِأَمۡرِنَا وَأَوۡحَيۡنَآ إِلَيۡهِمۡ فِعۡلَ

ٱلۡخَيۡرَٰتِ وَإِقَامَ ٱلصَّلَوٰةِ وَإِيتَآءَ ٱلزَّكَوٰةِ وَكَانُواْ لَنَا

عَٰبِدِينَ ﴿٧٣﴾

7. **Surat al-Furqan** 25:74

وَٱلَّذِينَ يَقُولُونَ رَبَّنَا هَبۡ لَنَا مِنۡ أَزۡوَٰجِنَا وَذُرِّيَّٰتِنَا قُرَّةَ

أَعۡيُنٍ وَٱجۡعَلۡنَا لِلۡمُتَّقِينَ إِمَامًا ﴿٧٤﴾

8. **Surat al-Qasas** 28:5

وَنُرِيدُ أَن نَّمُنَّ عَلَى ٱلَّذِينَ ٱسۡتُضۡعِفُواْ فِي ٱلۡأَرۡضِ وَنَجۡعَلَهُمۡ

أَئِمَّةً وَنَجۡعَلَهُمُ ٱلۡوَٰرِثِينَ ﴿٥﴾

9. **Surat al-Qasas** 28:41

وَجَعَلْنَٰهُمْ أَئِمَّةً يَدْعُونَ إِلَى ٱلنَّارِ وَيَوْمَ ٱلْقِيَٰمَةِ لَا يُنصَرُونَ ﴿٤١﴾

10. **Surat al-Sajdah** 32:24

وَجَعَلْنَا مِنْهُمْ أَئِمَّةً يَهْدُونَ بِأَمْرِنَا لَمَّا صَبَرُوا۟ وَكَانُوا۟ بِـَٔايَٰتِنَا يُوقِنُونَ ﴿٢٤﴾

11. **Surat Ya-Seen** 36:12

إِنَّا نَحْنُ نُحْىِ ٱلْمَوْتَىٰ وَنَكْتُبُ مَا قَدَّمُوا۟ وَءَاثَٰرَهُمْ وَكُلَّ شَىْءٍ أَحْصَيْنَٰهُ فِىٓ إِمَامٍ مُّبِينٍ ﴿١٢﴾

12. **Surat al-Ahqaf** 46:12

وَمِن قَبْلِهِۦ كِتَٰبُ مُوسَىٰٓ إِمَامًا وَرَحْمَةً وَهَٰذَا كِتَٰبٌ مُّصَدِّقٌ لِّسَانًا عَرَبِيًّا لِّيُنذِرَ ٱلَّذِينَ ظَلَمُوا۟ وَبُشْرَىٰ لِلْمُحْسِنِينَ ﴿١٢﴾

Indeed, this is one of the miracles of the Holy Qur'an and signifies the hadith of Holy Prophet (pbuh) mentioning "**twelve**" leaders for his true followers;

The Prophet (pbuh) said: *"The religion will continue to be established till there are **twelve caliphs/ rulers** over you, and the whole community will agree with each of them."* I then heard from the Prophet (pbuh) some remarks, which I could not understand. I asked my father: What is he saying: He said: *"All of them will belong to Quraysh."*

Narrated by Jabir Ibn Samurah:

Sources:

Sunan Abu Dawood (English) Book 37, Hadith 4266. http://sunnah.com/abuDawood/38

Sahih Muslim (Arabic) Hadith# 1818 a. (English) Book 20, Hadith 4473. http://sunnah.com/muslim/33

Sahih Bukhari Book 93, Hadith 82. http://sunnah.com/bukhari/93

Sunan al-Tirmidhi, Book 33, Hadith 66. http://sunnah.com/tirmidhi/33

Musnad of Ahmad Ibn Hanbal, Vol 1, P. 398 and Vol 5, P. 106

The Names of Twelve leaders after the Holy Prophet (pbuh) according to School of Ahlul Bayt (as)

1. Ali Ibn Abi Talib al Murtadha (as) (son of Hazrat Imran Ibn Abdul Muttalib *AKA* Abu Talib and Lady Fatima bint Asad as)
2. Hassan Ibn Ali al Mujtaba (as) (elder son of Imam Ali and Lady Fatima as)
3. Hussain Ibn Ali Sayed as-Shuhada (as) (second son of Imam Ali and Lady Fatima as)
4. Ali Ibn Hussain al Sajjad, Zain al Abideen (as) (son of Imam Hussain and Lady Shahr Bano as)
5. Muhammad Ibn Ali al Baqir (as) (son of Imam Zain al Abideen and Fatima bint Hassan as)
6. Jafar Ibn Muhammad al Sadiq (as) (son of Imam al Baqir and Farwah bint al-Qasim as)
7. Musa Ibn Jafar al Kadhim (as) (son of Imam al Sadiq and Lady Hamidah as)
8. Ali Ibn Musa al Reza (as) (son of Imam al Kadhim and Lady Najma as)
9. Muhammad Ibn Ali al Jawad, al Taqi (as) (son of Imam al Reza and Lady Sabeeka as)
10. Ali Ibn Muhammad al Hadi, al Naqi (son of Imam al Jawad and Lady Sumanah as)
11. Hassan Ibn Ali al Askari (as) (son of Imam al Naqi and Lady Hadithah as)

12. Muhammad Ibn Hassan al Qaim, al Mahdi (atf) (son of Imam al-Askari and Lady Narjis as)

Similar to Prophet's (pbuh) hadith, in the Old Testament, the significance of the '**twelve leaders**' is mentioned:

> "*As for Ishmael, I have heard you; behold, I will bless him, and will make him fruitful and will multiply him exceedingly. He shall become the father of **twelve rulers**, and I will make him a great nation.*"

Source: Bible, *Book of Genesis* 17:20

Imam al Baqir (as): "*We are the remnant of progeny* (of Prophet Ibrahim as). *And that was the prayer of Ibrahim (as) was regarding us* (the twelve Imams)."

Source: Sayyid Murtada al-Askari, *The Twelve Successors of the Holy Prophet*. Chapter: The Twelve Imams in the Old Testament *http://www.al-islam.org/twelve-successors-holy-prophet-sayyid-murtada-al-askari*

In Qur'an, Allah (swt) mentions the similar prayer of Prophet Ibrahim (as):

Surat Ibrahim14:37

$$\text{رَّبَّنَآ إِنِّىٓ أَسْكَنتُ مِن ذُرِّيَّتِى بِوَادٍ غَيْرِ ذِى زَرْعٍ عِندَ بَيْتِكَ الْمُحَرَّمِ رَبَّنَا لِيُقِيمُوا الصَّلَوٰةَ فَاجْعَلْ أَفْئِدَةً مِّنَ النَّاسِ تَهْوِىٓ إِلَيْهِمْ وَارْزُقْهُم مِّنَ الثَّمَرَٰتِ لَعَلَّهُمْ يَشْكُرُونَ ۝}$$

Our Lord!
I have settled part of my descendants
in a barren valley,
by Your sacred House, our Lord,
that they may maintain the prayer.
So make the hearts of a part of the people

fond of them,
and provide them with fruits,
so that they may give thanks.

Imam Baqir (as): *"We the Ahlul Bayt are meant by 'them' whom Ibrahim (as) mentioned in his prayer when he said: 'Make You (O Allah) therefore the hearts of some of the people to yearn/ fond towards them."*

The people mentioned in his prayer are those who remain faithfully attached to the Ahlul Bayt, known as their Shi'ahs (devout followers).

Source: Ayatollah Agha Mahdi Puya, *Tafsir of Holy Qur'an* Surat 14, P. 73. *http://www.islamicmobility.com/elibrary_14.htm*

As previously stated in the introduction of this book, all **of** the stories mentioned in the Holy Qur'an have a purpose to send a strong message to the people around the Holy Prophet (pbuh) and for the generations to come.

The Holy Prophet (pbuh): *"You will follow the ways of those nations who were before you, span by span and cubit by cubit (i.e., inch by inch) so much so that even if they entered a hole of a lizard, you would follow them."* We said: O Allah's Messenger (pbuh) (Do you mean) the Jews and the Christians?" He (pbuh) said: *"Whom else?"*

Narrated by Abu Said Al-Khudri

Source: Sahih Bukhari, vol. 9, Book 92, Hadith 422, *http://sunnah.com/bukhari/96*

As the above tradition in *Sahih Bukhari* confirms, the Prophet (pbuh) stated that the history of the Children of Israel would be repeated for Muslims. In fact, Qur'an has mentioned the stories of the Children of Israel to give us a way to understand the true history of Islam itself. There are many striking similarities in this regard written in the Qur'an, including the similarities of the leaders and the similarities of the people.

In **Surat al-Ma'ida, 5:12-13**, Allah (swt) is sending a very strong message to the Muslims, using the story of Prophet Moses (as):

﴿ وَلَقَدْ أَخَذَ اللَّهُ مِيثَاقَ بَنِي إِسْرَءِيلَ وَبَعَثْنَا مِنْهُمُ اثْنَىْ عَشَرَ نَقِيبًا وَقَالَ اللَّهُ إِنِّي مَعَكُمْ لَئِنْ أَقَمْتُمُ الصَّلَوٰةَ وَءَاتَيْتُمُ الزَّكَوٰةَ وَءَامَنتُم بِرُسُلِي وَعَزَّرْتُمُوهُمْ وَأَقْرَضْتُمُ اللَّهَ قَرْضًا حَسَنًا لَّأُكَفِّرَنَّ عَنكُمْ سَيِّئَاتِكُمْ وَلَأُدْخِلَنَّكُمْ جَنَّٰتٍ تَجْرِي مِن تَحْتِهَا الْأَنْهَٰرُ فَمَن كَفَرَ بَعْدَ ذَٰلِكَ مِنكُمْ فَقَدْ ضَلَّ سَوَآءَ السَّبِيلِ ﴿١٢﴾

Certainly Allah took a pledge (a covenant)
from the Children of Israel,
and We raised among them twelve chiefs.
And Allah said, 'I am with you!
Surely, if you maintain the prayer and give the zakat
and have faith in My apostles and support them
and lend Allah a good loan,
I will surely absolve you of your misdeeds,
and I will surely admit you into gardens
with streams running in them.
But whoever of you disbelieves after that
has certainly strayed from the right way.'

فَبِمَا نَقْضِهِم مِّيثَٰقَهُمْ لَعَنَّٰهُمْ وَجَعَلْنَا قُلُوبَهُمْ قَٰسِيَةً يُحَرِّفُونَ الْكَلِمَ عَن مَّوَاضِعِهِ وَنَسُوا حَظًّا مِّمَّا ذُكِّرُوا بِهِ وَلَا تَزَالُ تَطَّلِعُ عَلَىٰ خَآئِنَةٍ مِّنْهُمْ إِلَّا قَلِيلًا مِّنْهُمْ فَاعْفُ عَنْهُمْ وَاصْفَحْ إِنَّ اللَّهَ يُحِبُّ الْمُحْسِنِينَ ﴿١٣﴾

Then, because of their breaking their covenant
We cursed them and made their hearts hard:
they pervert words from their meanings,
and have forgotten a part of what they were reminded.
You will not cease to learn of some of their treachery,
excepting a few of them.
Yet excuse them and forbear.
Indeed Allah loves the virtuous.

In the above mentioned verses, Allah (swt) is telling us, Allah (swt) will make another 'Covenant' with the Muslims at the time of the Holy Prophet (pbuh) regarding **'Twelve Leaders'**. Also, using this story Allah (swt) is reminding Muslims to 'believe in the last messenger' and 'support him with everything he mentions.' Despite Allah's (swt) command to the people, Allah (swt), prophesized that the 'people will break their pledge.' Allah (swt) knew that people would change the meaning of the words of the Qur'an and the Prophet (pbuh) (*i.e. Maula and Wali*) and continue with their treacherous behavior until the end of times.

Ayatollah Agha Mahdi Puya wrote under the interpretation of this verse:

"If the righteous (as defined in this verse and in Surat al-Baqirah, 2:177) is adopted and put in practice Allah (swt) absolves man of his sins, but whosoever deviates, after coming into the fold of the religion of Allah (swt), shall go astray into the camp of Shaytan; a warning to those who had broken the covenant taken by the Holy Prophet (pbuh) at Ghadir Khum, and their followers till the day of resurrection."

Allah (swt) curses the people who break their pledge. So the Muslims should take precaution and avoid acting like the Jews. It is incumbent upon the Muslims to remain attached to the covenant the Holy Prophet bound them with at Ghadir Khum. They must also safeguard themselves from misinterpreting the Quran in order to keep away the curse of Allah which will certainly be upon them if they, like the Jews, distort the true meanings of the book of Allah to serve their worldly interests.

Source: Ayatollah Agha Mahdi Puya, _Tafsir of Holy Qur'an_ Surat 5, P. 430. _http://www.islamicmobility.com/elibrary_14.htm_

Note: In the _Tafseer of Qur'an by Ibn e Kathir_ (Arabic and Urdu), he mentioned narrations about Caliphate under the commentary of this verse (5:12), available on _http://qurango.com/tafseer.html_

> Ibn e Kathir mentioned that Imam Mahdi (atf) is the 12 caliphs. Ibn e Kathir tried his best to provide the list of those 12 Caliphs of Islam, but he could only come-up with six names and suggested that the rest of the caliphs will come before the Day of Judgment.

This is the big question for all Muslims as they still don't know, up until today **who their twelve caliphs are?**

If the Muslims cannot find those 12 Caliphs after Prophet Mohammad (pbuh) then they need to acknowledge '**the twelve**' who are from the progeny of Prophet Mohammad (pbuh), and they announced about themselves that they are the Caliphs of Prophet Mohammad (pbuh), and they are the _WALI_ (master) of his Ummah.

Here is the segment with the words of Imam Ali (as), the middle part of **Sermon 143 from Nahjul Balagha.**

> _"Where are those who falsely and unjustly claimed that they are deeply versed in knowledge, as against us, although Allah raised us in position and kept them down, bestowed upon us knowledge, but deprived them, and entered us (in the fortress of knowledge) but kept them out. With us guidance is to be sought and blindness (of misguidance) is to be changed into brightness. Surely Imams (divine leaders) will be from the Quraysh. They have been planted in this line through Hashim. It would not suit others, nor would others be suitable as heads of affairs."_

End of Chapter Notes:

Here are some of the other Ahadith of the Holy Prophet (pbuh) regarding 'twelve leaders' for his true followers:

1. *"The (Islamic) religion will continue until the Hour (day of resurrection), having **twelve Caliphs** for you, all of them will be from Quraysh."*

Source:

Sahih Muslim, Book 33, Hadith 11 *http://sunnah.com/muslim/33/11*

2. *"The affairs of people will continue to be conducted (well) as long as they are governed by the **twelve men**, all of them from Quraysh."*

Source:

Sahih Muslim, Book 33, Hadith 9, *http://sunnah.com/muslim/33/9*

3. *"Islam will continue to be triumphant until there have been **twelve Caliphs**, all of them from Quraysh."*

Source:

Sahih Muslim, Book 33, Hadith 8, *http://sunnah.com/muslim/33/8*

4. *"There will be after me **twelve Amir** (Prince/Ruler), all of them from Quraysh."*

Source:

Sunan at Tirmidhi, Book 33, Hadith 66
http://sunnah.com/tirmidhi/33/66

5. *"The religion will continue to be established till there are **twelve caliphs** over you, and the whole community will agree on each of them. All of them will belong to Quraysh.*

Source:

Sunan Abu Dawood, Book 38, Hadith 1,
http://sunnah.com/abuDawood/38/1

6. *"This religion will remain till **twelve Imams** from Quraysh (will pass), then when they expire the earth will swallow its inhabitants."*

Source:

Ali Ibn Abd-al-Malik Al-Muttaqi al-Hindi, *Kanz al-'Ummal*, Vol. 13, P. 27

Books on this topic:

Shorter Shi'a Encyclopedia *Chapters: The Twelve Imams Parts 1 and 2* by Hasan ul Amins.

Shi'a Anthology. *Chapter: The Twelve Imams* by Allama Sayyid Muhammad Hussain Tabataba'i

The Twelve Successors of the Holy Prophet by Sayyid Murtada al-Askari: http://www.al-islam.org/twelve-successors-holy-prophet-sayyid-murtada-al-askari

Who Are These Twelve Successors of the Prophet(s)? By Ahlul Bayt Digital Islamic Library Project

Chapter 6

The word Shi'a and its meaning from Qur'an

The word *Shi'a*, which means a 'follower', is used in the holy Qur'an at several places:

Surat al Saffat, 37:83

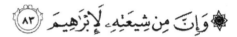

Indeed Abraham was among his followers

(Notice that the word "*Shi'a*" is explicitly used, letter-by-letter, in the above verse as well as the following verse).

Surat al Qasas 28:15

وَدَخَلَ ٱلْمَدِينَةَ عَلَىٰ حِينِ غَفْلَةٍ مِّنْ أَهْلِهَا فَوَجَدَ فِيهَا رَجُلَيْنِ
يَقْتَتِلَانِ هَٰذَا مِن شِيعَتِهِ وَهَٰذَا مِنْ عَدُوِّهِ ۖ فَٱسْتَغَاثَهُ ٱلَّذِى مِن
شِيعَتِهِ عَلَى ٱلَّذِى مِنْ عَدُوِّهِ فَوَكَزَهُ مُوسَىٰ فَقَضَىٰ عَلَيْهِ ۖ قَالَ هَٰذَا مِنْ
عَمَلِ ٱلشَّيْطَانِ ۖ إِنَّهُ عَدُوٌّ مُّضِلٌّ مُّبِينٌ ﴿١٥﴾

*[One day] he (Moses) entered the city
at a time when its people dwelt in distraction.
He found there two men fighting,
this one from among his followers,
and that one from his enemies.
The one who was from his followers sought his help
against him who was from his enemies.
So Moses hit him with his fist,
whereupon he expired.
He said, 'This is of Satan's doing.*

Indeed he is an enemy, manifestly misguiding.'

In the above verse of the Qur'an, one is mentioned as the Shi'a (follower) of Moses (as) and the other one is mentioned as the enemy of Moses (as). Thus Shi'a is an official word used by Allah (swt) in the holy Qur'an for the highest ranked prophets (as) and their followers.

If somebody calls himself a Shi'a, it is not due to any innovation or sectarianism. It is because Qur'an has used the phrase for the Prophets (as) of Allah (swt) and their followers. Therefore, according to the holy Qur'an the word **'Shi'a'** has a special meaning (i.e. The Shi'a of Noah (as), The Shi'a of Moses (as), Also in the History of Islam, Shi'a has been specially used for the 'followers of Ali Ibn Abu Talib (as))'. The first individual who used this term was the Messenger of Allah himself:

Prophet Muhammad (pbuh) said to Ali (as):

'Glad tiding O 'Ali! Verily you and your companions and your Shi'a (followers) will be in Paradise.'

Sources: (Ahle Sunnah books)

1. Ahmad Ibn Hanbal, *Kitab al-Fada'il Sahaba*: Virtues of the Companions (Arabic) Vol 2, P. 655

2. Shaykh Abu Nuaym Ahmad Isfahani, *Hilyatul Awliyaawa Tabaqaatul Asfiya:* The Adornment of the Saints and the Ranks of the Spiritual Elite (Arabic) Vol 4, P. 329. Urdu version URL:

https://ia700508.us.archive.org/16/items/HilyatulAwliyaWaTabaqat ulAsfiyaByShaykhAbuNuaymAhmadIsfahanir.a/HilyatulAwliyaWaT abaqatulAsfiyaByShaykhAbuNuaymAhmadIsfahanir.a_text.pdf

3. Abu Bakr Ahmad Ibn Ali Ibn Thabit *AKA* al-Khatib al-Baghdadi, *Ta'rikh Baghdad*: The History of Baghdad (Arabic) Vol. 12, P. 289

Also

Narrated by Jabir Ibn Abdullah al-Ansari (ra)

Prophet Muhammad (pbuh):

> *"The Shi'a of Ali are the real victorious in the day of resurrection/rising"*

Source: (Ahle Sunnah book) Sulayman al-Qunduzi, *Yanabi al-Muwadda*, P. 62

This clearly shows that the word "**Shi'a**" was used by Prophet Muhammad (pbuh) himself for the followers of Imam Ali (as) and was NOT invented by anyone else later on (as most believe).

Who are the Shi'as according to the Imams of Ahlul Bayt (as)?

Imam Muhammad al Baqir (as) to his student Jabir:

> *"Does it suffice for one who claims to be our Shi'a (follower) to just express his friendship with the members of the Holy Household? I swear by God that no one is our true follower unless he fears God and obeys Him. Our followers are known for their humbleness and frequent remembrance of God; fasting; praying; helping the orphans, the needy, the ones in debt, and needy neighbors; reading the Quran; and talking properly with the people. They have always been trustworthy in their tribes. O' Jabir! Do not let the various sects affect you. Do you think that it suffices for one to say that he likes Imam Ali and he is his follower, but does not do anything to support his claim? Or he says that he likes the Prophet, who is even better than Imam Ali, but does not take his example and follow his deeds and act according to the Prophet's tradition? Just having love for the Prophet is of no use for him. Therefore, fear God, and act in such a way as to attain what is near God, since there is no relation of kin between God and anyone. The one most loved by God is the one who is the most pious, and the noblest one is the one who fears God and obeys Him. I swear by God that it is not possible to get close to God, unless by His obedience, and we do not hold the key to relief from the Fire of Hell, and no one has any authority over God. Whoever is obedient to God is our friend, and whoever disobeys God is our*

enemy. No one can attain our friendship unless by having nobility and piety"

Source:

1. Sheikh Muhammad Ibn Ya'qub Ibn Ishaq al-Kulayni, *Al-Kafi*, Vol 2, P. 74

2. Abu Mohammed Al-Hasan bin Ali bin Al-Hussain bin Shu'ba Al-Harrani *Tuhaf ul Uqool: The Masterpiece of the Mind.* *http://www.hilmi.eu/islam/books/books/TuhafulUqool.pdf*

Imam al Baqir (as) to his Shi'as:

"Your strong one should help your weak one. Your rich one should be kind to your poor one. The man should be loyal to his brother as he is loyal to himself. Keep our secrets. Do not force the people to follow us. Consider carefully our affair and what has been mentioned on our authority. If you find it in agreement with the Qur'an, then put it into effect. If you find it contrary to the Qur'an, then leave it. If you doubt the affair, then stop and ask us to explain it to you."

Imam al Baqir (as):

"Our followers are of three kinds, one who follows us, but depends on others, another who is, like a glass involved in his own reflections, but the best are those who are like gold, the more they suffer the more they shine"

Imam al Baqir (as) describing signs of his Shi'as:

"Humility, fear of Allah, trustworthiness, remembrance of Allah, fasts, prays Salat, is good to parents, good to neighbors, is responsible towards widows, orphans & children, fulfills his/her vows, pays back his/her debts, & recites the Qur'an"

Imam Jafar al Sadiq (as) describing signs of his Shi'as:

"Our Shi'a are the people of piety and diligence, loyalty and honesty, and asceticism and worship. They perform fifty-one rak'as in a single day and night. They pass their nights with worship and their days with fasting. They pay the zakat from their wealth, perform the hajj, and refrain from committing any forbidden thing"

Imam Jafar al Sadiq (as) warns his Shi'as:

"O Shi'a community, be an adornment for us (amongst people), and not a disgrace to us. Say good words to people, guard your tongues, and restrain yourselves from mindless chatter and offensive speech."

Imam Jafar al Sadiq (as):

"One who claims to follow us with his tongue, but does the opposite of our actions and deeds is not from among our Shi'a"

Imam Ali al Murtadha (as):

"Fear Allah in relation to your prayers. It is the pillar of your religion"

Imam Jafar al Sadiq (as):

"Verily our intercession will not avail one who takes his prayer lightly"

"Test our followers at three occasions: during the prayer times to see how much importance they give it; and by our secrets to see how they protect our secrets from our enemies; and with their wealth to see how they help their brothers in faith with it"

Imam Ali Reza (as):

"Our (true) Shi'a are those who submit to our orders, carry out

our directives, and dissent from our enemies. He who does not enjoy such characteristics is not one of us"

Imam Muhammad al Jawad (as):

"The Shi'a of Ali (as) are surely those who meet the needs of each other for the sake of (their loyalty to) our leadership, love each other for the sake of our cherishment, and exchange visits for the sake of proclaiming our affairs. They do not oppress when they are enraged and do not exaggerate when they are pleased. They are blessings for their neighbors and peace for their associates"

Imam Muhammad al Baqir (as):

"The Shi'a of Ali (as) are only those whose voices do not exceed their hearings and detestation does not exceed their bodies. They do not praise those who abhor us, regard those who hate us, or associate with those who revile at us. The true Shi'a of Ali (as) do not bark like dogs, or beg people openly even if they starve. Their living is hardly sufficient. Their dwellings are roving..."

Imam Jafar al Sadiq (as):

"On the Day of Resurrection, all the creatures will be called with the names of their mothers. We, as well as our Shi'a, are not bound by this act, because we are saved from adultery (real Shi'as do not commit adultery)"

Imam Zainul Abideen (as):

"Our Shi'a are characterized by their worship and shagginess. Their noses are impaired due to worship, and their foreheads, as well as organs of prostration, are effaced. Their stomachs are atrophied, and their lips are withered. Worship has changed their faces, staying up at nights has fatigued them, and

hot weather has affected their bodies. They praise Allah when people are silent, offer prayers when people are asleep, and are sad when people are happy. Their distinctive feature is asceticism. Their wording is mercy and their main concern is Paradise"

Source for all of the above narrations:

Sheikh Sudooq, *Fadhail ush Shia: The Merits of the Shi'a.* *http://www.najaf.org/english/book/23/*

Abu Abd Allah Muhammad Ibn Muhammad Ibn al-Nu'man al Ukbari al-Baghdadi *AKA* **Shaykh al-Mufid** and **Ibn al-Mu'allim,** *Al-Amali, The Dictations of Shaykh al-Mufid.* *http://www.al-islam.org/al-amali-dictations-shaykh-al-mufid*

End of Chapter notes:

Origination of Shi'a Islam

The friends and followers of Ali (as) believed that after the demise of the Prophet (pbuh) the caliphate and religious authority (*marja'iyat-i 'ilmi*) belonged to Ali (as). This belief came from their consideration of Ali's position and station in relation to the Prophet (pbuh), his relation to the chosen among the companions, as well as his relation to Muslims in general. It was only the events that occurred during the few days of the Prophet's final illness that indicated that there was opposition to their view. Contrary to their expectation, at the very moment when the Prophet (pbuh) passed away and his body lay still unburied, while his household and a few companions were occupied with providing for his burial and funeral service, the friends and followers of Ali (as) received news about the activity of another group who had gone to the mosque where the community was gathered faced with this sudden loss of their leader. This group, which was later to form the majority, set forth in great haste to select a caliph for the Muslims with the aim of ensuring the welfare of the community and solving its immediate problems. They did this without consulting the Household of the Prophet, his relatives or many of his friends, who were busy with the funeral, and without providing them with any information. Thus Ali (as) and his companions were presented with an undeniable fact.

Ali (as) and his friends - such as Salman, Bilal, Abu Dhar, Miqdad and Ammar, after finishing with the burial of the body of the Prophet (pbuh) became aware of the proceedings by which the caliph had been selected. They protested against the act of choosing the caliph by consultation or election, and also against those who were responsible for carrying it out. They even presented their own proofs and arguments, but the answer they received was that the welfare of the Muslims was at stake and an immediate selection of a caliph was the only solution.

It was this unwarranted and forced selection of the caliphate that separated the majority from the minority. Those who followed Ali (as) were known to the society as the 'partisans' or

'Shi'ah' of Ali (as). The caliphate of the time was anxious to guard against this appellation being given to the Shi'ah minority and thus to have a Muslim society divided into sections comprised of a majority and a minority. The supporters of the caliph considered the caliphate being a matter of the consensus of the community (*ijma*) and called those who objected the 'opponents of allegiance'. They claimed that the Shi'ah stood, therefore, opposed to Muslim society. Since that time, over 1400 years ago up until today, the Shi'ah were given other pejorative and degrading names such as *Rafidha*, the ones who reject.

Shia'ism was condemned from the first moment because of the political situation of the time and thus it could not accomplish anything through mere political protest. Ali (as) did not up rise against the caliphate. However, his reasons to remain patient while his rightfully appointed position was taken were: 1.) he lacked sufficient military power and support at the time and 2.) he wanted to safeguard the well-being of the Muslim *Umma* and Islam. Yet those who protested against the established caliphate refused to surrender to the majority in certain questions of faith and continued to hold that the succession to the Prophet (pbuh) and religious authority belonged by right to Ali (as). They believed that all spiritual and religious matters should be referred to him and invited people to become his followers.

Source:

Allamah Sayyid Muhammad Hussain Tabatabi, *Shi'a*, P. 4-5

Books on this topic

Al-Amali, *The Dictations of Shaykh al-Mufid* by Shaykh al-Mufid:
http://www.al-islam.org/al-amali-dictations-shaykh-al-mufid

Asl al-Shia wa Usuluh: The Origin of the Shi'ite Islam and its Principles by al-Shaykh Muhammad Hussain aal Kashiful-Ghita

Fadhaail Ush-Shi'a: The Merits of the Shi'a by Abu Jafar Muhammad Ibn Ali Ibn Babawaih al-Qummi Shaykh Sudooq

Haqqul Yaqeen by al-Shaykh Muhammad Baqir al-Majlisi

Let Us Understand Each Other (Shia - Sunni Dialogue) by Abdul Hadi Abdul Hameed Saleh

Peshawar Nights by Sultanul Waizin Shirazi

Saqifa, the First Manifestations of the Emergence of the Shi'i Viewpoint by al-Syed Hussain Muhammad Jafari

Shi'aism in the View of Imam Al-Baqir (as): The Attributes of the Shia person (web article)
http://english.bayynat.org/infallibles/baqir.htm

Shi'ism in the View of Imam al Baqir (as) by Sayed Fadhlallah

Shi'ism And The Shi'a by Aytoallah Muhammad Shirazi

Shia by Allama Sayyid Muhammad Hussain Tabataba'i

Shia by al-Syed Iqbal Husain Rizvi

Shorter Shi'a Encyclopedia *Chapter: The Term "Shia" in Quran and Hadith* by Hasan ul Amins

The Glad Tidings of Mustafa for the Shia of Murtaza by Shaykh Emadul Deen Abu Jaafar Mohammad Bin Abi Qasem Al-Tabari

The Shia of Al-Baqir (web article) by Arsalan Rizvi http://www.islamicinsights.com/religion/religion/the-shia-of-al-baqir.html

The Shia Are the Real Ahl al-Sunnah (Followers of the Prophet's Tradition) by al-Syed Muhammad al-Tijani al-Smaoui

Then I was Guided by al-Syed Muhammad al-Tijani al-Smaoui

Truth about Shi'ah Ithna Ashari Faith by Asad Wahid al-Qasim

Chapter 7

Those vested with Authority

Surat al Nisa 4:59

يَـٰٓأَيُّهَا ٱلَّذِينَ ءَامَنُوٓا۟ أَطِيعُوا۟ ٱللَّهَ وَأَطِيعُوا۟ ٱلرَّسُولَ وَأُو۟لِى ٱلْأَمْرِ مِنكُمْ ۖ فَإِن
نَـٰزَعْتُمْ فِى شَىْءٍ فَرُدُّوهُ إِلَى ٱللَّهِ وَٱلرَّسُولِ إِن كُنتُمْ تُؤْمِنُونَ بِٱللَّهِ وَٱلْيَوْمِ
ٱلْأَخِرِ ۚ ذَٰلِكَ خَيْرٌ وَأَحْسَنُ تَأْوِيلًا ﴿٥٩﴾

O you who have faith!
Obey Allah and obey the Apostle
and those vested with authority among you.
And if you dispute concerning anything,
refer it to Allah and the Apostle,
if you have faith in Allah and the Last Day.
That is better and more favorable in outcome.

When we comes across the above verse of the holy Qur'an, we must ponder over the following questions:

- What qualities do the *Ulil Amr* "those vested with authority" need to have? *especially if they are to be obeyed as to obey*

  the Holy Prophet (pbuh) as 'and' or 'و' represents
- How do we identify the *Ulil Amr*?
- Does it mean political, military or spiritual leadership or all? Should you obey them unconditionally?
- What is the barometer of their obedience?
- If Allah (swt) meant here 'the scholars', then what is the criteria of such scholar? Can anyone with a long beard who memorizes few verses of the Qur'an and ahadith becomes an *Ulil Amr*?
- Who is the *Ulil Amr* today? Which scholars, political or

military leaders?
- Who is my *Ulil Amr*? Whom I must follow and obey similarly to an infallible Holy Prophet (pbuh).

Interpretation by Ayatollah Agha Puya:

The command to obey is infinite-total obedience in all material, religious and spiritual matters. Therefore, as this verse clearly signifies, the *Ulil Amr* must also be as just, wise and merciful as Allah (swt) and the Holy Prophet (pbuh) are, and he who administers the affairs of mankind should be the *Khalifa-tullah* (vicegerent of Allah) and the *Waliallah* (representative of Allah whom Allah chooses after equipping him with His wisdom).

It is a grave danger to Islam to accept any ruler as an *Ulil Amr*, except those leaders that Allah (swt) has chosen amongst the divine progeny. The grave danger extends to men like Yazid bin Muawiya to be included in the category of *Ulil Amr*. Considering that Yazid martyred Husain (as) and members of the Ahlul Bayt (as), it would be difficult to reason that Allah (swt) has enjoined to obey men like Yazid, just as one must obey Allah (swt) and the Holy Prophet (pbuh). (*One can easily find prototypes of Yazid in abundance throughout the history of Islam until today, i.e. ISIS, al-Qaida, Taliban etc.*)

From the event of *Ashira* (feast of the near relatives to carry out the divine command of 'warn your tribe of near relatives') to the day at *Ghadir Khum*, the Holy Prophet (pbuh) repeatedly announced the successorship of Ali (as), therefore, the first step a Muslim must take to obey the messenger of Allah is to obey and follow Ali Ibn abi Talib (as). It is in following the rightfully appointed Imams' that Muslims will be able to preserve Islam and Allah's (swt) message in its true essence. A deviation from the divinely appointed leadership, leads to the grave risk of Islam being high jacked by unfit Caliphates. Caliphate's who misuse the name of Islam to implement their own agendas.

Source: Ayatollah Agha Mahdi Puya, *Tafsir of Holy Qur'an* Surat 4, verse 59 P. 378-379.
http://www.islamicmobility.com/elibrary_14.htm

By the explanation of the Holy Prophet Muhammad (pbuh), this verse is also one of the Qur'anic references to the leadership of Imam Ali (as). When this verse was revealed to the Holy Prophet (pbuh), one of his great companions, Jabir Ibn Abdullah al-Ansari (ra) asked:

O Messenger of Allah (pbuh)! We are aware of Allah (swt) and His Messenger, but who are meant by the words (of this verse) <u>Persons vested with Authority</u>, whose obedience is made mandatory along with you and Allah? The Prophet (pbuh) replied:

O Jabir, they are the leaders over the Muslims after me, the first of them being Ali Ibn Abi Talib, the al-Hassan and al-Hussain followed by Ali Ibn Hussain, then Muhammad Ibn Ali, who is mentioned in the Torah as Baqir and you, O Jabir, would meet him; convey my salutation (greetings) to him. After him is Jafar Ibn Muhammad, Musa Ibn Jafar, Ali Ibn Musa, Muhammad Ibn Ali, Ali Ibn Muhammad, al-Hassan Ibn Ali followed by my namesake, who would be Allah's (swt) Mandate on Earth, who would disappear and go into occultation and it is through him that mankind would be put to test whether they steadfast in their belief regarding Imammat.

Source: Shaykh Sudooq, *Kamal al Deen wa Tamam Neymaat(Arabic)* P. 253

The Holy Prophet Muhammad (pbuh) told the Muslims both about the succession of the designated members of his family (*Ahlul Bayt*). The Messenger of Allah said:

You are in the same position with relation to me as Aaron was with Moses, except that there will be no prophet after me

Source: S*ahih Bukhari, Book* 62, Hadith 57:
      http://sunnah.com/bukhari/62

Surat al-Maidah 5:55-56

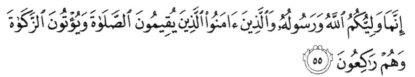

Your guardian is only Allah, His Apostle,
and the faithful who maintain the prayer
and give zakat while bowing down.

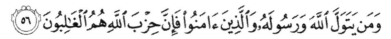

Whoever takes for his guardians Allah,
His Apostle and the faithful
The confederates of Allah are indeed the victorious.

Narrated by Abu Dhar al Ghafari (ra):

> *Both of my ears may turn deaf and both my eyes may become*
> *blind if I speak a lie. I heard the Holy Prophet (pbuh) saying:*
> *"Ali is the guide of the righteous and the slayer of the infidels.*
> *He who has helped him is victorious and he who has abandoned*
> *him is forsaken."*

> *One day I said my prayers in the company of the Holy Prophet;*
> *a beggar came to the mosque and begged for alms, but nobody*
> *gave him anything.*

> *Ali (as) was in a state of ruku (bowing down) in the prayer. He*
> *pointed out his ring to the beggar, who approached him and*
> *removed the ring from his finger. Thereupon the Holy Prophet*
> *(pbuh) implored Allah (swt), by saying: 'O Allah! My brother*
> *Musa begged You saying: My Lord, delight my heart and make*
> *my task easy and undo the knot in my tongue so that they may*
> *understand me, and appoint from among my kinsmen, Harun,*
> *my brother, as my vizier, and strengthen my back with him and*
> *make him participate in my mission so that we may glorify You*
> *and remember You more frequently. Certainly You see us, and*
> *You inspired him:*

"O Musa! All your requests have been granted. The Holy Prophet (pbuh) continued… Delight my heart and make my task easy and appoint from among my kinsmen Ali as my vizier and strengthen my back with him"

(Abu Dhar proceeds) By Allah, the Holy Prophet (pbuh) had not yet finished his supplication when the trustworthy Jibraeel descended to him with this verse".

Source: Ayatollah Agha Mahdi Puya, *Tafsir of Holy Qur'an* Surat 5, verses 55 – 56, P. 453.
   http://www.islamicmobility.com/elibrary_14.htm

Surat al Nisa 4:83

وَإِذَا جَآءَهُمۡ أَمۡرٌ مِّنَ ٱلۡأَمۡنِ أَوِ ٱلۡخَوۡفِ أَذَاعُواْ بِهِۦ وَلَوۡ رَدُّوهُ إِلَى ٱلرَّسُولِ وَإِلَىٰٓ أُوْلِي ٱلۡأَمۡرِ مِنۡهُمۡ لَعَلِمَهُ ٱلَّذِينَ يَسۡتَنۢبِطُونَهُۥ مِنۡهُمۡ وَلَوۡلَا فَضۡلُ ٱللَّهِ عَلَيۡكُمۡ وَرَحۡمَتُهُۥ لَٱتَّبَعۡتُمُ ٱلشَّيۡطَٰنَ إِلَّا قَلِيلًا ۝٨٣

When a report of safety or alarm comes to them,
they immediately broadcast it;
but had they referred it to the Apostle
or to those vested with authority among them,
those of them who investigate would have ascertained it.
And were it not for Allah's grace upon you
and His mercy,
you would have surely followed Satan,
[all] except a few.

In this verse, Allah again invites people to refer to the Holy Prophet (pbuh) and his Ahlul Bayt (as), their affairs and problems because they alone know the truth and are authorized to guide; and if they do not, surely they will go astray in the direction of Satan.

And had there not been Allah's grace (*fadl*) and mercy (*rahmat*) present among the Muslims, they would also have lived in total darkness of infidelity. *Fadl* and *rahmat* stand for the Holy Prophet (pbuh) and Ali Ibn Abi Talib (as).

In the *Dawat Dhul Ashira* (feast of the near relatives) when the Holy Prophet (pbuh) had said that he had been commanded by Allah (swt) to call them to His worship, therefore, who would, among them, testify to his Prophethood and join him to support his mission and be his brother, lieutenant, and successor, it was Ali (as) who stood up and offered his services unconditionally. Then the Holy Prophet said, *"Verily Ali is my brother and my successor. From this day it has been made obligatory upon everyone to obey the authority of Ali."*

Source: Ahmad Ibn Hanbal, *Musnad,* annotated by Ahmad Muhammad Shakir in 15 volumes, Dar al-Maarif, Cairo, 1949-1958, hadith 883.

So, from the 'feast of the near relatives' to 11ᵗʰ Hijra, Ali (as) stood by the Holy Prophet (pbuh) and supported him in his divine mission. In 11ᵗʰ Hijra the Holy Prophet (pbuh) declared at Ghadir Khum that:

"Of whomsoever he was the Master, this Ali (while raising Imam Ali's arm) was his Master!"

Source: Ahmad Ibn Hanbal, *Musnad,* English Vol 1. Darussalam Publishers. Hadith 950, P. 460, Hadith 961, P. 465, and Hadith 1311 592

As it is clearly mentioned in all history books (whether Shi'a or Sunni) the decisive role Ali (as) played in the battles of Badr, Uhud, Khandaq (Trench), Khaybar, Hunayn and many other wars, to confirm that it was Ali (as) who saved the Muslim Ummah from total destruction. The Holy Prophet (pbuh) showed the right path and Ali (as) guarded it. Ali (as) has been described as the '**total faith**' by the Holy Prophet (pbuh) in the battle of Khandaq (Trench). Also, after his decisive victory over Amr bin Abduwad which created terror in the hearts of a very large army of 12000 opposition soldiers, who all together took to flight, the Holy Prophet (pbuh) declared that:

"One strike of Ali, on the day of Khandaq, is superior to all worship of both the worlds (humans and angels combined)"

If this one strike were not to occur, there would have been no Muslims on the face of the earth.

Sources: Ayatollah Agha Mahdi Puya, *Tafsir of Holy Qur'an* Surat4, verse 83P. 390.
http://www.islamicmobility.com/elibrary_14.htm

Allama Muhammad Baqir Al-Majlisi, *Hayat al Qulub,* Vol 2: Battle of Khandaq. *http://www.al-islam.org/hayat-al-qulub-vol-2-allamah-muhammad-baqir-al-majlisi/battle-khandaq*

Witness of the Prophethood

Surat Ar Ra'ad 13:43

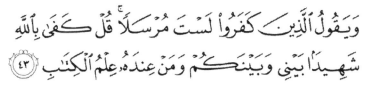

The faithless say,
You have not been sent [by Allah].
Say, 'Allah suffices as a witness between me
and you,
and he who possesses the knowledge of the Book.

Q. Who possesses the knowledge of the book? To whom does it refer to?

Abdullah Bin Bakeyr asked Imam Jafar al Sadiq (as) about Prophet Sulayman (as) (Soloman) and what he had been given from the knowledge and what he had been given from the kingdom?

Imam al Sadiq (as) said:

"And Prophet Sulayman Bin Dawood (as) had not been given all of the knowledge, but he had with him one letter from the Great Name (Ism Aazam), and your Imam is the one about whom Allah (swt) said:

Say, 'Allah suffices as a witness between me and you,

and he who possesses the knowledge of the Book (13:43).

…And by Allah (swt), Ali (as) was the one with the knowledge of the Book.

Imam al Sadiq (as) when asked about this verse by Muhammad Bin Suleiman Bin Sudeyr, Abu Baseer, Maysar, Yahya Al-Bazaaz, and Dawood Al-Raqy:

The Imam (as) puts his finger on his chest and said *"Knowledge of the Book, all of it, by Allah (swt) is with us (meaning the Imams of Ahlul Bayt as)."* The Imam (as) said this <u>three times.</u>

Source:

Abu Jafar Muhammad bin al-Hassan bin al-Farooq al-Saffar (companion of Imam Hassan al Askari AS) *Basaair Al Darajaat:An Insight Into The Levels* (English) Part 5, Ch 1, P. 4-5. <u>http://hubeali.com/online-books/online-english-books/basaair-al-darajaat</u>

More in the Knowledge of the Book

One can do many extraordinary things by having 'the knowledge of the Book', with the permission of Allah (swt). For example, the Qur'an mentions that at the time of the Prophet Sulayman (as), a person by the name of *Asaf Ibn Barkhiya*, who was the Minister of Prophet Sulayman (as) and had only a very small part of 'the knowledge of the Book', was able to bring the throne of Queen Bilqis (Sheeba) from another place of the world within the twinkling of an eye in:

Surat al Naml 27:40

قَالَ الَّذِى عِندَهُۥ عِلْمٌ مِّنَ الْكِتَبِ أَنَا۠ ءَاتِيكَ بِهِۦ قَبْلَ أَن يَرْتَدَّ إِلَيْكَ طَرْفُكَ

فَلَمَّا رَءَاهُ مُسْتَقِرًّا عِندَهُۥ قَالَ هَٰذَا مِن فَضْلِ رَبِّى لِيَبْلُوَنِىٓ ءَأَشْكُرُ أَمْ

أَكْفُرُ وَمَن شَكَرَ فَإِنَّمَا يَشْكُرُ لِنَفْسِهِۦ وَمَن كَفَرَ فَإِنَّ رَبِّى غَنِىٌّ كَرِيمٌ ۝

The one who had knowledge of the Book said,
I will bring it to you
in the twinkling of an eye.
So when he saw it set near him,
he said, 'This is by the grace of my Lord,
to test me if I will give thanks or be ungrateful.
And whoever gives thanks,
gives thanks only for his own sake.
And whoever is ungrateful [should know that]
my Lord is indeed all-sufficient, all-generous.

End of Chapter Notes

Surat al Nisa 4:59

يَٰٓأَيُّهَا ٱلَّذِينَ ءَامَنُوٓاْ أَطِيعُواْ ٱللَّهَ وَأَطِيعُواْ ٱلرَّسُولَ وَأُوْلِى ٱلْأَمْرِ مِنكُمْ فَإِن تَنَٰزَعْتُمْ فِى شَىْءٍ فَرُدُّوهُ إِلَى ٱللَّهِ وَٱلرَّسُولِ إِن كُنتُمْ تُؤْمِنُونَ بِٱللَّهِ وَٱلْيَوْمِ ٱلْأَخِرِ ذَٰلِكَ خَيْرٌ وَأَحْسَنُ تَأْوِيلًا ﴿٥٩﴾

O you who have faith!
Obey Allah and obey the Apostle
*and **those vested with authority among you**.*

Typically, there are three categories of *Ulul-Amr* (those vested with authority) specified by the Sunni scholars.

1. Those in army authority positions.
2. Political Leaders
3. The Ulema – Scholars of Deen.

Analysis of each category:

1. Those in army authority positions.

1.1   Qur'anic view on this category
Surah Nisa 4:95
Is he who fights equal to he who stays at home?

1.2 Excellences of Imam Ali (as)
Gibrael (as) stated at Uhud, *'There is no brave young man but Ali, and there is no sword but Dhulfiqar'*
Source: History of al-Tabari Volume 7 pages 120-121

1.3 Weaknesses amongst the previous Caliphs

Abu Jafar (al Tabari) says: The army had fled and abandoned the Messenger of God, some of them getting as far as al-Munaqqa near al-A'was. ''Uthman bin Affan, together with Uqbah b. Uthman and Sa'd bin Uthman, two men of the Ansar fled as far as Jal'ab, a mountain in the neighborhood of Medina near al-A'was. They stayed there for three days, and then came back to the Messenger of God. They claimed that he said to them, 'On that day you were scattered far and wide''.
Source: History of Tabari Volume 7 pages 126-127

2. Political Leaders

2.1 Qur'anic view on this category
Surah Ahzab: 33:6
The Prophet is Awla to the believers than their own selves

2.2 Excellences of Imam Ali (as)
Prophet (pbuh) said "do I have more authority over you than you have over yourselves? To which the people said 'Yes'. He then said of whomsoever I am Mawla Ali is his Mawla"
Source: Musnad, by Ahmad bin Hanbal, Vol 3, P.116 Sader Printing 1969

2.3 Weaknesses amongst the previous Caliphs
Abu Bakr: "Now then: O people, I have been put in charge of you, although I am not the best of you. Help me if I do well; rectify me if I do wrong"
Source: History of Tabari: English translation Volume 9 p 201

3. The Ulema/scholars of Deen

3.1 Qur'anic view on this category
Surah Zumar 39:9

Are those who have knowledge and those who do not 'alike?

3.2 Excellences of Imam Ali (as)

The Prophet (s) said 'I am the City of Knowledge and 'Ali is its Gate

Source: Sharh Mishkaath Volume 4 page 666, Sawaqih al Muhriqa page 418, taken from Tabrani and Hakim

3.3 Weaknesses amongst the previous Caliphs

Umar Ibn al Khattab said: 'Ali is the best judge among our people. Umar used to invoke the protection of Allah upon an intricate question if Abu Hasan was not there.

Source: Tabaqat Ibn Saad, Vol 2, Page 438

Books on this topic:

Imam Ali and Political Leadership by al-Shaykh Muhammad Reyshahri

Shorter Shi'a Encyclopedia *Chapters:* Leadership and Infallibility *Parts 1 and 2* by Hasan ul Amins.

Wilayah by Ayatollah Murtadha Mutahhari

Ayah of Wilaya by Ayatollah Syed Murtadha al-Shirazi

Hayat Al-Qulub Vol. 2: *A Detailed Biography of Prophet Muhammad (pbuh) by* Allama Muhammad Baqir Al-Majlisi *http://www.al-islam.org/hayat-al-qulub-vol-2-allamah-muhammad-baqir-al-majlisi*

It Removes the Misconception about Caliphs' Caliphate by Shah Walyullah Dehlavi

Shi'a Encyclopedia by Ahlul Bayt Digital Islamic Library Project Team *http://www.al-islam.org/shiite-encyclopedia-ahlul-bayt-dilp-team*

Chapter 8

The most important message in Qur'an

The Prophet's (pbuh) sermon at *Ghadir Khum* (the pond of Khum) is an utmost important sermon, which has been forgotten by the majority of the Muslim *Ummah*. This sermon and the traditions related to this sermon have been narrated by **110 companions** (*Sahaba*) of the Holy Prophet (pbuh) and it is recorded in **185 books** by Sunni scholars and authors, the list of the names of these books is available on:

http://www.al-islam.org/ghadir/books.asp

Background

The 'Farewell pilgrimage' ceremony was completed in the last month on the 10ᵗʰ A.H. The Muslims learned pilgrimage activities from the Prophet (pbuh), and then, the Prophet (pbuh) decided to leave Mecca to Medina. He instructed for departure, when the caravan reached an area called "*Rabegh*" (a place located between Mecca and Medina), which is three miles far from *Juhfah* (a place where paths towards Medina, Egypt and Iraq diverged), Arch angel Gabriel (the inspiration angel), revealed in a point called "*Ghadir Khum*", and addressed the Prophet (pbuh) with the following verse:

Surat al Maidah 5:67

﴿ يَٰٓأَيُّهَا ٱلرَّسُولُ بَلِّغۡ مَآ أُنزِلَ إِلَيۡكَ مِن رَّبِّكَ وَإِن لَّمۡ تَفۡعَلۡ فَمَا بَلَّغۡتَ رِسَالَتَهُۥ وَٱللَّهُ يَعۡصِمُكَ مِنَ ٱلنَّاسِ إِنَّ ٱللَّهَ لَا يَهۡدِي ٱلۡقَوۡمَ ٱلۡكَٰفِرِينَ ۝٦٧ ﴾

O Apostle!
Communicate that which has been sent down to you

from your Lord,
and if you do not,
you will not have communicated His message,
and Allah shall protect you from the people.
Indeed Allah does not guide the faithless lot.

This verse begins with Allah (swt) addressing his most beloved Prophet (pbuh) by his title, which puts an emphasis on the importance of this verse. The tone of the verse indicates that Allah (swt) has assigned Prophet Muhammad (pbuh) a critical mission, which equals with his prophetic mission, and caused despair of the enemies of Islam, these enemies performed the last pilgrimage with the Prophet (pbuh) and were present at this sermon. Thus, one has to ask: was there any matter more critical and important than the appointment of Ali (as) to the rank of caliphate, guardianship and succession in front of more than hundred thousand people?

Upon receiving the verse, the Prophet (pbuh) stopped at the pond of Khum, and it is reported to have been extremely hot on that day. Then he sent to all people who had been ahead in the way, to come back and waited until all pilgrims who fell behind to arrive and gather.

The Prophet (pbuh) ordered Salman (ra) to use rocks and camel saddles to make a pulpit (*Minbar*) so he could make his announcement. It was around noon-time, and due to the extreme heat in that valley, people were wrapping their robes around their feet and legs, and were sitting around the pulpit, on the hot rocks.

On this day the Messenger of Allah (pbuh) spent approximately five hours in this place; **three hours** of which he was on the pulpit. He recited nearly one hundred verses from The Glorious Quran, and for seventy-three times reminded and warned people of their deeds and future. Then he gave them a long speech. The following is a part of his speech, which has been widely narrated by the Sunni traditionalists.

Note: The full sermon with English translation and references is available at:
http://islamicblessings.com/upload/SermonOfGhadir.pdf

and

http://www.imamshirazi.com/ghadir_sermon.pdf

The Messenger of Allah (pbuh) declared:

> *"Praise belongs to God. We seek help from Him, and believe in Him, and trust in Him. We turn to Him for our evil and unrighteous deeds. The Lord, save whom there is no guide. Whoever is guided by Him, there will be no deviator for him. I testify that there is no God, save Him, and Mohammad is his servant and prophet. O people! Soon, I will die, and leave you. I am responsible and you too!*

Then the Prophet (pbuh) added: *What do you think about me? (Have I fulfilled my responsibility against you?)*

The crowd all said: *We testify that you have accomplished your prophetic mission, and endeavored. God may grant you good rewards.*

Then the Prophet (pbuh) said: *Do you testify that the Lord of the world is one, and Mohammad is His servant and prophet, and there is no doubt about paradise, hell, the everlasting life in the other world?*

All replied: *Yes, that is right. We testify!*

Prophet (pbuh) added: *O people, I leave among you two precious things. I shall see how you treat with my two heritages?*

One stood up and asked loudly: *What are these two precious things?*

Prophet (pbuh) said: *One is a divine book, one side of which is in the powerful hand of God, and the other is with you. And the next is my Household (Ahlul Bayt). God has informed me that these two will never separate! Beware, O People, do not surpass Quran and my Household. Do not fail to follow both of them. Otherwise, you will perish!*

Then, the Prophet (pbuh) took Ali's (as) hand, and raised it so high that the armpit of both of them was seen by the people, and introduced him to the people and asked: *Who is more authorized and rightful to the believers than themselves?*

All replied: *God and His messenger are more aware.*

The Prophet (pbuh) said: *God is my master and I am the master of believers, and I am more authorized and rightful than themselves! Beware, O People! Whoever I am his master and authority, this 'Ali will be his master and authority.* (Prophet pbuh repeated this three times) and then added:

O God, be friend with whoever is friend with Ali, and be the enemy with whoever is an enemy of Ali. Help whoever helps him, and leave whoever leaves him, make him the criteria of right!

Right after the Prophet (pbuh) finished his speech Allah (swt) revealed the following verse to the Prophet (pbuh)

Surat al Maidah 5:3

ٱلْيَوْمَ أَكْمَلْتُ لَكُمْ دِينَكُمْ وَأَتْمَمْتُ عَلَيْكُمْ نِعْمَتِى وَرَضِيتُ لَكُمُ ٱلْإِسْلَٰمَ دِينًا فَمَنِ ٱضْطُرَّ فِى مَخْمَصَةٍ غَيْرَ مُتَجَانِفٍ لِّإِثْمٍ فَإِنَّ ٱللَّهَ غَفُورٌ رَّحِيمٌ ﴿٣﴾

Today the faithless have despaired of your religion.
So do not fear them, but fear Me.
Today I have perfected your religion for you,
and I have completed My blessing upon you,
and I have approved Islam as your religion.

The above verse clearly indicates that Islam without clearing up matter of leadership after the Prophet was not complete, and completion of religion was due to the announcement of Prophet's (pbuh) immediate successor.

Afterward, the Messenger of Allah (pbuh) asked everybody to give the oath of allegiance to Ali (as) and congratulate him. Zeid Ibn Arqam narrates: Abu Bakr, Umar, Uthman, Talha and Zubayr from among the immigrants were the first who paid homage to Ali (as), and the congratulation and paying homage ceremonies continued until sunset.

It is narrated that Umar and Abu Bakr said:

"Well done Ibn Abi Talib! Today you become the leader (Mawla) of all believing men and women."

Sources:

Ahmad Ibn Hanbal, *Musnad*, V. 4, P. 281, narration # 17749

Khatib al-Baghdadi, *Tarikh*, V. 8, P. 290 & 596 from Abu Hurayra

The news spread quickly all over urban and rural areas. When Harith Ibn Numan al-Fahri (or Nadhr Ibn Harith according to another tradition) came to know about it, he rode his camel and came to Medina and went to the Prophet Muhammad (pbuh) and said to him:

"You commanded us to testify that there is no deity but Allah and that you are the Messenger of Allah. We obeyed you. You ordered us to perform the prayers five times a day and we obeyed. You ordered us to observe fasts during the month of Ramadhan and we obeyed. Then you commanded us to offer pilgrimage to Mecca and we obeyed. But you are not satisfied with all this and you raised your cousin by your hand and imposed him upon us as our master by saying Ali is the MAWLA of whom I am MAWLA. Is this imposition from Allah or from You?"

The Prophet (pbuh) said: *"By Allah (swt) who is the only deity! This is from Allah, the Mighty and the Glorious."*

On hearing this Harith turned back and proceeded towards his camel saying: *"O Allah! If what Muhammad said is correct, then fling at us a stone from the sky and subject us to severe pain and torture."*

He had not reached his camel when Allah (swt), who is above all defects flung at him a stone that struck him on his head, penetrated his body, and resulted in his death. It was on this occasion that Allah (swt), the exalted, caused to descend the following verses:

Surat al Ma'arij (70:1-3)

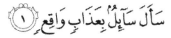

1 An asker asked for a punishment bound to befall

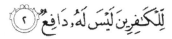

2 which none can avert from the faithless

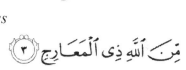

3 from Allah, Lord of the lofty stations.

Reminders by Imam Ali (as)

Imam Ali (as) in person, reminded others who witnessed the event of Ghadir and the tradition of the Messenger of Allah (pbuh), these are some of the events:

- On the day of Shura (Election Day for Uthman) (*Sermon 73*)
- During the days of Uthman's caliphate
- The Day of Rahbah (year 35) was 24 companions stood up and swore that they attended and heard the tradition of the Prophet (pbuh) first hand, twelve of whom were the warriors of Badr (*Sermon 3, on next page is the sermon, also known as the sermon as ash-Shaqshaqiyya*)
- The Day of Jamal (the battle of Camel, year 36) where he reminded Talha (*Sermon 6*)
- The Day of the Riders where 9 witnesses testified.

Source:

Hasan ul Amins, (1995) *Shorter Shi'a Encyclopedia, Chapters: Ghadir Khum (Parts 1-3)* P. 246 – 285

Sermon ash-Shaqshaqiyya (the roar of a camel) in

Nahjul Balagha (Peak of Eloquence) Sermons of Imam Ali (as) during his Caliphate:

> *Beware! By Allah, the son of Abu Quhafah (Abu Bakr) dressed himself with it (the caliphate) and he certainly knew that my status in relationship to it was the same as the status of the axis in relationship to the hand-mill. The floodwater flows down from me and the bird cannot fly up to me. I put a curtain against his caliphate and kept myself detached from it.*

> *Then I began to think whether I should assault or endure calmly the blinding darkness of tribulations wherein the grown up are feeble and the young grow old and the true believer acts under strain till he meets Allah (on his death). I found that endurance there on was wiser. So I adopted patience, although there was pricked in the eye and suffocation (of mortification) in the throats. I watched the plundering of my inheritance till the first one went his way, but handed over the Caliphate to Ibn al-Khattab after himself.*

> *My days are now passed on the camel's back (in difficulty) while there were days (of ease) when I enjoyed the company of Jabir's brotherhood. It is strange that during his lifetime, he wished to be released from the caliphate, but he confirmed it for the other one after his death. No doubt these two shared its udders strictly among themselves. This one puts the caliphate in a tough enclosure where the utterance was haughty and the touch was rough. Mistakes were in plenty and also the excuses therefore. One in contact with it was like the rider of an unruly camel. If he pulled up its rein the very nostril would be slit, but if he let it loose he would be thrown. Consequently, by Allah, people got involved in recklessness, wickedness, unsteadiness and deviation.*

Nevertheless, I remained patient despite a length of period and stiffness of trial, until when he went his way (of death) he put the matter (of Caliphate) in a group and regarded me to be one of them. But good Heavens! What had I to do with his "consultation"? Where was any doubt about me with regard to the first of them that I was now considered akin to these ones? But I remained low when they were low and flew high when they flew high. One of them turned against me because of his hatred and the other got inclined the other way due to his in-law relationship and this thing and that thing, till the third man of these people stood up with heaving breasts between his dung and fodder. With him his children of the grandfather (Umayyah) also stood up, swallowing up Allah's wealth like a camel devouring the foliage of spring, till his rope broke down, his actions finished him and his gluttony brought him down prostrate.

At that moment, nothing took me by surprise, but the crowd of people rushing to me. It advanced toward me from every side like the mane of the hyena so much so that Hassan and Hussain were getting crushed and both the ends of my shoulder garment were torn. They collected around me like the herd of sheep and goats. When I took up the reins of government, one party broke away and another turned disobedient while the rest began acting wrongfully as if they had not heard the word of Allah saying:

That abode in the hereafter, We assign it for those who intend not to exalt themselves in the earth, nor (to make) mischief (the rein), and the end is (best) for the pious. (Holy Qur'an 28:83)

Yes, by Allah, they had heard it and understood it, but the world appeared to glitter in their eyes and its embellishments seduced them. Behold, by Him who split the grain (to grow) and created living beings, if people had not come to me and supporters had not exhausted the argument and if there had been no pledge of Allah with the learned to the effect that they should not acquiesce in the gluttony of the oppressor and the hunger of the oppressed, I would have cast the rope of Caliphate on its own shoulders and would have given the last one the same treatment as to the first one. Then you would have seen that in my view this world of yours is not better than the sneezing of a goat.

It is said that when Amir al-Mu'minin (as) reached this point in his sermon, a man from Iraq stood up and handed him something in writing. Amir al-Mu'minin (as) began looking at it, whereupon Ibn Abbas said, "O Amir al-Mu'minin (as), I wish you resumed your sermon from where you broke it." Thereupon, he replied, "O Ibn Abbas, it was like the foam of a camel which gushed out, but subsided." Ibn Abbas said that he never grieved over any utterance as he did over this one because Amir al-Mu'minin (as) could not finish it as he wished to.

Source: *Nahjul Balagha* (The Peak of Eloquence) by Imam Ali Ibn Abu Talib (as) With Commentary By Martyr Ayatollah Murtada Mutahhari (2009) 7th Edition, Tahrike Tarsile Qur'an, Inc. NY. Sermon # 3. P. 314-316.

Why we must remember Ghadir?

Prophet Muhammad (pbuh) said: *"O assembly of Muslims – those who are present must convey the following to those who are not, "I advise the person who believes in me and has confirmed me (as being the final Prophet) to accept the Wilayat (mastership of 'Ali). Now surely the mastership of 'Ali is my mastership, and my mastership is the mastership of my Lord. This is a pledge from my Lord, which He commanded me to convey to all of you."*

Source: Mulla Muhammad Baqir *AKA* Allama Majlisi, *Biharul Anwar,* Volume 37, Page 131, Hadith 35

Ameer ul Momineen Imam Ali (as) said: *"... when you meet each other (on the Day of 'Eid Ghadir), shake hands with one another with greetings (of peace) and exchange gifts on this day and let those who are present convey this to those who are not, and let the rich person give something to the poor, and the powerful one to the weak, as the Messenger of Allah (blessings of Allah be upon him and his family) commanded me to (also) do this."*

Source: Shaykh Muhammad bin Hasan al-Hurr al-Amili, *Wasa'il ash-Shi'a*, Volume 7, Page 327

Imam Jafar al Sadiq (as) was asked if there was an Eid for Muslims besides Friday, Eid al Adha and Eid al Fitr?

The Imam (as) replied, *"Yes, there is one more Eid, which is greater in holiness (a'adhamuha hurmatan)."*

The person asked the Imam (as) which Eid that was?

Imam (as) said: *"It is the day when the Messenger of Allah (pbuh) declared Amirul Mu'mineen (as) his vicegerent, saying: "whomever I am his Master, this Ali is his Master" And it is the 18th of Dhil-Hijjah."*

Source: Abu Jafar Muhammad Ibn Hassan Tusi *AKA* Sheikh At-Tusi, *Misbahul Mutahajjid*, P. 736.

Imam al Sadiq (as) said: *"... and surely this is the day when the Messenger of Allah (blessings of Allah be upon him and his family) appointed Ali (peace be upon him) as the flag for the people and made known his greatness and successorship; and he fasted on this day as a sign of thanks to Allah, the Glorious and Noble. This day should be taken as one of fasting, feeding others, establishing ties with brothers (in faith), and on this day is the pleasure of the Most Merciful (al-Rahman) and the rubbing in the dust (humiliation) of the face of Shaitan."*

Source: Shaykh Muhammad bin Hasan al-Hurr al-Amili, *Wasa'il* *ash-Shi'a*, Volume 7, Page 328, Hadith 12

Imam al Sadiq (as) said: *"The worth of (good) actions performed on this day (18th of Dhul Hijjah) is equivalent to 80 months (of good deeds) and one is advised to frequently remember Allah, the Noble and Grand, and send prayers upon the Prophet (blessings of Allah be upon him and his family) and that a man be generous to his family (by presenting them with gifts)."*

Source: Shaykh Muhammad bin Hasan al-Hurr al-Amili, *Wasa'il ash-Shi'a*, Volume 7, Page 325, Hadith 6

Imam Ali al Reza (as) said: *"One who worships on the Ghadir day, and cares his family and his Islamic brothers, God will increase his wealth and property."*

Imam Ali al Reza (as) said: *"Allah (swt) will grant a person who visits a true believer on it (the Day of 'Eidul Ghadir) seventy types of Divine Light in his grave and will expand his grave. Every day, 70,000 Angels will visit him in the grave and they will grant him the glad tidings of Paradise."*

Source: Ali Ibn Musa Ibn Tawus al-Hilli, Iqbal *al-A'mal*, Page 778

End of Chapter Notes

Question: *If indeed, the Holy Prophet (pbuh) appointed Ali (as) as his successor in clear terms, then why did the companions of the Holy Prophet (pbuh) still disobey him right after his demise and appointed a caliph by themselves?*

Answer. This can be answered in a number of stages:

1. Not all companions were pious and righteous, amongst them were hypocrites who were not pleased with the announcement of Imam Ali (as) as a successor as it is evident in the verse itself **"and Allah shall protect you from the people" Surat al Maidah 5:67.**Why does the Prophet (pbuh) need any protection, if all of the people in the crowd were all contented with this decision of appointed Ali (as) as his successor? And Surat al Tawbah, which is one of the last chapters of the Quran to be revealed, (numbered as 109 out of 114) in Madina, in which Allah (swt) clearly states:

Surat al Tawbah 9:101

وَمِمَّنْ حَوْلَكُم مِّنَ ٱلْأَعْرَابِ مُنَٰفِقُونَ وَمِنْ أَهْلِ ٱلْمَدِينَةِ

مَرَدُوا۟ عَلَى ٱلنِّفَاقِ لَا تَعْلَمُهُمْ نَحْنُ نَعْلَمُهُمْ سَنُعَذِّبُهُم مَّرَّتَيْنِ ثُمَّ

يُرَدُّونَ إِلَىٰ عَذَابٍ عَظِيمٍ ﴿١٠١﴾

There are hypocrites among the Bedouins around you
and among the towns people of Madina,
steeped in hypocrisy.
You do not know them;

We know them,
and We will punish them twice,
then they shall be consigned to a great punishment.

This verse clearly shows: there were hypocrites in Medina steeped in hypocrisy, the Prophet (pbuh) doesn't know them, and they will be punished twice.

Both, Imam Bukhari and Imam Muslim narrate this famous hadith at multiple places of their Sahih books (authentic books of Ahle Sunnah):

The Prophet (pbuh) said, *"I am your predecessor at the Lake-Fount, and some of you will be brought in front of me till I will see them and then they will be taken away from me and I will say, O Lord, my companions!' It will be said, You do not know what they did after you had left.*

Sources:

Sahih Bukhari, Book 81, Hadith 164
   http://sunnah.com/bukhari/81/164

Sahih Bukhari, Book 92, Hadith 2 *http://sunnah.com/bukhari/92/2*

Sahih Bukhari, Book 81, Hadith 172
   http://sunnah.com/bukhari/81/172

Sahih Bukhari, Book 81, Hadith 181
   http://sunnah.com/bukhari/81/181

With slight variation in *Sahih Muslim*

".....My Lord, they are my followers and belong to my Umma, and it would be said to me: ***Do you know what they did after you? By Allah, they did not do good after you, and they turned back upon their heels..."***

Sources:

Sahih Muslim, Book 43, Hadith 33 *http://sunnah.com/muslim/43/33*

Sahih Muslim, Book 43, Hadith 34 *http://sunnah.com/muslim/43/34*

Sahih Muslim, Book 43, Hadith 31 *http://sunnah.com/muslim/43/31*

These hadiths are another proof that there were several so-called companions of the Holy Prophet (pbuh) who disregarded his teachings and performed treacherous deeds after his (pbuh) demise. This topic is further discussed in detail in **Chapter 13 *Shi'a view of the companions of the Holy Prophet (PBUH) with the Qur'an of*** this book.

Also in *Sunan Jami al-Tirmidhi*, Muhammad Ibn Isa at-Tirmidhi has recorded:

Prophet Muhammad (pbuh) said:

"Ali is from me and I am from Ali. And none should represent me except myself or Ali."

Then how can anyone else other than Ali (as) represents the Islam after Prophet Muhammad (pbuh)?

Source: *Sunan Jami al-Tirmidhi,*Vol. 1, Book 46, Hadith 3719: *http://sunnah.com/urn/635990*

2. Not all 120,000 Muslims who were present at Ghadir were in Madina at the time of appointment of Abu Bakr as the caliph. According to many narrations, only a few thousand returned to Madina. Out of those who returned, many were Bedouins, financially poor, or slaves. Although the Prophet (pbuh) gave women their rights and freedom of speech, that right was taken away after his demise and this deprivation of womens' rights still exist until today in modern day. For example, in Saudi Arabia women can't voice their opinion about their affairs.

3. At first, a few of the Ansaar (the helpers at Medina) gathered at Saqifa to appoint Sa'd Ibn Ubadah (the leader of the Khazraj) Abu Nakr and Umar Ibn Khattab followed them and gathered at Saqifa,

where Abu Bakr gave an influencial speech to which Umar bin Khatab, Bashir Ibn Sad, Usayd Ibn Hudayr, Abu Ubaydah Ibn al-Jarrah and Salim mawla Abi Hudhayfah gave their allegiance and chose Abu Bakr as a caliph without the consensus of the Muslims, nor they followed Qur'an or tradition of the Holy Prophet (pbuh) by doing so. Soon after, they walked into the city of Medina and grabbed people's hands forcefully and took the oath of allegiance; Sa'd Ibn Ubadah was the first one who opposed Abu Bakr as a caliph to which he was severely beaten. When the average folks saw what the group supporting Abu Bakr did to the leader of the Khazraj (Sa'd Ibn Ubadah) they couldn't dare to oppose. The very next day Abu Bakr gave this speech at Prophet's (pbuh) mosque: *"O Men! Here I have been assigned the job of being a ruler over you **while I am not the best among you**. If I do well in my job, help me. If I do wrong, redress me. Truthfulness is fidelity, and lying is treason. The weak shall be strong in my eyes until I restore to them their lost rights, and the strong shall be weak in my eye until I have restored the rights of the weak from them. No people give up fighting for the cause of God, but God inflicts upon them abject subjection; and no people give themselves to lewdness but God envelops them with misery. Obey me as long as I obey God and His Prophet. But if I disobey God's command or His Prophet's, then no obedience is incumbent upon you. Rise to your prayer, that God may bless you"*

- How can Abu Bakr declare himself as a ruler when a majority of the righteous companions of the Holy Prophet (pbuh) didn't recognize him as a caliph?
- How can Abu Bakr admit himself that 'he is not the best' for the Caliphate, yet not acknowledge the position of Ali Ibn Abi Talb (as)?

4. Amongst those who did NOT give their allegiance to Abu Bakr were: Ali Ibn Abi Talib (as), Abbas Ibn Abdul Muttalib, Fadhl Ibn Abbas, Salman al Muhammadi, Abu Dhar al-Ghifari, Ammar Ibn Yasir, Miqdad Ibn Aswad, Bilal Ibn Rabah, Khalid Ibn Sa'id, Buraida Aslami, Uthman Ibn Hunaif,

Hudhayfah ibn al-Yaman, Zubayr Ibn al Awam, Abu Ayyub Ansari, Khuzaymah bin Thabit, Ubayy bin Kab, Khalid Ibn Sa'id, Qays Ibn Sa'd, Buraydah Ashami, Abul Haytham bin al Tayyihan, and several others as were recorded in history.

When Abbas Ibn Abdul Muttalib and Abu Sufyan Ibn Harb offered to swear allegiance to Imam Ali (as), he said:

O People! Steer clear through the waves of mischief by boats of deliverance, turn away from the path of dissension and put off the gowns of pride. Prosperous is one who rises with wings (i.e. When he has power) or else he remains peaceful and others enjoy ease. It (i.e. The aspiration for Caliphate) is like turbid water or like a morsel that would suffocate the person who swallows it. One who plucks fruits before ripening is like one who cultivated in another's field.

If I speak out they would call me greedy towards power, but if I keep quiet, they would say I was afraid of death. It is a pity that after all the ups and downs (I have been through). By Allah, the son of Abu Talib is more familiar with death than an infant with the breast of its mother. I have hidden knowledge; if I disclose it, you will start trembling like ropes in deep wells...

Source: *Nahjul Balagha* (The Peak of Eloquence) by Imam Ali Ibn Abu Talib (as) With Commentary By Martyr Ayatollah Murtada Mutahhari (2009) 7th Edition, Tahrike Tarsile Qur'an, Inc. NY. Sermon 5, P. 333

5. Communication system and circulation of information was not strong in those days. By the time everyone came to know about the selection of Abu Bakr against the verdict of the Holy Prophet (pbuh) it was too late. Abu Bakr had already become too powerful in material terms. He appointed Khalid bin Waleed as the General of the Army and anyone who opposed the ruling caliph, he was silenced either through temptation or through intimidation. The murder of Malik Ibn Nuwayrah is a glaring example in this respect (*Discussed in details in Chapter 13*).

6. Every Muslim accepts that the Holy Prophet (pbuh) had said to Ali that:

"*You are to me as Haroon (Aaron) was to Musa (Moses) except that there shall be no prophet after me.*"

Source:

Sahih Bukhari, Book 62, Hadith 57 *http://sunnah.com/bukhari/62/57*

Sahih Muslim, Book 44, Hadith 47 *http://sunnah.com/muslim/44/47*

If one were to analyze the similarities between Prophet Aaron (as) and Imam Ali (as) to understand how it is possible for the companions of a Prophet to disobey and disregard the clear appointment of the vicegerent. The Holy Qur'an in Chapter 7, Surat al A'raf verses 142 onwards describes when Prophet Moses (as) appointed Prophet Aaron (as) as his successor, he gathered round him the Bani Isra'il (according to some reports, 70,000 people). Moses (as) emphasized that in his absence, they should obey Aaron (as), his successor. Moses (as) then went up to the mountain to be alone with Allah (swt). Samiri incited dissension among the Israilis. He fashioned a golden calf and Bani Israil, having left Aaron (as), gathered round the treacherous Samiri in large numbers. It was a short time before this that the Bani Israil had heard Moses say that during his absence Aaron (as) was to be the leader and they should obey him. Nevertheless, 70,000 people followed Samiri. The Prophet Aaron (as) loudly protested this action and forbade them from indulging in such sinful acts, but no one listened to him. The verse 150 of Chapter 7, Surat A'raf states that when Moses came back, Aaron said to him:

"O son of my mother, indeed the people oppressed me and were about to kill me, so let not the enemies rejoice over me and do not place me among the wrongdoing people."

The Bani Israil themselves heard the clear instruction from the Prophet Moses (as), but when Moses (as) went up to the mountain, Samiri seized his opportunity. He fashioned a golden calf and misguided the Bani Israil. Similarly, after the demise of Prophet Muhammad (pbuh), some people who had heard him say that Ali (as) was his successor, turned against Ali (as). Imam Ghazali referred to this fact in the beginning of his fourth treatise in *Sirru'l-Alamin*. Ghazali states that some people returned to the state of their former ignorance. In this respect, there is great similarity between the situation of Aaron and that of Ali. Umar bin Khattab along with several prominent personalities of both Mecca and Medina came to Ali's (as) house and threatened to burn down the house. They took him to the mosque by force, and threatened to kill him unless he swore allegiance to Abu Bakr. Imam Ali (as) went to the sacred grave of the Prophet (pbuh) and repeated the same words of the Holy Qur'an where Aaron (as) spoke to Moses (as): *[Aaron] said, "O son of my mother, indeed the people oppressed me and were about to kill me..."*

Thus fulfills the prophecy of the Holy Prophet (pbuh) when he said:

> *"You will follow the ways of those nations who were before you, span by span and cubit by cubit (i.e., inch by inch) so much so that even if they entered a hole of a lizard, you would follow them."* We said: O Allah's Messenger (pbuh) (Do you mean) the Jews and the Christians?" He (pbuh) said: *"Whom else?"*

Source: Sahih Bukhari,Vol. 9, Book 92, Hadith 422,
http://sunnah.com/bukhari/96

Is Abu Bakr an *Awliya* (a custodian, protector, helper, one in authority) according to the Qur'an?

According to Surah Yunus 10:62

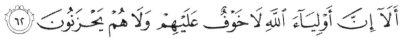

*Look! The Awliya of Allah will indeed have no fear
nor will they grieve.*

Where as, ALL interpreters of the Qur'an agree that Abu Bakr was in the cave with the Holy Prophet (pbuh) and showed fear and grief in:

Surat al Tawbah 9:40

إِلَّا نَصُرُوهُ فَقَدْ نَصَرَهُ ٱللَّهُ إِذْ أَخْرَجَهُ ٱلَّذِينَ كَفَرُواْ

ثَانِيَ ٱثْنَيْنِ إِذْ هُمَا فِى ٱلْغَارِ إِذْ يَقُولُ لِصَحِبِهِ لَا

تَحْزَنْ إِنَّ ٱللَّهَ مَعَنَا فَأَنزَلَ ٱللَّهُ سَكِينَتَهُ عَلَيْهِ

وَأَيَّدَهُ بِجُنُودٍ لَّمْ تَرَوْهَا وَجَعَلَ كَلِمَةَ ٱلَّذِينَ

كَفَرُواْ ٱلسُّفْلَىٰ وَكَلِمَةُ ٱللَّهِ هِىَ ٱلْعُلْيَا وَٱللَّهُ

عَزِيزٌ حَكِيمٌ ﴿٤٠﴾

If you do not help him,
then Allah has already helped him
when the faithless expelled him,
as one of two [refugees],
when the two of them were in the cave,
he said to his companion,
'Do not grieve; Allah is indeed with us.'
Then Allah sent down His composure upon him,
and strengthened him with hosts you did not see,
and He made the word of the faithless the lowest;
and the word of Allah is the highest;
and Allah is all-mighty, all-wise.

And in the battle of Uhud, even Hind the wife of Abu Sufyan knew who the real protectors of the religion of Islam were, as she asked Wahshi to specifically kill Muhammad (pbuh), Ali (as) and Hamza (as), as she knew not to worry about the rest of the Muslims at that time. When Hamza Ibn Abdul Muttalib (as) was martyred, all of the companions of the Holy Prophet (pbuh) left him alone in the battlefield and ran far away from the battlefield in cowardice and fear, except for Imam Ali (as), Miqdad al Aswad (ra), Abu Dhar al Ghaffari (ra), Abu Dujanahal Ansari, and a lady by the name of Harathia (ra) who picked up a spear and defended the Prophet of Allah (swt).

Surat Aly Imran 3:153

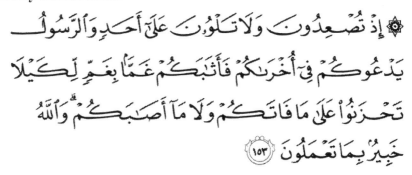

When you were fleeing
without paying any attention to anyone,
while the Apostle was calling you from your rear,
He requited you with grief upon grief,
so that you may not grieve for what you lose
nor for what befalls you,
and Allah is well aware of what you do.

Therefore, according to the holy Qur'an: Abu Bakr, Umar or Uthman does not fit the criteria to be the leader of a Muslim nation. The above three companions were known to run away in fear from the battlefields, not just at Uhud, but also at Khandaq, Khaybar and Hunayn.

In fairness, it is narrated by Abu Bakr that he said: *"When people left the Messenger of God on the day of Uhud, I was the first one to come back to the Messenger of God..."*

Source:

Allama Mohamad Jawad Chirri, *The Brother of the Prophet Mohammad: The Imam Ali, Chpater 9: Battle of Uhud.* *http://www.al-islam.org/articles/battle-uhud-shaykh-muhammad-jawad-chirri#footnote7_rnng622*

Books on this topic

40 Ahadith Series - Completion of Islam Ghadeer by World Federation of Khoja Shia Ithna-Asheri Muslim Communities

A Victom Lost in Saqifah by Ali Labbaf

Al-Ghadir and its Relevance to Islamic Unity by Ayatollah Murtadha Mutahhari

Ahl al-Bayt and Caliphate by Ayatollah Murtadha Mutahhari

Ayatul Ghadir: Verses of Ghadir by Ayatollah Sayed Ali al-Hussaini al-Sistani

Ayah of Wilaya by al-Syed Murtadha al-Shiraz

Black Thursday by Muhammad al-Tijani al-Smaoui

Did the Prophet Appoint a Successor? by Ahlul Bayt Digital Islamic Library Project

Ghadir by Ayatollah Muhammad Baqir al-Sadr

Ghadir Sermon by Muhammad Baqir Ansari:
http://www.imamshirazi.com/ghadir_sermon.pdf

Ghadir As Reflected from the Quran and Traditions by Dr Majid Maaref

Ghadir Khum by Hossein Najafi

Ghadir in the Light of the Book and Tradition by Majid Ma'aref

Ghadir Tradition, the Expressive Evidence for Guardianship by Islamic Sciences and Researches Group

Glimpses of Shi'ism in the Musnad of Ibn Hanbal by Kadhim al-Tabatabai

Imammat and Wilayat by Sayyid Muhammad Rizvi

Imammat and Wilayat by Hussain Dargahee

Kamaaluddin wa Tamaamul Ni'ma (Perfection of Faith and Completion of Divine Favor) Parts 1 and 2 by Shaykh Muhammad Ibn Ali al-Saduq

Nahjul Balagha (Peak of Eloquence) Prophet's Historic Ghadir Sermon (English) Ver 7. P. 208 By Tahrike Tarsile Qur'an, Inc. NY

Necessity of Divine Leadership by al-Syed Hussain Murtaza
Saqifa by al-Shaykh Muhammad Ridha al-Muthaffar

Shiism: Imamate and Wilayat by Sayyid Muhammad Rizvi

Shorter Shi'a Encyclopedia Chapters: Ghadir Khum (Parts 1-3) by Hasan ul Amins.

The Voice Of Human Justice by George Jordac

To Be with the Truthful by al-Syed Muhammad al-Tijani al-Smaoui

The story of Ghadir by Dr. Nadir Fazli

What happened in Ghadir? by Mohammad Bagher Ansari

Wilayah The Station of the Master by Murtada Mutahhari

Chapter 9

Qur'an and the 'Great Sacrifice'

Only fifty years after the demise of Prophet Muhammad (pbuh), the so-called Muslims oppressed his grandson Hussain (as). Under the Caliphate of Yazid, his army forced Husain (as) out of his homeland, surrounded him in the middle of a desert and cut-off water from him and his family and friends. The army of Yazid brutally killed all of Husain's (as) male relatives and friends. Then they beheaded the grandson of the Prophet (pbuh) and killed him. Even after, they killed him, their torture continued. They snatched the clothes off his holy body, mutilated his body and trampled his holy body with their horses. The army of Yazid plundered and burned the camps, snatched the veil from the granddaughter of Holy Prophet (pbuh), and imprisoned the grandchildren of the Holy Prophet (pbuh).

There is no oppression or tragedy that can compare to the one underwent by the household of the Prophet (pbuh) in Karbala. Through this sacrifice, Imam Hussain (as) revived the true practical Islam by establishing clear criteria between 'truth' and 'falsehood'. Therefore, the remembrance of this 'Great Sacrifice', which saved the religion of Allah (swt), is extremely important to those who adhere to the traditions of the Holy Prophet (pbuh). This 'Great Sacrifice' was prophesized in the holy Quran in:

Surat as Saffat, 37:104-107

وَنَٰدَيۡنَٰهُ أَن يَٰٓإِبۡرَٰهِيمُ ﴿١٠٤﴾

104 We called out to him, 'O Abraham!

قَدۡ صَدَّقۡتَ ٱلرُّءۡيَآ إِنَّا كَذَٰلِكَ نَجۡزِى ٱلۡمُحۡسِنِينَ ﴿١٠٥﴾

105 You have indeed fulfilled the vision!
Thus indeed do We reward the virtuous!

إِنَّ هَٰذَا لَهُوَ ٱلۡبَلَٰٓؤُاْ ٱلۡمُبِينُ ﴿١٠٦﴾

106 This was indeed a manifest test.

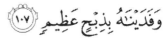

107 Then We ransomed him with a great sacrifice,

Note: In the above verses of the holy Qur'an, Allah (swt) has stated that He (swt) **ransomed** Prophet Ismael's (as) life with a 'Great Sacrifice', almost all non-Shi'a interpreters of the Qur'an have mentioned that the 'Great Sacrifice' in this verse refers to a 'Lamb'. This seems improbable that 'a life of a Prophet of God can be ransomed for nothing but a lamb?' Is this, what they value a life of a Prophet (as) for?

Therefore, one must turn to *'Ulul Amr'* and ask them for the meaning behind this verse. Imam Ali al-Reza (as) was asked about the interpretation of these verses (37:100-107) and He (as) said:

When Allah (swt) the High, commanded Prophet Ibrahim (as) that he should slaughter instead of his son Ismail (as), the lamb, which had descended to him, he wished that he could slaughter his son Ismail (as) with his own hands, and he had yet to be commanded to slaughter the lamb instead. There occurred in his heart what occurs in the heart of a parent who has to slaughter his dear son by his own hands. So he deserved, due to that, the highest levels of the people of the rewards, upon the difficulties.

So Allah (swt) revealed: *O Ibrahim! Who is the most beloved of the creatures, to you?* So he (as) said: *O Lord! No creature has been created who is more beloved to me than Your Beloved, Muhammad (pbuh).* So Allah (swt) revealed to him: *So is he more beloved to you than yourself?* Prophet Ibrahim (as) said: *Yes, he (pbuh) is more beloved to me than my own self.* Allah (swt) then revealed: *So is his son more beloved to you, or your own son?* Prophet Ibrahim (as) said: *His (pbuh) son.*

Allah (swt) revealed: *His son would be slaughtered unjustly at the hands of his enemies, is that more hurtful to your heart, or the slaughter of your son by your own hands in My obedience?* Prophet Ibrahim (as) said: *O Lord! His slaughter by the hands of his enemies is more hurtful to my heart.* Allah (swt) revealed: *O Ibrahim! A group of people who would claim that they are from the community of Muhammad (pbuh), would be killing Al-Hussain (as), and his sons after him, unjustly and aggressively, just like the slaughter of the lamb, so due to that, they would be obligating My wrath upon themselves.*

Prophet Ibrahim (as) was horrified by this, it was very painful to his heart, and he started to weep. So Allah (swt) revealed unto him: *I have ransomed your anxiety for your son; had you slaughtered him by your own hands, by your anxiety over al-Hussain (as) and his killing, and have obligated for you the highest levels for the people of the rewards upon the difficulties.* So these are the words of Allah the Mighty and Majestic

Then We ransomed him with a great sacrifice (37:107).

Source: Sheikh Sudooq, *Uyun Akhbar Al Reza* (The Source of Traditions on Imam Reza) Vol 1. Chapter 25, P. 224 *http://www.feedbooks.com/userbook/29089/uyun-akhbar-al-reza-vol-1*

Surat Maryam 19:1

كهيعص ﴿١﴾

Kaf, Ha, Ya, Ayn, Saad

Imam Hassan al Askari (as) was asked the meaning of verse: ***Kaf, Ha, Ya, Ayn, Saad?***

The Imam (as) replied:

These letters are from the unseen information that the Almighty Allah (swt) conveyed to His servant, Zakariya (as). Then He related the story to Muhammad (pbuh). It was that when Zakariya (as) implored his Lord to teach him the names of *Panjetan* (the holy five, but); the Almighty Allah (swt) sent Jibraeel to him and he taught him their names. Thus, whenever Zakariya (as) mentioned or remembered the names of Muhammad, Ali, Fatima or Hassan (as) his sorrow and grief used to go away, but whenever he thought of Hussain (as) a terrible grief used to beset him and he was very much astonished why it was so. Thus, one day he prayed to Allah (swt): O my God, how is it so that when I remember the four names I obtain peace, but when I think of Hussain, tears flow from my eyes and I begin to wail?

Allah, the Mighty and the High informed him about the tragedy of Imam Hussain (as) and told him that in ***Kaaf Ha Ya Ayn Saad***:

- ***Kaaf*** is for *Karbala*,
- ***Ha*** stands for *Halakat* (getting killed) of '*Itrat*' (progeny) the Holy Prophet (pbuh),
- ***Ya*** implies *Yazid* who would oppress Hussain (as),
- ***Ayn*** denotes '*Atash*' (thirst) of Husain (as) and
- ***Saad*** indicates '*Sabr*' (patience) from Imam Hussain (as) and those in Karbala.

Thus, when Zakariya heard this he did not leave the Masjid for three days and did not allow anyone to meet him and continued to weep and wail. He lamented on Hussain (as) and prayed to Allah: *My God, will they make the best of Your creatures sit in mourning for his son? O Lord, would this tremendous tragedy befall him? My God, would they make Ali and Fatima put on the dress of mourning? Would they make the shock of this calamity reach their abode?* Then he said: *Bestow me a son so that I can be pleased in my old age and that his love affects my heart. After that make me sit in his mourning as You would make Muhammad, Your beloved sit.* So the Almighty Allah gave him Yahya (John the Baptist) and later his martyrdom made him aggrieved. And the period of Yahya's pregnancy was six months like in the case of Husain (as)."

Source: Sheikh Sudooq, *Kamaaluddin wa Tamaamun Ni'ma*
(Perfection of faith and completion of divine favor) Chapter 43,
P. 116 – 117. Available at: *http://umaa-
library.org/content/kamal-al-deen-wa-tamam-al-nimah-volume-
1-2*

Similarities between Prophet Yahya Ibn Zakariya (as) (*John the Baptist*) and Imam Hussain (as)

- Both Prophet Yahya Ibn Zakariya (as), and Imam Hussain Ibn Ali (as) were born in a premature birth; their pregnancy was about 6 months.
- Both Prophet Yahya Ibn Zakariya (as), and Imam Hussain Ibn Ali (as) were given unique names, which no one else was named before.
- Both had firm belief in Allah (swt), and held a high esteem for themselves.
- They both chose death with dignity over submitting to the tyrant.
- Both were martyred, were beheaded and their heads were presented to the tyrants of their time.

Imam al Sadiq (as) said:

"...For no one the heavens wept for forty days except Yahya and Hussain..."

Source: Ayatollah Agha Mahdi Puya, *Tafsir of Holy Qur'an,* Surah
19, verse 2, P. 83.
http://www.islamicmobility.com/elibrary_14.htm

End of Chapter Notes:

Imam Hussain's (as) Sermon on the 10ᵗʰ of Muharram

On the 10th of Moharram in 61 A.H.; in the plains of Karbala, Imam Hussain (as) admonished the army of the Banu Umayyad by giving this eloquent Sermon.

The Holy Prophet (pbuh) raised me up by feeding the Divine Prophecies. I am the son of the Prophet (pbuh) and my mother is Batool (sa). I have been created as infallible Imam. I have the privilege of being the son of Amir ul Momineen (as). I am the son of that who holds the key to the future events and sustenance of the whole Universe. Hassan (as) has brought me up to his customs. I am the Divine authority; recognize me prior to declaring war against me. Be aware! You will close all the doors of forgiveness by killing me.

You are doing this for the attraction of your leader's promised rewards? But if you ask me, I can bless you thousands' time more than that. I know collecting filth is in your genes. You are unable to comprehend and debate with doubts that we regularly travel through the milky ways. Be aware! The stars are nothing else but the aftermath of footprints. North Pole finds its direction from us. Our destination is in *'Qabah Quosaan'* and *'Bait-ul-Mamoor'* (highest points in the heavens) is our residence. *'Bismillah'* refers to our beginning and *'Yakhamah'* concludes with our attributes.*'Innamah'* describes our Divinity and Purity, *'Allif-lam'* is on our introduction, *'Wal Asr'* is about our glandular status, The Verse of *'Fi'l'* is the narration of our past, *'Wal fajr'* has borrowed colours from us, *'Fil qurbah'* is the means to seek nearness to us, the verse of *'Dahr'* is on our generosity, *'Min Yashra'* defines our rights, *'Al-Taha'* is about our way of life, the Verse of *'Muzimmil'* is our outfit, the verse of *'Al Qadr'* authenticate our Divine rights.

It is in our jurisdiction to change the direction of *'Qabateen'*we attend to the needs of others in *'Rukku'* of prayers. Our traditions became the principles of religion; we are the *'Ibrahimy'*.

Source: Islamic Mobility, *Historical Sermons: Imam Hussain's (as) Last Sermon - To Umayyad Army in Karbala* *http://islamicmobility.com/pdf/Historical%20Sermons%20Imam %20Hussain%20Mola%20Abbas%20bibi%20Sakina%20syeda %20Zainab.pdf*

Sermon of Syeda Zainab (sa) in the court of Yazid

Praise be to Allah, the Lord of the worlds and blessings on my grandfather, the seal of divine prophets. O Yazid, Allah (swt) says, and his word is true, that: *Then evil was the end of those who did evil because they rejected the communications of Allah and used to mock them* (30:10)

O Yazid, do you believe that you have succeeded in closing the sky and the earth for us and that we have become your captives just because we have been brought before you in a row and that you have secured control over us?

Do you believe that we have been afflicted with insult and dishonor by Allah and that you have been given the honor and respect by Him? You have become boastful of this apparent victory that you have secured and you have started feeling jubilant and proud over this prestige and honor. You think that you have achieved worldly good that your affairs have become stabilized and our rule has fallen into your hands. Wait for a while! Do not be so joyful. Have you forgotten Allah's saying: The unbelievers should not carry the impression that the time allowed to them by us is good for them. *Surely we give them time so that they may increase their evil deeds, and eventually they will be given insulting chastisement* (3:178).

O son of freed slaves, is this your justice that you keep your own daughters and slave maids veiled, while the daughters of the Messenger of Allah (pbuh) are being paraded from place to place exposed?

You have dishonored us by unveiling our faces. Your men take us from town to town where all sorts of people, whether they be residents of the hills or of riversides have been looking at us. The near as well as the distant ones, the poor as well as the rich, the low as well as the high - all casting their glances at us, while our position is such that there is no male relative of ours to render us help or support.

O Yazid, whatever you have done, proves your revolt against Allah (swt) and your denial of His Prophet (pbuh) and of the Book and Sunnah that the Holy Prophet (pbuh) brought from Allah (swt). Your deeds should not cause amazement because one whose ancestors chewed the livers of the martyrs, whose flesh grew up with virtuous people, who fought against the Master of divine prophets, who mobilized parties for fighting against him and drew swords against him, would obviously excel all Arabs in unbelief, sinfulness, excesses, and hatred against Allah and His Prophet (pbuh).

Remember that the evil deeds and sinful actions that you have committed are the result of 'kufr' (disbelief) and the hatefulness you bear because of your ancestors who were killed in Badr.

One who cast his glance of enmity, malice and hatred upon us does not lag behind in practicing enmity against us. He proves his unbelief, declares it with his tongue and jubilantly proclaims: I have killed the sons of the Prophet of Allah (pbuh) and made his progeny captive, and wishes that his ancestors had lived to see his achievement and to have exclaimed, O Yazid, may your hands not lose their strength, and you have wreaked good vengeance on our behalf.

O Yazid, you are striking the lips of Imam Hussain (as) with your stick in front of this crowd, while these very lips used to be kissed by the Prophet (pbuh) of Allah (swt), and yet your face reflects pleasure and happiness.

By my life, by killing the master of youths of Paradise, the son of the Master of Arabs (Ali as) and the shining sun of the progeny of Abdul Muttalib (as), you have deepened our wound and uprooted us completely.

By killing Hussain Ibn Ali (as) you have gained nearness to the state of your disbelieving ancestors. You proclaim your deed with pride and if they were to see you they would approve of your action and pray that Allah may not paralyze your arms.

O Yazid! If you had heard enough to take account of your heinous deeds, you yourself would surely wish your arms to be paralyzed and severed from your elbow and you would wish that your parents had not given birth to you, because you would know that Allah has become displeased with you. Allah, Grant us our rights. Avenge those who have oppressed us.

O Yazid! You did what you wished, but remember that you have cut your own skin and your own flesh to pieces. Soon you will be brought before the Holy Prophet (pbuh). You will be overburdened with the weight of your sins committed by shedding the blood of his progeny and by dishonoring his family. The place to which you will be taken will be before all the members of his family. The oppressed will be avenged and the enemies will be punished.

O Yazid! It is not becoming for you to swell with joy after slaying the Prophet's progeny. *Reckon not those who are killed in Allah's way as dead; nay, they are alive and are provided sustenance from their Lord; rejoicing in what Allah has given them out of His grace* (3:169-170).

Allah (swt) is sufficient to deal with you. Prophet Muhammad (pbuh) is your adversary and Hazat Jibraeel (as) is our support and help against you.

Those who have made you the head of state and burdened the Muslims with your leadership will soon find out what awaits them. The end of all tyrants is agony.

O Yazid! I speak not to you thus to warn you of the severe chastisement in store for you so that you should be regretful for you are one of those whose hearts are hardened, souls are rebellious and whose bodies are busy in Allah's disobedience while they are under the curse of the Prophet of Allah (pbuh). You are from among those in whose heart, Satan has made his abode and has been breeding his offspring.

How amazing it is that the virtuous people, sons of the divine prophets and successors are killed at the hands of liberated slaves, evildoers and sinners? Our blood is shed by their hands and our flesh serves as food for them. We feel grieved for those whose bodies are lying un-shrouded and unburied in the battlefield, wounded with arrows.

O Yazid, if you consider our defeat as your achievement, then you will have to pay its price. Allah (swt) does not commit an injustice to His servants.

Our reliance is for Allah (swt). He alone is our relief and place of protection, and in Him alone do we repose our hope. You may contrive and try however much you can. By Him who honored us with revelation, the book and Prophethood, you cannot achieve our status, nor reach our position, nor can you affect our mention, nor remove from yourself that shame and dishonor that is now your fate, because of perpetrating excess and oppression on us. Your word now is weak and your days are counted. Beware of the day when the announcer would announce the curse of Allah (swt) on the oppressors and the unjust.

Praise be to Allah (swt) who gave a good end to His friends and granted them success in their aims, and thereafter called them back to His mercy, pleasure and bliss, while you hurled yourself into evil and mischief by committing injustice against them. We pray to Allah (swt) to favor us with full recompense through them and grant us the good of the Caliphate and Imamate. Surely Allah is Kind and the Most Merciful over His creatures.

Among the gathering was a red haired Syrian who saw Syeda Fatima (sa) Kubra, daughter of Imam Hussain (as) and asked Yazid to give her to him. When the girl heard this she clung to Syeda Zainab (sa) and started to weep. She now feared that after the loss of her father, she was to be made a slave girl. Syeda Zainab (sa) was not afraid. She turned to Yazid and told him that he had neither right nor authority to give the young girl away like that, at which he bristled, retorting that he could do so. Syeda Zainab (sa) replied, *"You are abusing me because of your authority and power."* At this Yazid was shamed into silence.

To the Syrian she said:

"May the curse of Allah be upon you. May hell be your eternal abode. May your eyes be blinded and your limbs paralyzed." Immediately paralysis gripped the man and he fell to the ground dead.

Source: Islamic Mobility, *Historical Sermons:* Sermon of Syeda Zainab (SA) in Court of Yazid
http://islamicmobility.com/pdf/Historical%20Sermons%20Imam %20Hussain%20Mola%20Abbas%20bibi%20Sakina%20syeda %20Zainab.pdf

Imam Zain al Abideen's (as) Sermon in Yazid's court

Yazid permitted all the people to come to his palace, so the hall of his palace became full of people who came and congratulated him on the false victory. He was pleased and happy, because the world yielded to him, and the kingdom belonged to him only. So he ordered the orator to ascend the pulpit and to defame Imam Hussain (as) and his father, the Commander of the faithful Imam Ali (as). The orator ascended the pulpit and went too far in slandering the pure family (of the Prophet pbuh), and then he lauded in a false way Yazid and his father Muawiya. Thus, Imam Zain al Abidin, peace be on him, interrupted him, saying: *"Woe unto you, orator! You have traded the pleasure of the creature for the wrath of the Creator, so take your place in the fire (of Hell)."*

Then the Imam turned to Yazid and asked him, saying: *"Do you permit me to ascend this pulpit to deliver a speech that will please Allah, the Almighty, and that will bring good rewards for these folks?"*

The attendants were astonished at this sick lad, who interrupted the orator and the governor while he was a captive. Yazid refused, but the people begged him. He said to them: *"If he ascends the pulpit, he will not descend (from it) till he expose me and the family of Abi Sufyan."*

The people asked him: *"What will this sick lad do?"*

The people did not know the Imam (as). They thought that he was like the other people, but the tyrant, Yazid, knew him, so he said to them: *"These are people who have been spoon-fed with knowledge."*

They kept pressuring him till he agreed. So the Imam (as) ascended the pulpit and delivered the most wonderful speech in history in eloquence. He made the people weep. The folks were confused because the Imam's (as) speech controlled their hearts and feelings. The following is some of what he said:

"O people, we were granted six things and favored with seven: We were granted knowledge, clemency, leniency, fluency, courage, and love for us in the hearts of the believers. We were favored by the fact that from among us came the chosen Prophet Mohammed, may Allah bless him and his family, al-Siddiq (the very truthful one), al-Tayyar (the one who flies in the heaven), the Lion of Allah and of the Prophet, may Allah bless him and his family, the doyenne of the women of the world Fatima the chaste, and both lords of the youths of Heaven from among this nation"

Having introduced his family, the Imam (as) continued his speech explaining their outstanding merits, saying:

Whoever recognizes me knows me, and whoever does not recognize, let me tell him who I am and to what family I belong: I am the son of Mecca and Mina; I am the son of Zamzam and al-Safa; I am the son of the one who carried Zakat in the ends of the mantle; I am the son of the best man who ever put on a loincloth and clothes; I am the son of the best man who ever put on sandals and walked barefooted; I am the son of the best man who ever made tawaf (the procession round the Kaaba) and Sa'i (ceremony of running seven times between Safā and Marwa); I am the son of the best man who ever offered the hajj and pronounced talbiya (Here I am at your service); I am the son of the one who was transported on the buraq in the air; I am the son of the one who was made to travel from the Sacred Mosque to the Remote Mosque, so glory belongs to Him Who made (His Servant) travel; I am the son of the one who was taken by Gabriel to sidrat al-muntaha ; I am the son of the one who drew near (his Lord) and suspended, so he was the measure of two bows or closer still; I am the son of the one who led the angels of the heavens in prayer; I am the son of the one to whom the Almighty revealed what He revealed; I am the son of Mohammed al-Mustafa ; I am the son of Ali al-Murtada ; I am the son of the one who fought against the creatures till they said: There is no god but Allah. I am the son of the one who struck (the enemies) with two swords before Allah's Apostle, may Allah bless him and his family, and stabbed (them) with two spears, emigrated twice, pledged allegiance twice (to the Prophet), prayed in the two qiblas, and fought (against the unbelievers) at Badr and Hunayn and never disbelieved in Allah, not even as much as the twinkling of an eye. I am the son of the best of the believers, the heir of the prophets, the destroyer of the unbelievers, the Commander of the Muslims, the light of the mujahidin, the ornament of the worshippers, the crown of the weepers, the most patient of the patient, and the best of the steadfast from among the family of Yasin, and the Messenger of the Lord of the world's inhabitants. I am the son of the one who was backed by Gabriel, supported by Mikael. I am the son of the one who defended the Muslims, killed the oath breakers of allegiance and the unjust and the renegades, struggled against his tiring enemies, the most excellent one of those who walked (to war) from among Quraysh, the first to respond to Allah from among the believers, the prior to all the previous ones, the breaker of the aggressors, the destroyer of the atheists, an arrow from among the shooting-places of Allah against the hypocrites, the tongue of the wisdom of worshippers, the supporter of the religion of Allah, the protector of the affair of Allah, the garden of the wisdom of Allah, the container of the knowledge of Allah, tolerant, generous, benevolent, pure, satisfied, easily satisfied, intrepid, gallant, patient, fasting, refined, steadfast, courageous, honored, the severer of the backbones, the scatterer of the allies, the calmest of them, the best of them in giving free rein (to his horse), the boldest of them in tongue, the firmest of them in determination, the most powerful of them, a lion, brave, pouring rain, the one who destroyed them at the battles and dispersed them in the wind, the lion of al-Hijaz, the possessor of the miracle, the ram of Iraq, the Imam through the text and worthiness, Makki, Madani, Abtahi, Tuhami, Kha'yani, Uqbi, Badri, Uhdi, Shajari, Muhajiri, the Lord of the Arabs, the Lion of war, the inheritor of al-Mash'arayn, the father of the two grandsons (of the Prophet) al-Hasan and al-Hussain, the one who manifested miracles, the one who scattered the phalanxes, the piercing meteor, the following light, the victorious Lion of Allah, the request of every seeker, the victorious over every victorious, such is my grandfather, Ali ibn Abi Talib. I am the son of Fatima, the chaste. I am the son of the doyenne of women. I am the son of the purified, virgin (lady). I am the son of the part of the Messenger, may Allah bless him and his family. I am the son of the one who was covered with blood. I am the son of the one who was slaughtered at Karbala. I am the son of the one for whom the Jinns wept in the dark and for whom the birds in the air cried."

The Imam (as) continued saying *'I am....'* until the people wailed.

Yazid thought that a discord would occur, for the Imam (as) made a cultural revolt through his speech when he introduced himself to the Syrians and made them know what they did not know, so Yazid ordered the muazzin to call for prayer (say the adhan) and he said: "Allahu Akbar!"

The Imam (as) turned to him and said: *"You have made great the Great One who cannot be measured and cannot be perceived by the senses, there is nothing greater than Allah."*

The muazzin said: "Ashhadu an la ilaha illa Allah!"

Imam Zain al Abideen (as) said: *"My hair, my skin, my flesh, my blood, my brain, and my bones bear witness that there is no god but Allah."*

The muazzin said: "Ashhadu anna Mohammedan

rasool Allah!"

The Imam (as) turned to Yazid and asked him: *"Yazid, is Mohammed your grandfather or mine? If you say that he is yours, then you are a liar, and if you say that he is mine, then why did you kill his family?"*

Yazid became silent and was unable to answer, for the great Prophet was Imam Zain al Abidin's (as) grandfather. As for Yazid's grandfather, he was Abu Sufyan, the mortal enemy of the Prophet, may Allah bless him and his family. The Syrians understood that they were drowning in sin, and that the Umayyad government spared no effort to delude and mislead them.

The Imam confined his speech to introducing the Prophet's Household to the Syrians. He indicated to them that the Prophet's Household had a great position with Allah, that they waged jihad against the enemies of Islam, and that they suffered persecutions. The Imam mentioned nothing other than these matters. The Imam's (as) speech had a great effect on the Syrians, who secretly told each other about the Umayyad false mass medium, and about the disappointment and loss at which they reached, so their attitudes toward Yazid changed and they looked at him with disdain.

Source: Allama Baqir Sharif al-Qarashi. *The life of Imam Zayn al Abidin (as).* Chapter 7, P. 155-157. Available on *http://www.maaref-foundation.com/english/index.htm*

Books on this topic:

There is no other personality other than Imam Hussain (as) and no event other than the tragedy of Karbala on which the MOST number of books have been written. Below is a very small list of the books in English which I know of and are available for free on the websites mentioned in the introduction of this book.

40 Ahadith on Mourning (For Imam al-Hussain as) by al-Shaykh Jawad Muhaddathi

A Probe into the History of Ashura by Dr. Ibrahim Ayati

Al-Hussain in Prophetic Sunnah by Muhammad Nassirudin Arif

Al-Hussain's Martyrdom by Muhammad Nassirudin Arif

An Everlasting Instruction by Abu Muhammad Zain al-Aabideen

Arabic Accounts of Al- Hussain's Martyrdom by I.K.A Howard of Edinburg University

Ashura by Ayatollah Murtadha Mutahhari

Ashura Encyclopedia by I.K.A Howard of Edinburg University

Abul Fazl al Abbas: Eminence and Status by Syed Mohammad Masoom

Azadari 40 Ahadith by Agha Jawad Muhaddathi - Shahnwaz Mahdav

Event & Circumstances of the Martyrdom of Al Hussain Ibn Ali (as) by I.K.A Howard of Edinburg University

History of Karbala by Abu Ammar

Hussain: The sacrifice for mankind by Ayatollah Muhammad Shirazi

Hussain the Savior of Islam by SV Mir Ahmed Ali

Imam al- Hussain (as) – Taken from Kitab al-Irshad by al-Shaykh Muhammad Ibn Muhammad al-Mufeed

Imam Hasan (as) by Revolt and Silence Imam Hussain (as) by Silence and Revolt by Hassan Saeed

Imam Hussain's Revolution by Yusuf Fadhl

Karbala and Ashura by al-Syed Ali Hosayn Jalali

Karbala by al-Shaykh Muhammad Ibn Muhammad al-Mufeed

Karbala, the Chain of Events by Ramzan Sabir

Karbala Historical Resourses by Sheikh Al Mufid

Karbala and Beyond by Yasin T. al-Jibouri

Kitab Maqtal al-Hussain Compiled by al-Shaykh Abu Mikhnaf

Lectures on Ashura by Ayatullah Murtaza Mutahhari

Lohoof - Sighs of Sorrow by Seyed Ibn Tawus

Maqtal al-Hussain (as) by al-Shaykh Abd al-Razzaq al-Muqarram

Nafasul Mahmoom by Sheikh Abbas Qummi

Our Hussain (as), Mourning Him and His Karbala by al-Shaykh Abd al-Hussain al-Ameeni

Roots of the Karbala Tragedy by al-Syed Imdad Iman

Saving Monotheism in the Sands of Karbala by SV Mir Ahmed Ali

Tears and Tributes by Zakir

The Cause of the Ashura Uprising – A Qur'anic Perspective by Ismat Yazdi

The Fast of Ashura by Ayatollah Sayyid Saeed Akhtar Rizvi

The Hidden Truth about Karbala by A. K. Ahmed

The History of al Tabari: The Caliphate of Yazid b. Muawiyah by al Tabari, available at:
http://www.sunypress.edu/details.asp?id=50398

The Infallibles – #5 Imam al-Hussain (as) by al-Syed Mehdi Ayatollahi

The Journey of Imam Hussain by al-Shaykh Muhammad Ibn Muhammad al-Mufeed

The Journey of Tears by Bashir Hassanali Rahim

The Limits of Azadari by Ayatollah Naser Makarem Shirazi

The Martyr For Mankind by Allama Ali Naqi Naqvi

The Master of the Martyrs by Sayyid Ibn Tawoos

The Nature of Imam Hussain's Movement by Ayatollah Murtadha Mutahhari

The Probe into the History of Ashura by Dr. Ibrahim Ayati

The Revolution of al-Hussain (as) – It's Impact on the Consciousness of Muslim Society by al-Shaykh Muhammad Mahdi Shams al-Din

The Rising of al-Hussain by Shaykh Muhammad Mehdi Shams al Din

The Story of Karbala by Ayatollah Ali Nazari Munfarid

The Truth about al-Hussain's Revolt by Ayatollah Murtadha Mutahhari

The Tragedy of Karbala by Syed-Mohsin Naquvi

The Virtues of Imam Hussain (as) and His Companions by al-Shaykh Mohammad Ali Shomali

The World Finally Speaks at Karbala Tribunals by Dr. Hatem Abu Shahba

Tragedy of Karbala by al-Shaykh Muhammad Ibn Jarir al-Tabari

Understanding Karbala by al-Syed Saeed Akhtar Rizvi

We Cry for Hussain, So Did the Prophet of Islam by Yasser al-Madani

Why Imam Hussain Took a Stand by Mohammad Taqi Shariati

Chapter 10

Roots of the Shi'a faith (Usool al Deen) from the Qur'an

It is imperative that a Muslim's belief in the roots or the fundamentals of religion should be based on reasoning and proof. There are five **Fundamental Principles of Shi'a faith** or religious pillars or roots also known as *Usool al Deen* in Arabic, are as follow:

1. *Tawheed* or Oneness of God

2. *Ad'l* or Divine Justice

3. *Nabuwwat* or Prophethood

4. *Imamate* or Divinely Appointed Leadership

5. *Qiyamat* or Day of Judgement

Although, a person may not follow anyone regarding the fundamentals of religion, in the sense of accepting someone's words on this without reason, explanation, and rationale; Allah (swt) the Almighty, the most Beneficent to guide mankind has mentioned the five Fundamentals which Shi'a Muslims believe in, in the Holy Qur'an.

1. Tawheed (The Oneness of God)

The first fundamental principle of Shi'a Islam is Tawheed. Tawheed is the belief in the Indivisible Oneness of God, the Creator of the universe and all existence who has no partners and/or associates; in Arabic this indivisible one God is called Allah. Allah (swt) has no contender, rival or challenger.

Tawheed is the belief that Allah does not have an equal, and there is no being who remotely comes close to Allah in the attributes. Allah is the originator, maintainer and sustainer of everything that exists. Allah brought everything into existence from nonexistence and He sustains and maintains everything.

The proper name, which we use for God in the religion of Islam, is 'ALLAH' and that also needs some explanations. Although other monotheistic religions such as Christianity and Judaism in the Arabic speaking regions/countries (i.e. Lebanon, Egypt etc.) also use Allah as God, that Allah is driven out of *Al' Allah* (Eliahi) which is the word for "the God." Whereas, in the religion of Islam, 'ALLAH' means the 'One who deserves to be loved' and 'into Whom everyone seeks refuge.'

This word (ALLAH), grammatically speaking, is unique. It has no plural and no feminine. So this name itself reflects light upon the fact that Allah is one and only one; He has neither any partner nor any equal. Therefore, this name (Allah) cannot be translated by the word 'GOD' because God can be transformed into 'gods' and 'goddess' whereas, Allah cannot.

Sources:

Ayatollah Muhammad Shirazi, *Fundamentals of Islam*, P.1
   http://www.imamshirazi.com/fundamentalsofislam.pdf

Sayed Saeed Akhtar Rizvi, *Islam*, P. 11

Tawheed, the oneness of Allah (swt) is mentioned in the Holy Qur'an at several places, following are some of those verses:

Suratal Ikhlas 112

In the Name of Allah,
the All-beneficent, the All-merciful.

قُلْ هُوَ ٱللَّهُ أَحَدٌ ﴿١﴾

1 Say, 'He is Allah, the One.

ٱللَّهُ ٱلصَّمَدُ ﴿٢﴾

2 Allah is the All-embracing.

لَمْ يَلِدْ وَلَمْ يُولَدْ ﴿٣﴾

3 He neither begat, nor was begotten,

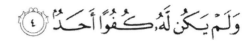

4 nor has He any equal.'

Surat Ta Ha 20:8

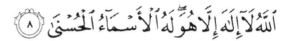

Allah - there is no god except Him
to Him belong the Best Names.

Surat Ta Ha 20:98

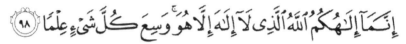

Indeed, your God is Allah.
There is no god except Him.
He embraces all things in [His] knowledge.

Surat al Saffat 37:35

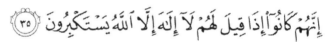

Indeed, it was they who,
when they were told,
'There is no god except Allah,'
used to be disdainful,

Surat al Baqirah 2:163

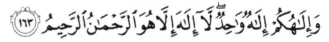

Your god is the One God,
there is no god except Him,
the All-beneficent, the All-merciful.

Surat al Anbiya 21:87

وَذَا ٱلنُّونِ إِذ ذَّهَبَ مُغَـٰضِبًا فَظَنَّ أَن لَّن نَّقْدِرَ عَلَيْهِ فَنَادَىٰ فِي ٱلظُّلُمَـٰتِ أَن لَّا إِلَـٰهَ إِلَّا أَنتَ سُبْحَـٰنَكَ إِنِّي كُنتُ مِنَ ٱلظَّـٰلِمِينَ ﴿٨٧﴾

And the Man of the Fish, when he left in a rage,
thinking that We would not put him to hardship.
Then he cried out in the darkness,
'There is no god except You!
You are immaculate!
I have indeed been among the wrongdoers!

Surat al Nahl 16:2

يُنَزِّلُ ٱلْمَلَـٰٓئِكَةَ بِٱلرُّوحِ مِنْ أَمْرِهِۦ عَلَىٰ مَن يَشَآءُ مِنْ عِبَادِهِۦٓ أَنْ أَنذِرُوٓا۟ أَنَّهُۥ لَآ إِلَـٰهَ إِلَّآ أَنَا۠ فَٱتَّقُونِ ﴿٢﴾

He sends down the angels
with the Spirit of His command
to whomever He wishes of His servants:
'Warn [the people] that there is no god except Me;
so be wary of Me.'

Surat al Maidah 5:73

لَّقَدْ كَفَرَ ٱلَّذِينَ قَالُوٓا۟ إِنَّ ٱللَّهَ ثَالِثُ ثَلَـٰثَةٍ وَمَا مِنْ إِلَـٰهٍ إِلَّآ إِلَـٰهٌ وَٰحِدٌ وَإِن لَّمْ يَنتَهُوا۟ عَمَّا يَقُولُونَ لَيَمَسَّنَّ ٱلَّذِينَ كَفَرُوا۟ مِنْهُمْ عَذَابٌ أَلِيمٌ ﴿٧٣﴾

They are certainly faithless who say,

'Allah is the third [person] of a trinity,'
while there is no god except the One God.
If they do not relinquish what they say,
there shall befall the faithless among them
a painful punishment.

Surat al Araf 7:65

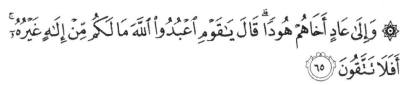

And to [the people of] Aad, Hud, their brother.
He said, 'O my people, worship Allah!
You have no other god besides Him.
Will you not then be wary [of Him]?'

Surat al Muminum 23:91

Allah has not taken any offspring,
neither is there any god besides Him,
for then each god would take away what he created,
and some of them would surely rise up against others.
Clear is Allah of what they allege!

Surat al Nisa 4:171

يَـٰٓأَهۡلَ ٱلۡكِتَٰبِ لَا تَغۡلُواْ فِى دِينِكُمۡ وَلَا تَقُولُواْ عَلَى

ٱللَّهِ إِلَّا ٱلۡحَقَّ إِنَّمَا ٱلۡمَسِيحُ عِيسَى ٱبۡنُ مَرۡيَمَ رَسُولُ ٱللَّهِ

وَكَلِمَتُهُۥٓ أَلۡقَىٰهَآ إِلَىٰ مَرۡيَمَ وَرُوحٌ مِّنۡهُ فَـَٔامِنُواْ بِٱللَّهِ

وَرُسُلِهِۦ وَلَا تَقُولُواْ ثَلَٰثَةٌ ٱنتَهُواْ خَيۡرًا لَّكُمۡ إِنَّمَا ٱللَّهُ إِلَٰهٌ

وَٰحِدٌ سُبۡحَٰنَهُۥٓ أَن يَكُونَ لَهُۥ وَلَدٌ لَّهُۥ مَا فِى ٱلسَّمَٰوَٰتِ وَمَا فِى

ٱلۡأَرۡضِ وَكَفَىٰ بِٱللَّهِ وَكِيلًا ﴿١٧١﴾

O People of the Book!
Do not exceed the bounds in your religion,
and do not attribute anything to Allah
except the truth.
The Messiah, Jesus son of Mary, was only
an apostle of Allah,
and His Word that He cast toward Mary
and a spirit from Him.
So have faith in Allah and His apostles,
and do not say, '[God is] a trinity.'
Relinquish [such a creed]! That is better for you.
Allah is but the One God.
He is far too immaculate to have any son.
To Him belongs whatever is in the heavens
and whatever is on the earth,
and Allah suffices as trustee.

Surat al Kahf 18:110

قُلْ إِنَّمَا أَنَا بَشَرٌ مِّثْلُكُمْ يُوحَىٰ إِلَيَّ أَنَّمَا إِلَٰهُكُمْ إِلَٰهٌ وَاحِدٌ فَمَن كَانَ يَرْجُو لِقَاءَ رَبِّهِ فَلْيَعْمَلْ عَمَلًا صَالِحًا وَلَا يُشْرِكْ بِعِبَادَةِ رَبِّهِ أَحَدًا ﴿١١٠﴾

Say, 'I am just a human being like you.
It has been revealed to me
that your God is the One God.

Surat al Anam 6:19

قُلْ أَيُّ شَيْءٍ أَكْبَرُ شَهَادَةً قُلِ اللَّهُ شَهِيدٌ بَيْنِي وَبَيْنَكُمْ وَأُوحِيَ إِلَيَّ هَٰذَا الْقُرْآنُ لِأُنذِرَكُم بِهِ وَمَن بَلَغَ أَئِنَّكُمْ لَتَشْهَدُونَ أَنَّ مَعَ اللَّهِ آلِهَةً أُخْرَىٰ قُل لَّا أَشْهَدُ قُلْ إِنَّمَا هُوَ إِلَٰهٌ وَاحِدٌ وَإِنَّنِي بَرِيءٌ مِّمَّا تُشْرِكُونَ ﴿١٩﴾

Say, 'What thing is greatest as witness?'
Say, 'Allah!
[He is] witness between me and you,
and this Qur'an has been revealed to me
that I may warn thereby you
and whomever it may reach.'
'Do you indeed bear witness
that there are other gods besides Allah?'
Say, 'I do not bear witness [to any such thing].'
Say, 'Indeed He is the One God,
and I indeed disown what you associate [with Him].'

Surat al Saffat 37:4

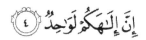

إِنَّ إِلَٰهَكُمْ لَوَاحِدٌ ﴿٤﴾

indeed your God is certainly One,

2. *Ad'l* (Justice of Allah swt)

The second fundamental principle of Shi'a faith is believing in '*Ad'l*' or "Justice of Allah (swt)."This is one of the biggest and decisive differences between the school of Ahlul Bayt (as) known as the Shi'a and the various schools of thought in *Ahle Sunnah Wal Jam'a.*

Therefore, the existence and unity of God falls under the first fundamental principle, which is *Tawheed,* whereas, the actions of Allah (swt) fall under the second fundamental principle of *Ad'l.*

The School of Ahlul Bayt (as) believes that one of Allah's (swt) attributes is that He is Just beyond all injustice (*adil ghayr zalim*). Allah (swt) does not treat His creatures without justice, nor does He rule them unfairly or cruelly, He rewards His obedient servants and punishes those who fall into sin. Allah (swt) does not compel His servants to do things, which are not within their capabilities, nor does he punish them for more than the sins they have committed.

Source:

Sayed Saeed Akhtar Rizvi, *Islam*, P. 12

Ayatollah Muhammad Rida al-Muzaffar, *The Faith of Shi'a Islam*, P. 9

Allah's (swt) **justice (*ad'l*)** is mentioned at several places in the holy Qur'an, below are few of those verses:

Surat al Nisa 4:40

$$إِنَّ ٱللَّهَ لَا يَظْلِمُ مِثْقَالَ ذَرَّةٍ وَإِن تَكُ حَسَنَةً يُضَٰعِفْهَا وَيُؤْتِ مِن لَّدُنْهُ أَجْرًا عَظِيمًا ﴿٤٠﴾$$

Indeed Allah does not wrong [anyone]
[even to the extent of] an atom's weight,

and if it be a good deed He doubles it[s reward],
and gives from Himself a great reward.

Surat al Anbiya 21:47

وَنَضَعُ ٱلْمَوَٰزِينَ ٱلْقِسْطَ لِيَوْمِ ٱلْقِيَٰمَةِ فَلَا نُظْلَمُ نَفْسٌ شَيْئًا ۖ وَإِن كَانَ مِثْقَالَ حَبَّةٍ مِّنْ خَرْدَلٍ أَتَيْنَا بِهَا ۗ وَكَفَىٰ بِنَا حَٰسِبِينَ ﴿٤٧﴾

We shall set up the scales of justice
on the Day of Resurrection,
and no soul will be wronged in the least.
Even if it be the weight of a mustard seed
We shall produce it
and We suffice as reckoners.

Surat al Nahl 16:90

۞ إِنَّ ٱللَّهَ يَأْمُرُ بِٱلْعَدْلِ وَٱلْإِحْسَٰنِ وَإِيتَآئِ ذِى ٱلْقُرْبَىٰ وَيَنْهَىٰ عَنِ ٱلْفَحْشَآءِ وَٱلْمُنكَرِ وَٱلْبَغْىِ ۚ يَعِظُكُمْ لَعَلَّكُمْ تَذَكَّرُونَ ﴿٩٠﴾

Indeed Allah enjoins justice and kindness
and generosity towards relatives,
and He forbids indecency, wrong,
and aggression.
He advises you,
so that you may take admonition.

Surat Yunus 10:52

ثُمَّ قِيلَ لِلَّذِينَ ظَلَمُوا۟ ذُوقُوا۟ عَذَابَ ٱلْخُلْدِ هَلْ تُجْزَوْنَ إِلَّا بِمَا كُنتُمْ تَكْسِبُونَ ﴿٥٢﴾

Then it will be said to those who were wrongdoers,
'Taste the everlasting punishment.
Shall you be requited
except for what you used to earn?'

Surat al Ankabut 29:40

فَكُلًّا أَخَذْنَا بِذَنْبِهِۦ فَمِنْهُم مَّنْ أَرْسَلْنَا عَلَيْهِ حَاصِبًا وَمِنْهُم مَّنْ أَخَذَتْهُ الصَّيْحَةُ وَمِنْهُم مَّنْ خَسَفْنَا بِهِ الْأَرْضَ وَمِنْهُم مَّنْ أَغْرَقْنَا وَمَا كَانَ اللَّهُ لِيَظْلِمَهُمْ وَلَٰكِن كَانُوٓا أَنفُسَهُمْ يَظْلِمُونَ ﴿٤٠﴾

So We seized each [of them] for his sin:
among them were those
upon whom We unleashed a rain of stones,
and among them were those
who were seized by the cry,
and among them were those
whom We caused the earth to swallow,
and among them were those
whom We drowned.
It was not Allah who wronged them,
but it was they who used to wrong themselves.

Surat Hud 11:100

ذَٰلِكَ مِنْ أَنۢبَاءِ الْقُرَىٰ نَقُصُّهُۥ عَلَيْكَ مِنْهَا قَآئِمٌ وَحَصِيدٌ ﴿١٠٠﴾

These are from the accounts of the townships
which We recount to you.
Of them there are some that still stand,
and some that have been mown down.

Surat Hud 10:44

$$\text{إِنَّ ٱللَّهَ لَا يَظْلِمُ ٱلنَّاسَ شَيْئًا وَلَكِنَّ ٱلنَّاسَ أَنفُسَهُمْ}$$
$$\text{يَظْلِمُونَ ﴿٤٤﴾}$$

Indeed Allah does not wrong people in the least;
rather it is people who wrong themselves.

3. *Nabuwwat* (Prophethood)

The School of Ahlul Bayt (as) believes that the Prophethood is a divine duty and a mission from Allah (swt). Allah (swt) appoints this Prophethood to those whom He selects from among His good servants, from those who are exalted among mankind. Allah (swt) sends them to the rest of humanity to be a guide to what is of benefit to them and is in their interest in this world and the next; to purify them from immorality, evil deeds, harmful customs, and also to teach people wisdom and knowledge and the ways of happiness and goodness until they attain to the perfection for which they were created, and reach the highest position in both worlds.

The School of Ahlul Bayt (as) believes that the Grace of Allah (*lutf*) requires that He send His messengers to His servants to guide them, to carry out reforming work, and to be intermediaries (*sufara*) between Allah (swt) and his vicegerents (*khulafa*). Therefore, the School of Ahlul Bayt (as) believes that Allah (swt) does not allow mankind to appoint, nominate or select a person as a prophet; indeed only Allah can choose and appoint someone as a prophet, because in

Surat al Anam 6:124

$$\text{وَإِذَا جَآءَتْهُمْ ءَايَةٌ قَالُواْ لَن نُّؤْمِنَ حَتَّى نُؤْتَى مِثْلَ مَآ أُوتِىَ رُسُلُ}$$
$$\text{ٱللَّهِ ٱللَّهُ أَعْلَمُ حَيْثُ يَجْعَلُ رِسَالَتَهُۥ سَيُصِيبُ ٱلَّذِينَ أَجْرَمُواْ}$$
$$\text{صَغَارٌ عِندَ ٱللَّهِ وَعَذَابٌ شَدِيدٌۢ بِمَا كَانُواْ يَمْكُرُونَ ﴿١٢٤﴾}$$

Allah knows best where to place His apostleship!

Allah (swt) sent 124,000 Prophets to guide mankind; believing in all of them is a third fundamental principle in the school of Ahlul bayt (as). The Prophets are of two kinds of status:

1. The Mursal Prophets: They were those prophets who were commissioned to guide people out of darkness to light, out of falsehood to the truth, from myths and superstition to reality and out of ignorance to knowledge.

2. The non-Mursal Prophets: They were those prophets who just received divine revelations for themselves only and they had not received orders to preach such revelations to the people.

The first of the prophets was Prophet Adam (as) and the last of them was Prophet Muhammad (pbuh).

The *Ulul-Azm* Prophets; who are Universal Prophets that received divine orders to preach to and lead the whole of mankind. They were:

1. Abraham (*Ibrahim*),
2. Noah, (*Nuh*)
3. Moses, (*Musa*)
4. Jesus (*Issa*)
5. Muhammad, peace be upon them all.

Source:

Ayatollah Muhammad Rida al-Muzaffar, *The Faith of Shi'a Islam*, P. 15

Ayatollah Muhammad Shirazi, *Fundamentals of Islam*, P.6 *http://www.imamshirazi.com/fundamentalsofislam.pdf*

The **Prophethood (***Nabuwwat***)** is mentioned in the holy Qur'an at several places; some of them are as follows:

Surat Aly Imran 3:79

مَاكَانَ لِبَشَرٍ أَن يُؤْتِيَهُ ٱللَّهُ ٱلْكِتَبَ وَٱلْحُكْمَ وَٱلنُّبُوَّةَ ثُمَّ يَقُولَ لِلنَّاسِ كُونُوا۟ عِبَادًا لِّى مِن دُونِ ٱللَّهِ وَلَكِن كُونُوا۟ رَبَّنِيِّنَ بِمَا كُنتُمْ تُعَلِّمُونَ ٱلْكِتَبَ وَبِمَا كُنتُمْ تَدْرُسُونَ ﴿٧٩﴾

It does not behoove any human
that Allah should give him the Book,
judgement and Prophethood,
and then he should say to the people,
'Be my servants instead of Allah.'
Rather [he would say], 'Be a godly people,
because of your teaching the Book
and because of your studying it.'

Surat al Jumuah 62:2

هُوَ ٱلَّذِى بَعَثَ فِى ٱلْأُمِّيِّنَ رَسُولًا مِّنْهُمْ يَتْلُوا۟ عَلَيْهِمْ ءَايَتِهِ وَيُزَكِّيهِمْ وَيُعَلِّمُهُمُ ٱلْكِتَبَ وَٱلْحِكْمَةَ وَإِن كَانُوا۟ مِن قَبْلُ لَفِى ضَلَلٍ مُّبِينٍ ﴿٢﴾

It is He who sent to the unlettered [people]
an apostle from among themselves,
to recite to them His signs, to purify them,
and to teach them the Book and wisdom,
and earlier they had indeed been
in manifest error.

Surat Yunus 10:57

يَٰٓأَيُّهَا ٱلنَّاسُ قَدْ جَآءَتْكُم مَّوْعِظَةٌ مِّن رَّبِّكُمْ وَشِفَآءٌ لِّمَا فِى ٱلصُّدُورِ وَهُدًى وَرَحْمَةٌ لِّلْمُؤْمِنِينَ ﴿٥٧﴾

O mankind!
There has certainly come to you an advice
from your Lord,
and a cure for what is in the breasts,
and a guidance and mercy for the faithful.

Surat al Anam 6:124

وَإِذَا جَاءَتْهُمْ ءَايَةٌ قَالُوا لَن نُّؤْمِنَ حَتَّىٰ نُؤْتَىٰ مِثْلَ مَا أُوتِيَ رُسُلُ اللَّهِ اللَّهُ أَعْلَمُ حَيْثُ يَجْعَلُ رِسَالَتَهُۥ سَيُصِيبُ الَّذِينَ أَجْرَمُوا صَغَارٌ عِندَ اللَّهِ وَعَذَابٌ شَدِيدٌ بِمَا كَانُوا يَمْكُرُونَ ﴿١٢٤﴾

And when a sign comes to them, they say,
'We will not believe until we are given
the like of what was given to Allah's apostles.
Allah knows best where to place His apostleship!
Soon the guilty will be visited by
a degradation before Allah
and a severe punishment
because of the plots they used to devise.

Surat al Kahf 18:110

قُلْ إِنَّمَا أَنَا بَشَرٌ مِّثْلُكُمْ يُوحَىٰ إِلَىَّ أَنَّمَا إِلَٰهُكُمْ إِلَٰهٌ وَحِدٌ فَمَن كَانَ يَرْجُوا لِقَاءَ رَبِّهِۦ فَلْيَعْمَلْ عَمَلًا صَلِحًا وَلَا يُشْرِكْ بِعِبَادَةِ رَبِّهِۦ أَحَدَا ﴿١١٠﴾

Say, 'I am just a human being like you.
It has been revealed to me
that your God is the One God.
So whoever expects to encounter his Lord
let him act righteously,
and not associate
anyone with the worship of his Lord.'

Surat al Isra 17:55

وَرَبُّكَ أَعْلَمُ بِمَن فِي السَّمَٰوَٰتِ وَالْأَرْضِ وَلَقَدْ فَضَّلْنَا بَعْضَ النَّبِيِّنَ عَلَىٰ بَعْضٍ وَءَاتَيْنَا دَاوُۥدَ زَبُورًا ﴿٥٥﴾

Your Lord knows best whoever is in the heavens
and the earth.

Certainly We gave some prophets an advantage
over others,
and We gave David the Psalms.

Surat al Isra 17:94-95

وَمَا مَنَعَ ٱلنَّاسَ أَن يُؤْمِنُوٓا۟ إِذْ جَآءَهُمُ ٱلْهُدَىٰٓ إِلَّآ أَن قَالُوٓا۟ أَبَعَثَ ٱللَّهُ بَشَرًا رَّسُولًا ۝

94 Nothing kept the people from believing
when guidance came to them,
but their saying,
'Has Allah sent a human as an apostle?!

قُل لَّوْ كَانَ فِى ٱلْأَرْضِ مَلَٰٓئِكَةٌ يَمْشُونَ مُطْمَئِنِّينَ لَنَزَّلْنَا عَلَيْهِم مِّنَ ٱلسَّمَآءِ مَلَكًا رَّسُولًا ۝

95 Say, 'Had there been angels in the earth,
walking around
and residing [in it like humans do],
We would have sent down to them from the heaven
an angel as apostle.'

Surat Hud 11:25-26

وَلَقَدْ أَرْسَلْنَا نُوحًا إِلَىٰ قَوْمِهِۦٓ إِنِّى لَكُمْ نَذِيرٌ مُّبِينٌ ۝

25 Certainly We sent Noah to his people [to declare]:
'Indeed I am a manifest warner to you,

أَن لَّا تَعْبُدُوٓا۟ إِلَّا ٱللَّهَ إِنِّىٓ أَخَافُ عَلَيْكُمْ عَذَابَ يَوْمٍ أَلِيمٍ ۝

26 Worship none but Allah.
Indeed I fear for you the punishment
of a painful day.'

Surat al Ankabut 29:16

وَإِبْرَاهِيمَ إِذْ قَالَ لِقَوْمِهِ اعْبُدُوا اللَّهَ وَاتَّقُوهُ ذَلِكُمْ خَيْرٌ لَّكُمْ إِن كُنتُمْ تَعْلَمُونَ ﴿١٦﴾

And Abraham, when he said to his people,
'Worship Allah and be wary of Him.
That is better for you,
should you know.

Surat al Ankabut 29:27

وَوَهَبْنَا لَهُ إِسْحَقَ وَيَعْقُوبَ وَجَعَلْنَا فِي ذُرِّيَّتِهِ النُّبُوَّةَ وَالْكِتَابَ وَءَاتَيْنَاهُ أَجْرَهُ فِي الدُّنْيَا وَإِنَّهُ فِي الْآخِرَةِ لَمِنَ الصَّالِحِينَ ﴿٢٧﴾

And We gave him Isaac and Jacob,
and We ordained among his descendants
Prophethood and the Book,
and We gave him his reward in the world,
and in the Hereafter he will indeed be
among the Righteous.

Surat Hud 11:50

وَإِلَى عَادٍ أَخَاهُمْ هُودًا قَالَ يَا قَوْمِ اعْبُدُوا اللَّهَ مَا لَكُم مِّنْ إِلَهٍ غَيْرُهُ إِنْ أَنتُمْ إِلَّا مُفْتَرُونَ ﴿٥٠﴾

And to Aad [We sent] Hud, their brother.
He said, 'O my people!
Worship Allah.
You have no other god besides Him:
you merely fabricate [the deities that you worship].

Surat Hud 11:61

وَإِلَى ثَمُودَ أَخَاهُمْ صَالِحًا قَالَ يَا قَوْمِ اعْبُدُوا اللَّهَ مَا لَكُم مِّنْ إِلَهٍ غَيْرُهُ هُوَ أَنشَأَكُم مِّنَ الْأَرْضِ وَاسْتَعْمَرَكُمْ فِيهَا فَاسْتَغْفِرُوهُ ثُمَّ تُوبُوا إِلَيْهِ إِنَّ رَبِّي قَرِيبٌ مُّجِيبٌ ﴿٦١﴾

And to Thamud [We sent] Salih, their brother.
He said, 'O my people!
Worship Allah.
You have no other god besides Him.
He brought you forth from the earth
and made it your habitation.
So plead with Him for forgiveness,
then turn to Him penitently.
My Lord is indeed nearmost [and] responsive.'

Surat Hud 11:84

وَإِلَى مَدْيَنَ أَخَاهُمْ شُعَيْبًا قَالَ يَا قَوْمِ اعْبُدُوا اللَّهَ مَا لَكُم مِّنْ إِلَهٍ غَيْرُهُ وَلَا تَنقُصُوا الْمِكْيَالَ وَالْمِيزَانَ إِنِّي أَرَاكُم بِخَيْرٍ وَإِنِّي أَخَافُ عَلَيْكُمْ عَذَابَ يَوْمٍ مُّحِيطٍ ﴿٨٤﴾

And to Midian [We sent] Shuayb, their brother.
He said, 'O my people!
Worship Allah.
You have no other god besides Him.
Do not diminish the measure or the balance.
Indeed I see that you are faring well,
but I fear for you the punishment
of an all-embracing day.

Surat Maryam 19:30

قَالَ إِنِّي عَبْدُ اللَّهِ آتَانِيَ الْكِتَابَ وَجَعَلَنِي نَبِيًّا ﴿٣٠﴾

He (Jesus as) said, 'Indeed I am a servant of Allah!
He has given me the Book

and made me a prophet.

Surat Maryam 19:41

وَٱذْكُرْ فِى ٱلْكِتَٰبِ إِبْرَٰهِيمَ إِنَّهُۥ كَانَ صِدِّيقًا نَّبِيًّا ﴿٤١﴾

And mention in the Book Abraham.
Indeed he was a truthful one, a prophet.

Surat Maryam 19:49

فَلَمَّا ٱعْتَزَلَهُمْ وَمَا يَعْبُدُونَ مِن دُونِ ٱللَّهِ وَهَبْنَا لَهُۥٓ إِسْحَٰقَ وَيَعْقُوبَ
وَكُلًّا جَعَلْنَا نَبِيًّا ﴿٤٩﴾

So when he had left them
and what they worshipped besides Allah,
We gave him Isaac and Jacob,
and each We made a prophet.

Surat Maryam 19:53-54

وَوَهَبْنَا لَهُۥ مِن رَّحْمَتِنَآ أَخَاهُ هَٰرُونَ نَبِيًّا ﴿٥٣﴾

53 And We gave him out of Our mercy
his brother Aaron, a prophet.

وَٱذْكُرْ فِى ٱلْكِتَٰبِ إِسْمَٰعِيلَ إِنَّهُۥ كَانَ صَادِقَ ٱلْوَعْدِ وَكَانَ رَسُولًا نَّبِيًّا ﴿٥٤﴾

54 And mention in the Book Ishmael.
Indeed he was true to his promise,
and an apostle and a prophet.

Surat al Hadid 57:25-26

لَقَدْ أَرْسَلْنَا رُسُلَنَا بِالْبَيِّنَاتِ وَأَنزَلْنَا مَعَهُمُ الْكِتَابَ

وَالْمِيزَانَ لِيَقُومَ النَّاسُ بِالْقِسْطِ وَأَنزَلْنَا الْحَدِيدَ فِيهِ بَأْسٌ

شَدِيدٌ وَمَنَافِعُ لِلنَّاسِ وَلِيَعْلَمَ اللَّهُ مَن يَنصُرُهُ وَرُسُلَهُ بِالْغَيْبِ إِنَّ اللَّهَ

قَوِيٌّ عَزِيزٌ ﴿٢٥﴾

25 Certainly We sent Our apostles with manifest proofs,
and We sent down with them the Book
and the Balance,
so that mankind may maintain justice;
and We sent down iron,
in which there is great might
and uses for mankind,
and so that Allah may know those who help Him
and His apostles in [their] absence.
Indeed Allah is all-strong, all-mighty.

وَلَقَدْ أَرْسَلْنَا نُوحًا وَإِبْرَاهِيمَ وَجَعَلْنَا فِي ذُرِّيَّتِهِمَا النُّبُوَّةَ

وَالْكِتَابَ فَمِنْهُم مُّهْتَدٍ وَكَثِيرٌ مِّنْهُمْ فَاسِقُونَ ﴿٢٦﴾

26 Certainly We sent Noah and Abraham
and We ordained among their descendants
Prophethood and the Book.
Some of them are [rightly] guided,
and many of them are transgressors.

Surat Fatir 35:24

إِنَّا أَرْسَلْنَاكَ بِالْحَقِّ بَشِيرًا وَنَذِيرًا وَإِن مِّنْ أُمَّةٍ إِلَّا خَلَا فِيهَا

نَذِيرٌ ﴿٢٤﴾

Indeed We have sent you with the truth
as a bearer of good news and as a warner;
and there is not a nation
but a warner has passed in it.

4. *Imamat* (leadership)

It was a matter of divine choice or plan to appoint His messengers for the guidance of mankind. Similarly, appointing deputies and successors to those messengers was also a matter of divinity. Allah (swt), the Most High, appointed twelve distinguished personalities, one after the other, as successors of the Holy Prophet of Islam (pbuh)

Prophet Muhammad (pbuh) said:

'I leave with you the two momentous things, as long as you adhere to them you will never go astray - the book of Allah, and my kin the people of my household. Indeed, these two will never separate from one another until they arrive at the well (of Kawthar in Paradise).

Source: Ahmad Ibn Hanbal, *Musnad* vol. 3, pp 17, 26, 59, Dar-Sadir, Beirut.

Prophet Muhammad (pbuh) also said:

*"The religion will continue to be established till there are **twelve caliphs/ rulers** over you, and the whole community will agree on each of them."* I then heard from the Prophet (pbuh) some remarks, which I could not understand. I asked my father: What is he saying: He said: *"all of them will belong to Quraysh."*

Narrated by Jabir Ibn Samurah:

Sources:

Sunan Abu Dawood (English) Book 37, Hadith 4266. http://sunnah.com/abuDawood/38

Sahih Muslim (Arabic) Hadith# 1818 a. (English) Book 20, Hadith 4473. http://sunnah.com/muslim/33

Sahih Bukhari Book 93, Hadith 82. http://sunnah.com/bukhari/93

Sunan al-Tirmidhi, Book 33, Hadith 66. http://sunnah.com/tirmidhi/33

Musnad of Ahmad Ibn Hanbal, Vol 1, P. 398 and Vol 5, P. 106

The prominent Sunni scholar al-Hafiz al-Qanduzi al-Hanafi quotes Prophet Muhammad (pbuh) in his book, Yanaabee' al-Mawaddah, as saying:

I am the master of the prophets and Ali is the master of the successors, and indeed my successors after me are twelve, the first of whom is Ali and the last is al-Qa'em al-Mahdi.

Source:

Ayatollah Muhammad Rida al-Muzaffar, *The Faith of Shi'a Islam*, P. 15

Ayatollah Muhammad Shirazi, *Fundamentals of Islam*, P.6 *http://www.imamshirazi.com/fundamentalsofislam.pdf*

The succession (Leadership, Authority, Vicegerency, Imamate, Caliphate) after the Holy Prophet (pbuh) is to be assigned by Allah (swt) ONLY and only Allah (swt) sends guidance to mankind as stated in the holy Qur'an:

Surat al Ra'd 13:7

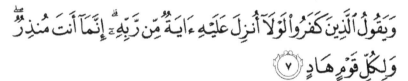

The faithless say,
'Why has not some sign been sent down to him
from his Lord?'
You are only a warner,
and there is a guide for every people.

Question: *Who is the guide after the Holy Prophet (pbuh) from Allah (swt)?*

Surat al Sajdah 32:24

وَجَعَلْنَا مِنْهُمْ أَئِمَّةً يَهْدُونَ بِأَمْرِنَا لَمَّا صَبَرُواْ وَكَانُواْ بِآيَٰتِنَا يُوقِنُونَ ﴿٢٤﴾

And amongst them We appointed imams
to guide [the people] by Our command,
when they had been patient
and had conviction in Our signs.

Note: Only, Allah (swt) appoints Imam, not people!

Surat al Baqirah 2:30

وَإِذْ قَالَ رَبُّكَ لِلْمَلَٰئِكَةِ إِنِّي جَاعِلٌ فِي ٱلْأَرْضِ خَلِيفَةً قَالُوٓاْ أَتَجْعَلُ فِيهَا مَن يُفْسِدُ فِيهَا وَيَسْفِكُ ٱلدِّمَآءَ وَنَحْنُ نُسَبِّحُ بِحَمْدِكَ وَنُقَدِّسُ لَكَ قَالَ إِنِّيٓ أَعْلَمُ مَا لَا تَعْلَمُونَ ﴿٣٠﴾

When your Lord said to the angels,
'Indeed I am going to set a viceroy (caliph) on the earth,'
they said, 'Will You set in it
someone who will cause corruption in it,
and shed blood,
while we celebrate Your praise
and proclaim Your sanctity?'
He said, 'Indeed I know what you do not know.'

Note: Only, Allah (swt) sets a Caliph/ Viceroy, not people!

Surat al Nisa 4:59

يَـٰٓأَيُّهَا ٱلَّذِينَ ءَامَنُوٓا۟ أَطِيعُوا۟ ٱللَّهَ وَأَطِيعُوا۟ ٱلرَّسُولَ وَأُو۟لِى ٱلْأَمْرِ مِنكُمْ ۖ فَإِن

نَـٰزَعْتُمْ فِى شَىْءٍ فَرُدُّوهُ إِلَى ٱللَّهِ وَٱلرَّسُولِ إِن كُنتُمْ تُؤْمِنُونَ بِٱللَّهِ وَٱلْيَوْمِ

ٱلْءَاخِرِ ۚ ذَٰلِكَ خَيْرٌ وَأَحْسَنُ تَأْوِيلًا ﴿٥٩﴾

O you who have faith!
Obey Allah and obey the Apostle
and those vested with authority among you.
And if you dispute concerning anything,
refer it to Allah and the Apostle,
if you have faith in Allah and the Last Day.
That is better and more favorable in outcome.

Note: Obey those vested with authority from Allah (swt)

Surat Aly Imran 3:33-34

۞ إِنَّ ٱللَّهَ ٱصْطَفَىٰٓ ءَادَمَ وَنُوحًا وَءَالَ إِبْرَٰهِيمَ وَءَالَ عِمْرَٰنَ عَلَى

ٱلْعَـٰلَمِينَ ﴿٣٣﴾

33 Indeed Allah chose Adam and Noah,
and the progeny of Abraham
and the progeny of Imran
above all the nations;

ذُرِّيَّةًۢ بَعْضُهَا مِنۢ بَعْضٍ ۗ وَٱللَّهُ سَمِيعٌ عَلِيمٌ ﴿٣٤﴾

34 some of them are descendants of the others,
and Allah is all-hearing, all-knowing.

Note: Allah (swt) made the progeny of Abraham and progeny of
Imran (Abu Talib as) above all the nations

Surat al Baqirah 2:247

وَقَالَ لَهُمْ نَبِيُّهُمْ إِنَّ ٱللَّهَ قَدْ بَعَثَ لَكُمْ طَالُوتَ مَلِكًا

قَالُوٓاْ أَنَّىٰ يَكُونُ لَهُ ٱلْمُلْكُ عَلَيْنَا وَنَحْنُ أَحَقُّ بِٱلْمُلْكِ مِنْهُ وَلَمْ

يُؤْتَ سَعَةً مِّنَ ٱلْمَالِ قَالَ إِنَّ ٱللَّهَ ٱصْطَفَىٰهُ عَلَيْكُمْ وَزَادَهُۥ

بَسْطَةً فِى ٱلْعِلْمِ وَٱلْجِسْمِ وَٱللَّهُ يُؤْتِى مُلْكَهُۥ مَن

يَشَآءُ وَٱللَّهُ وَٰسِعٌ عَلِيمٌ ﴿٢٤٧﴾

Their prophet said to them,
'Allah has appointed Saul as king for you.'
They said, 'How can he have kingship over us,
when we have a greater right to kingship than him,
as he has not been given ample wealth?'
He said, 'Indeed Allah has chosen him over you,
and enhanced him vastly
in knowledge and physique,
and Allah gives His kingdom
to whomever He wishes,
and Allah is all-bounteous, all-knowing.'

Note: It is not upto people to decide who has greater right of leadership.

Surat al Nisa 4:54

أَمْ يَحْسُدُونَ ٱلنَّاسَ عَلَىٰ مَآ ءَاتَىٰهُمُ ٱللَّهُ مِن فَضْلِهِۦ فَقَدْ ءَاتَيْنَآ ءَالَ

إِبْرَٰهِيمَ ٱلْكِتَٰبَ وَٱلْحِكْمَةَ وَءَاتَيْنَٰهُم مُّلْكًا عَظِيمًا ﴿٥٤﴾

Or do they envy the people
for what Allah has given them out of His grace?
We have certainly given the progeny of Abraham
the Book and wisdom,
and We have given them a great sovereignty.

5. *Qiyamat* (Resurrection)

The fifth fundamental of Shi'a faith is a firm belief in the Day of Judgment or '*Qiyamat.*' On this day Allah (swt) will bring every human being back to life and on that day every human be judged according to his or her faith and deeds. A person with true faith and righteous deeds will receive the grace of Allah (swt) and will be sent to Paradise where he will find contentment according to his spiritual qualities. On the other hand, a person who has deviated and engages in bad deeds will be punished in Hell.

A person who holds the right belief but engaged in wrong actions (except any wrong doing against a fellow human being) will be either forgiven by Allah (swt) and sent to Paradise straight away or punished at first and then sent to Paradise.

Source:

Sayed Saeed Akhtar Rizvi, *Islam*, P. 67

Note: It is impossible to deal with this topic here in detail, but it will be sufficient to say that the mercy and justice of Allah (swt) is beyond limits and he is the only judge in determining who is granted paradise or who is sent to hell.

Qiyamat (**Day of Judgement**) is the most discussed topic in the holy Qur'an; Allah (swt) has named a whole Chapter (75, Surat al Qiyamah) on this topic; here are some of the other verses, which discuss this topic:

Surat al Baqirah 2:212

$$ زُيِّنَ لِلَّذِينَ كَفَرُوا الْحَيَوٰةُ الدُّنْيَا وَيَسْخَرُونَ مِنَ الَّذِينَ ءَامَنُوا ۘ وَالَّذِينَ اتَّقَوْا فَوْقَهُمْ يَوْمَ الْقِيَـٰمَةِ ۗ وَاللَّهُ يَرْزُقُ مَن يَشَاءُ بِغَيْرِ حِسَابٍ ﴿٢١٢﴾ $$

Worldly life has been glamorized for the faithless,

and they ridicule the faithful.
But those who are Godwary
shall be above them on the Day of Resurrection,
and Allah provides for whomever He wishes
without any reckoning.

Surat Aly Imran 3:185

كُلُّ نَفْسٍ ذَآئِقَةُ ٱلْمَوْتِ وَإِنَّمَا تُوَفَّوْنَ أُجُورَكُمْ يَوْمَ
ٱلْقِيَـٰمَةِ فَمَن زُحْزِحَ عَنِ ٱلنَّارِ وَأُدْخِلَ ٱلْجَنَّةَ فَقَدْ فَازَّ وَمَا
ٱلْحَيَوٰةُ ٱلدُّنْيَآ إِلَّا مَتَـٰعُ ٱلْغُرُورِ ﴿١٨٥﴾

Every soul shall taste death,
and you will indeed be paid your full rewards
on the Day of Resurrection.
Whoever is delivered from the Fire
and admitted to paradise
has certainly succeeded.
The life of this world is nothing
but the wares of delusion.

Surat al Nisa 4:87

ٱللَّهُ لَآ إِلَـٰهَ إِلَّا هُوَ لَيَجْمَعَنَّكُمْ إِلَىٰ يَوْمِ ٱلْقِيَـٰمَةِ لَا رَيْبَ فِيهِ وَمَنْ
أَصْدَقُ مِنَ ٱللَّهِ حَدِيثًا ﴿٨٧﴾

Allah—there is no god except Him—
will surely gather you on the Day of Resurrection,
in which there is no doubt;
and who is more truthful in speech than Allah?

Surat al Anam 6:12

قُل لِّمَن مَّا فِى السَّمَوَاتِ وَالْأَرْضِ قُل لِلَّهِ كَتَبَ عَلَىٰ نَفْسِهِ
الرَّحْمَةَ لَيَجْمَعَنَّكُمْ إِلَىٰ يَوْمِ الْقِيَمَةِ لَا رَيْبَ فِيهِ الَّذِينَ
خَسِرُوٓا أَنفُسَهُمْ فَهُمْ لَا يُؤْمِنُونَ ﴿١٢﴾

Say, 'To whom belongs whatever is in the heavens
and the earth?'
Say, 'To Allah.
He has made mercy incumbent upon Himself.
He will surely gather you on the Day of Resurrection,
in which there is no doubt.
Those who have ruined their souls
will not have faith.'

Surat al Araf 7:187

يَسْـَٔلُونَكَ عَنِ السَّاعَةِ أَيَّانَ مُرْسَىٰهَا قُلْ إِنَّمَا عِلْمُهَا عِندَ رَبِّى لَا يُجَلِّيهَا
لِوَقْتِهَآ إِلَّا هُوَ ثَقُلَتْ فِى السَّمَوَاتِ وَالْأَرْضِ لَا تَأْتِيكُمْ إِلَّا بَغْتَةً يَسْـَٔلُونَكَ
كَأَنَّكَ حَفِىٌّ عَنْهَا قُلْ إِنَّمَا عِلْمُهَا عِندَ اللَّهِ وَلَٰكِنَّ أَكْثَرَ النَّاسِ لَا
يَعْلَمُونَ ﴿١٨٧﴾

They question you concerning the Hour,
when will it set in?
Say, 'Its knowledge is only with my Lord:
none except Him shall manifest it at its time.
It will weigh heavy on the heavens and the earth.
It will not overtake you but suddenly.'
They ask you as if you were in the know of it.
Say, 'Its knowledge is only with Allah,
but most people do not know.'
Surat Ibrahim 14:48-51

$$\text{يَوْمَ تُبَدَّلُ ٱلْأَرْضُ غَيْرَ ٱلْأَرْضِ وَٱلسَّمَوَاتُ ۖ وَبَرَزُوا لِلَّهِ ٱلْوَاحِدِ}$$

$$\text{ٱلْقَهَّارِ ﴿٤٨﴾}$$

48 The day the earth is transformed into another earth
and the heavens [as well],
and they are presented before Allah,
the One, the All-paramount.

$$\text{وَتَرَى ٱلْمُجْرِمِينَ يَوْمَئِذٍ مُّقَرَّنِينَ فِي ٱلْأَصْفَادِ ﴿٤٩﴾}$$

49 On that day you will see the guilty
bound together in chains,

$$\text{سَرَابِيلُهُم مِّن قَطِرَانٍ وَتَغْشَىٰ وُجُوهَهُمُ ٱلنَّارُ ﴿٥٠﴾}$$

50 their garments made of pitch,
and the Fire covering their faces,

$$\text{لِيَجْزِيَ ٱللَّهُ كُلَّ نَفْسٍ مَّا كَسَبَتْ ۚ إِنَّ ٱللَّهَ سَرِيعُ}$$

$$\text{ٱلْحِسَابِ ﴿٥١﴾}$$

51 so that Allah may reward every soul
for what it has earned.
Indeed Allah is swift at reckoning.

Surat al Ahzab 33:63

$$\text{يَسْأَلُكَ ٱلنَّاسُ عَنِ ٱلسَّاعَةِ ۖ قُلْ إِنَّمَا عِلْمُهَا عِندَ ٱللَّهِ ۚ وَمَا يُدْرِيكَ لَعَلَّ}$$

$$\text{ٱلسَّاعَةَ تَكُونُ قَرِيبًا ﴿٦٣﴾}$$

The people question you concerning the Hour.
Say, 'Its knowledge is only with Allah.'
What do you know,
maybe the Hour is near.

Surat al Mumtahanah 60:3

$$\text{لَن تَنفَعَكُمْ أَرْحَامُكُمْ وَلَا أَوْلَٰدُكُمْ يَوْمَ ٱلْقِيَٰمَةِ يَفْصِلُ بَيْنَكُمْ وَٱللَّهُ بِمَا تَعْمَلُونَ بَصِيرٌ ٣}$$

Your relatives and your children will not avail you
on the Day of Resurrection:
He will separate you [from one another],
and Allah sees best what you do .

Other Qur'anic references: 2:48, 2:113, 2:123, 2:141, 2:166, 2:212, 3:9, 3:30, 3:106, 3:185, 4:42, 4:87, 5:109, 5:119, 6:12, 6:22, 6:27, 6:30, 6:51, 6:128, 6:158, 7:38, 7:53, 9:34, 10:28, 10:45, 10:53, 10:61, 11:8, 11:103, 13:5, 14:21, 14:42, 14:47, 15:85, 16:77, 16:84, 16:111, 17:13, 17:52, 17:71, 17:97, 18:45, 18:51, 18:100, 19:66, 19:85, 19:93, 20:101-112, 20:124, 20:135,20:137, 21:39, 21:101, 22:1, 22:7, 22:17, 22:19, 22:55, 22:69, 23:101-115, 24:24, 25:10-16, 25:22-29, 26:90-104, 27:75, 27:78, 27:82, 27:87-90, 28:60-66, 28:74, 28:83, 29:54, 30:7, 30:11-16, 30:19, 30:43, 30:55, 31:28, 31:33, 32:5, 32:12, 32:28, 33:63-68, 34:3, 34:25, 34:29-33, 34:40, 34:51, 35:45, 36:32, 36:48-54, 36:63-67, 37:19-34, 39:15, 39:46, 39:56-61, 39:67-75, 40:10, 40:15-20, 40:47-52, 40:59, 41:19-25, 41:29, 41:48, 42:17, 42:20, 42:22, 42:44, 43:39, 43:66, 44:9-16, 44:38-42, 45:27-35, 46:35, 47:18, 50:20-30, 50:43, 51:1-6, 51:22, 52:1-16, 53:57, 54:6, 54:46, 55:35, 56:1-9, 57:12, 57:20, 58:6, 64:9, 66:6, 67:25, 69:1, 69:13-18, 70:5-14, 72:24, 73:11, 73:17, 75:1-35, 77:1-15, 77:24-40, 78:1, 78:17, 78:37, 79:6-14, 79:34:46, 80:33, 81:1-14, 82:1-9, 82:13-19, 83:7-12, 83:18, 83:34, 84:1-12, 86:9-17, 89:24, 99:1-9, 101:1-7, 102:1-8

End of chapter notes:

Rights of a Muslim by the Holy Prophet (pbuh)

The Holy Prophet (pbuh) said:

"Every believer has 30 obligations over his brother-in-faith, which could not be said to have been met unless he either performs them or is excused from performing them by his brother-in-faith."

1. Forgiving his mistakes
2. Being merciful and kind to him when he is in a strange land
3. Guarding his secrets
4. Giving him a hand when he is about to fall
5. Accepting his apology
6. Discouraging backbiting about him
7. Persisting giving him good advice
8. Treasuring his friendship
9. Fulfilling his trust
10. Visiting him when he is ill
11. Being with him at his death
12. Accepting his invitations and presents
13. Returning his favors in the same way
14. Thanking him for his favors
15. Being grateful for his assistance
16. Protecting his honor and property
17. Helping him meet his needs
18. Making an effort to solve his problems
19. Saying to him Yarhamuka Allah (May Allah have mercy on you) when he sneezes
20. Guiding him to the thing he has lost

21. Answering his greeting

22. Take him at his word

23. Accepting his bestowals

24. Confirming him if he swears to something

25. Being kind and friendly towards him

26. Helping him when he is unjustly by stopping him or when he is being a victim of injustice

27. Not being unsympathetic and hostile towards him

28. Refraining from feeling bored and fed up with him

29. Not forsaking him in the midst of troubles

30. Whatever good thing you like, you should also like for him and whatever you dislike, you should dislike it for him.

These are the morals we should live by and the way that we should treat each other. Just imagine if we lived by all of these how much better this world would be. The Prophet (pbuh) gave us the remedy for our social problems, but it is up to us to put them into practice.

Source: Allama Muhammad Mahdi Ibn Abi Zarr al-Naraqi, *Jami`al-Sa'adat* (The Collector of Felicities). P. 37-38

Books on the Fundamental Principles of Shi'a Faith

Divine (Allah's) Judgment (Hokm) versus Human Judgment (Hokm) by Dr. Hatem Abu Shahba

Divine Justice by Sayyid Mujtaba Musawi Lari

Early Shia Thought by Arzina Lalani

Essence of Shia Faith by al-Shaykh Muhammad Ibn Ali as Sudooq

Fifty Lessons on Principles of Belief for Youths by Ayatollah Nasir Makarem Shirazi

Faith and Reason by al-Shaykh Mahdi Hadavi Tehrani

Fundamentals of Islam by Ayatollah Muhammad Shirazi

Fundamentals of Islam, according to Quran by Ayatollah Mahdi Puya

General Concepts of Islam by Ayatollah Ali Khamenei

Inquiries about Islam by al-Shaykh Mohamad Jawad Chirri

Inquiries About Shi'a Islam by Sayed Moustafa al-Qazwini

Introduction to Islam by Ayatollah Muhammad Ridha Golpayghani

Introduction to Islamic Principles by al-Shaykh Jafar Subhani

Islam: Fundamental Principles and Teachings by Ayatollah Muhammad Shirazi
Islamic Beliefs for All by Ayatollah Muhammad Shirazi

Islam and Religious Pluralism by Ayatollah Murtadha Mutahhari

Islam and the Modern Age by al-Syed Muhammad Hussain Tabatabai

Islam for All by Reza Esfahani

Islam by al-Syed Saeed Akhtar Rizvi

Islamic Teachings – an Overview by al-Syed Muhammad Hussain Tabatabai

Islamic Teachings in Brief by al-Syed Muhammad Hussain Tabatabai

Justice of God by Ayatollah Nasir Makarem Shirazi

Let's Learn about Divine Justice by Ayatollah Nasir Makarem Shirazi

Levels of Submission by Ayatollah Murtadha Mutahhari

Man and His Destiny by Ayatollah Murtadha Mutahhari

Methods of Religious Thought in Islam by al-Syed Muhammad Hussain Tabatabai

Need of Religion by al-Syed Saeed Akhtar Rizvi

Rationality of Islam by Al-Khoei Foundation

Reason, Faith & Authority – A Shi'ite Perspective by al-Shaykh Mohammed Ali Shomali

Religion vs. Religion by Dr. Ali Shariati

Shi'a Creed by Abu Jafar Muhammad Ibn Ali Ibn Babawaih al-Qummi Shaykh Sudooq

Shiism, the Natural Product by Ayatollah Syed Muhammad Baqir al-Sadr

Shi'aism in Sunnism by Ayatollah Sayyid Muhammad Reza Mudarraisi Yazdi

Shiism in Relation to Various Islamic Sects by Dr. Abul Qasim Gorji

Shia Islam by Syed Hussain Nasr

Shia Islam in Sunni Traditions by Sultanul-Waizin al-Shiraz

Shiism and its Types during the Early Centuries Part 1 by al-Shaykh Rasul Ja'fariyan

Striving for Right Guidance by al-Syed Muhammad al-Tijani al-Smaoui

Tenets of Islam by al-Shaykh Muhammad Ibn al-Hasan al-Tusi

The Divine Invitation by al-Shaykh Muhammad Khalfan

The Faith of Shi'a Islam by Muhammad Rida al-Muzaffar

The Justice of God by Ayatollah Sayyid Saeed Akhtar Rizvi

The Origin of the Shi'ia Islam and its Principles by Allama Shaykh Muhammad Hussain Al-Kashiftul'Ghita

The Shi'a and their Beliefs by Ayatollah Sayed Muhammad Shirazi

The Truth about the Shi'a by Ayatollah Sayed Sadiq Hussain Shirazi

Theological Instructions by al-Shaykh Muhammad Taqi Mesbah Yazdi

This is Islam by Mohammad Hassan Ghadiri Abyaneh

Truth about Shi'ah Ithna 'Ashari Faith by Asad Wahid al-Qasim

Usul ud-Deen (Principles of Faith) by Ayatollah Wahid Khorasani

Why Shia – In a Nutshell by Ahlul Bayt Digital Islamic Library
Project

What is Islam by Ayatollah Sayed Muhammad Shirazi

Chapter 11

Branches of Shi'a faith (Furooh al Deen) from Qur'an

Islam is like a tree whose roots are its beliefs (*Usool al Deen*) and whose branches are its practices (*Furooh al Deen*). If the roots are not firm and healthy, the tree will not survive - but the roots only form the foundation of the tree.

The Islamic Practices are referred to as such because they are the ways in which the theory of Islam - the Beliefs are turned into reality. The different forms of outward worship translate a person's inner love and connection with the Almighty into a physical form.

Islam has ten **fundamental** Practices:

1. *Salah* or the daily obligatory prayers
2. *Sawm* or fasting
3. *Khums* or the one-fifth (20%) religious duty
4. *Zakat* or the duty applicable to certain commodity
5. *Hajj or* pilgrimage to the holy city of Mecca
6. *Jihad or* striving
7. *Amr bil-Ma'roof*– promoting virtue or enjoining good
8. *Nahy anil-Munkar*– prohibiting evil
9. *Tawalla*– supporting Allah's disciples
10. *Tabarra*– dissociating from the enemies of Allah, the Prophet (pbuh) and his holy household (as)

Source: Sayed Mustafa al-Qazwini, (2012). *Invitation to Islam.* Chapter 4, P. 33.

There are four sources for *Furooh al-Deen* or 'the essential rulings and practices of Islam'

1. The Holy Qur'an
2. Sunnah of the Holy Prophet (pbuh) and his Ahlul Bayt (as)
3. Reasoning and consensus (what benefit these practices have

on one's life?)

4. Following an expert in the field of Jurisprudence ~ doing *Taqlid* (following) of a *Marja* (an expert).

In this Chapter, I am only discussing the Qur'anic perspectives on the ten most important *Furooh al-Deen* or 'the practices of Islam'; they are as follows:

Note: For further sources from *Sunnah* and experts in the field of Jurisprudence, Please refer to the books mentioned at the end of this chapter.

1. *Salaat/Namaz* (Prayer):

Praying the five obligatory prayers every single day.

Prayers are the pillars of religion. Through prayer, people establish communication and dialogue with the Almighty, and they realize that they are not alone in this universe and that they have been created for a legitimate purpose. Allah created human beings to recognize and appreciate His grace and blessings. Just as the body needs food to survive and grow, so does the soul, and the food of the soul is prayer. So that people receive their necessary spiritual nourishment and maintain a strong connection to Allah, Islam orders them to pray at five particular times of the day:

i. The Dawn Prayer (*Fajr*)

Surat Hud 11:114

وَأَقِمِ ٱلصَّلَوٰةَ طَرَفَيِ ٱلنَّهَارِ وَزُلَفًا مِّنَ ٱلَّيْلِ إِنَّ ٱلْحَسَنَـٰتِ يُذْهِبْنَ ٱلسَّيِّـَٔاتِ ذَٰلِكَ ذِكْرَىٰ لِلذَّٰكِرِينَ ﴿١١٤﴾

Maintain the prayer at the two ends of the day,
and during the early hours of the night.
Indeed good deeds efface misdeeds.
That is an admonition for the mindful.

Surat al Nur 24:58

يَـٰٓأَيُّهَا ٱلَّذِينَ ءَامَنُوا لِيَسْتَـٔذِنكُمُ ٱلَّذِينَ مَلَكَتْ أَيْمَـٰنُكُمْ وَٱلَّذِينَ لَمْ

يَبْلُغُوا ٱلْحُلُمَ مِنكُمْ ثَلَـٰثَ مَرَّٰتٍ مِّن قَبْلِ صَلَوٰةِ ٱلْفَجْرِ وَحِينَ تَضَعُونَ ثِيَابَكُم

مِّنَ ٱلظَّهِيرَةِ وَمِنۢ بَعْدِ صَلَوٰةِ ٱلْعِشَآءِ ثَلَـٰثُ عَوْرَٰتٍ لَّكُمْ لَيْسَ

عَلَيْكُمْ وَلَا عَلَيْهِمْ جُنَاحٌۢ بَعْدَهُنَّ طَوَّٰفُونَ عَلَيْكُم بَعْضُكُمْ عَلَىٰ

بَعْضٍ كَذَٰلِكَ يُبَيِّنُ ٱللَّهُ لَكُمُ ٱلْـَٔايَـٰتِ وَٱللَّهُ عَلِيمٌ حَكِيمٌ ﴿٥٨﴾

O you who have faith!
Let your permission be sought by your slaves
and those of you who have not reached puberty
three times:
before the dawn prayer,
and when you put off your garments at noon,
and after the night prayer.
These are three times of privacy for you.
Apart from these, it is not sinful of you or them
to frequent one another [freely].
Thus does Allah clarify the signs for you,
and Allah is all-knowing, all-wise.

ii. The Noon Prayer (*Dhuhr*)

Surat al Isra 17:78

أَقِمِ ٱلصَّلَوٰةَ لِدُلُوكِ ٱلشَّمْسِ إِلَىٰ غَسَقِ ٱلَّيْلِ وَقُرْءَانَ ٱلْفَجْرِ إِنَّ

قُرْءَانَ ٱلْفَجْرِ كَانَ مَشْهُودًا ﴿٧٨﴾

Maintain the prayer from the sun's decline
till the darkness of the night,
and [observe particularly] the dawn recital.
Indeed the dawn recital is attended [by angels].

iii. The Afternoon Prayer – Middle Prayer (*Asr*)

Surat al Baqirah 2:238

حَٰفِظُوا۟ عَلَى ٱلصَّلَوَٰتِ وَٱلصَّلَوٰةِ ٱلْوُسْطَىٰ وَقُومُوا۟ لِلَّهِ قَٰنِتِينَ ﴿٢٣٨﴾

Be watchful of your prayers,
and [especially] the middle prayer,
and stand in obedience to Allah;

iv. The Sunset Prayer (*Maghrib*)

Surat Hud 11:114

وَأَقِمِ ٱلصَّلَوٰةَ طَرَفَىِ ٱلنَّهَارِ وَزُلَفًا مِّنَ ٱلَّيْلِ إِنَّ ٱلْحَسَنَٰتِ يُذْهِبْنَ ٱلسَّيِّـَٔاتِ ذَٰلِكَ ذِكْرَىٰ لِلذَّٰكِرِينَ ﴿١١٤﴾

Maintain the prayer at the two ends of the day,
and during the early hours of the night.
Indeed good deeds efface misdeeds.
That is an admonition for the mindful.

v. The Night Prayer (*Isha*)

Surat al Nur 24:58

يَٰٓأَيُّهَا ٱلَّذِينَ ءَامَنُوا۟ لِيَسْتَـْٔذِنكُمُ ٱلَّذِينَ مَلَكَتْ أَيْمَٰنُكُمْ وَٱلَّذِينَ لَمْ يَبْلُغُوا۟ ٱلْحُلُمَ مِنكُمْ ثَلَٰثَ مَرَّٰتٍ مِّن قَبْلِ صَلَوٰةِ ٱلْفَجْرِ وَحِينَ تَضَعُونَ ثِيَابَكُم مِّنَ ٱلظَّهِيرَةِ وَمِنۢ بَعْدِ صَلَوٰةِ ٱلْعِشَآءِ ثَلَٰثُ عَوْرَٰتٍ لَّكُمْ لَيْسَ عَلَيْكُمْ وَلَا عَلَيْهِمْ جُنَاحٌۢ بَعْدَهُنَّ طَوَّٰفُونَ عَلَيْكُم بَعْضُكُمْ عَلَىٰ بَعْضٍ كَذَٰلِكَ يُبَيِّنُ ٱللَّهُ لَكُمُ ٱلْءَايَٰتِ وَٱللَّهُ عَلِيمٌ حَكِيمٌ ﴿٥٨﴾

O you who have faith!

Let your permission be sought by your slaves
and those of you who have not reached puberty
three times:
before the dawn prayer,
and when you put off your garments at noon,
and after the night prayer.
These are three times of privacy for you.
Apart from these, it is not sinful of you or them
to frequent one another [freely].
Thus does Allah clarify the signs for you,
and Allah is all-knowing, all-wise.

Friday noon congregational prayer (*Jumuah Salat*)

Surat Jumuah 62:9

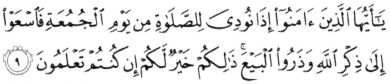

O you who have faith!
When the call is made for prayer on Friday,
hurry toward the remembrance of Allah,
and leave all business.
That is better for you,
should you know.

2. *Saum*: (Fasting):

Fasting during the Holy Month of Ramadan in order to gain Taqwa (Closeness to God).

Almost every religion on earth encourages some form of fasting. Prophet Muhammad (peace be upon him and his family) and the prophets before him (peace be upon them) all called upon their followers to fast, as mentioned in the holy Qur'an:

Surat al Baqirah 2:183

يَٰٓأَيُّهَا ٱلَّذِينَ ءَامَنُوا۟ كُتِبَ عَلَيْكُمُ ٱلصِّيَامُ كَمَا كُتِبَ عَلَى ٱلَّذِينَ مِن قَبْلِكُمْ لَعَلَّكُمْ تَتَّقُونَ ﴿١٨٣﴾

O you who believe! Fasting has been prescribed for you just as it was prescribed for those before you so that you may be pious and learn self-restraint.

Also in
Surat al Baqirah 2:185

شَهْرُ رَمَضَانَ ٱلَّذِىٓ أُنزِلَ فِيهِ ٱلْقُرْءَانُ هُدًى لِّلنَّاسِ وَبَيِّنَٰتٍ مِّنَ ٱلْهُدَىٰ وَٱلْفُرْقَانِ فَمَن شَهِدَ مِنكُمُ ٱلشَّهْرَ فَلْيَصُمْهُ وَمَن كَانَ مَرِيضًا أَوْ عَلَىٰ سَفَرٍ فَعِدَّةٌ مِّنْ أَيَّامٍ أُخَرَ يُرِيدُ ٱللَّهُ بِكُمُ ٱلْيُسْرَ وَلَا يُرِيدُ بِكُمُ ٱلْعُسْرَ وَلِتُكْمِلُوا۟ ٱلْعِدَّةَ وَلِتُكَبِّرُوا۟ ٱللَّهَ عَلَىٰ مَا هَدَىٰكُمْ وَلَعَلَّكُمْ تَشْكُرُونَ ﴿١٨٥﴾

The month of Ramadhan
is one in which the Qur'an was sent down
as guidance to mankind,
with manifest proofs of guidance
and the Criterion.
So let those of you who witness it fast [in] it,
and as for someone who is sick or on a journey,
let it be a [similar] number of other days.
Allah desires ease for you,
and He does not desire hardship for you,
and so that you may complete the number,
and magnify Allah for guiding you,
and that you may give thanks.

Islam prescribes complete fasting - complete abstinence from food, drink (including water), smoking, and sexual activity from *Imsak* (about 10 minutes before Fajr) until *Maghrib* prayer time (about twenty minutes after the sun actually sets).

Although fasting is recommended on many days, it is required during every day of the month of Ramadan, the ninth month of the Islamic lunar calendar.

As with prayer, the benefits of fasting are innumerable and can only be appreciated by those who practice it. Fasting strengthens the willpower, teaches discipline, encourages sympathy with the poor, breaks bad habits, improves the health, and establishes a sense of religious brotherhood and sisterhood. But the strongest benefits are spiritual; Fatima al-Zahra (peace be upon her), the daughter of Prophet Muhammad (peace be upon him and his family), has said: "Fasting is to deepen and strengthen faith." Fasting sharpens the spiritual awareness and imbues a sense of gratitude towards Allah.

3. *Khums* (Islamic Tax):

Paying one-fifth (20%) of one's yearly savings or profits go to the community.

Khums should be paid yearly on 20% of the excess profit that a person acquires. 'Excess profit' refers to the profit that remains after a person pays for food, clothing, shelter, and other necessities for himself and his family. *Khums* must also be paid on five other items, but some of these cases in the current society tend to be rare.

1. Minerals found from Earth
2. Found Treasure trove
3. Mixing of *Halal* wealth with *Haraam* (i.e. gambling wins, lottery, etc.).
4. Gems obtained from the sea diving.
5. Spoils of war. As commonly held, a land which a zimmi (a non-Muslim living under the protection of Islamic Government) purchases from a Muslim.

6.

Khums has been ordained in the Qur'an:

Surat al Anfal 8:41

$$۞ وَٱعْلَمُوٓاْ أَنَّمَا غَنِمْتُم مِّن شَىْءٍ فَأَنَّ لِلَّهِ خُمُسَهُۥ وَلِلرَّسُولِ وَلِذِى ٱلْقُرْبَىٰ وَٱلْيَتَـٰمَىٰ وَٱلْمَسَـٰكِينِ وَٱبْنِ ٱلسَّبِيلِ إِن كُنتُمْ ءَامَنتُم بِٱللَّهِ وَمَآ أَنزَلْنَا عَلَىٰ عَبْدِنَا يَوْمَ ٱلْفُرْقَانِ يَوْمَ ٱلْتَقَى ٱلْجَمْعَانِ وَٱللَّهُ عَلَىٰ كُلِّ شَىْءٍ قَدِيرٌ ﴿٤١﴾$$

Know that whatever thing you may come by,
a fifth of it is for Allah and the Apostle,
for the relatives and the orphans,
for the needy and the traveler,
if you have faith in Allah
and what We sent down to Our servant
on the Day of Separation,
the day when the two hosts met;
and Allah has power over all things.

One-Fifth or 20% of an amount will be divided in 6 parts: For example, for every $100 dollars received $16.66 will go to each part.

1. For Allah (swt)
1. The Messenger (pbuh)
2. Kinfolk
3. Orphans
4. Needy
5. Wayfarers

4. *Zakat* (Charity):

There are two categories of Charity

1. Obligatory charity or *Zakat*, and
2. General charity, which is known as *Sadaqa*

The Obligatory charity is mentioned in Qur'an in:

Surat al Baqirah 2:177

﴿ لَّيْسَ ٱلْبِرَّ أَن تُوَلُّوا۟ وُجُوهَكُمْ قِبَلَ ٱلْمَشْرِقِ وَٱلْمَغْرِبِ وَلَٰكِنَّ ٱلْبِرَّ مَنْ ءَامَنَ بِٱللَّهِ وَٱلْيَوْمِ ٱلْءَاخِرِ وَٱلْمَلَٰٓئِكَةِ وَٱلْكِتَٰبِ وَٱلنَّبِيِّۦنَ وَءَاتَى ٱلْمَالَ عَلَىٰ حُبِّهِۦ ذَوِى ٱلْقُرْبَىٰ وَٱلْيَتَٰمَىٰ وَٱلْمَسَٰكِينَ وَٱبْنَ ٱلسَّبِيلِ وَٱلسَّآئِلِينَ وَفِى ٱلرِّقَابِ وَأَقَامَ ٱلصَّلَوٰةَ وَءَاتَى ٱلزَّكَوٰةَ وَٱلْمُوفُونَ بِعَهْدِهِمْ إِذَا عَٰهَدُوا۟ۖ وَٱلصَّٰبِرِينَ فِى ٱلْبَأْسَآءِ وَٱلضَّرَّآءِ وَحِينَ ٱلْبَأْسِۗ أُو۟لَٰٓئِكَ ٱلَّذِينَ صَدَقُوا۟ۖ وَأُو۟لَٰٓئِكَ هُمُ ٱلْمُتَّقُونَ ﴿١٧٧﴾

Piety is not to turn your faces
to the east or the west;
rather, piety is [personified by] those who have faith
in Allah and the Last Day,
the angels, the Book,
and the prophets,
and who give their wealth, for the love of Him,
to relatives, orphans,
the needy, the traveller
and the beggar, and for [the freeing of] the slaves,
and maintain the prayer and give the zakat,
and those who fulfill their covenants,
when they pledge themselves,
and those who are patient in stress and distress,
and in the heat of battle.
They are the ones who are true [to their covenant],
and it is they who are the God wary.

Surat al Mujadilah 58:13

ءَأَشْفَقْتُمْ أَن تُقَدِّمُوا بَيْنَ يَدَىْ نَجْوَىٰكُمْ صَدَقَتٍ فَإِذْ لَمْ تَفْعَلُوا وَتَابَ ٱللَّهُ

عَلَيْكُمْ فَأَقِيمُوا ٱلصَّلَوٰةَ وَءَاتُوا ٱلزَّكَوٰةَ وَأَطِيعُوا ٱللَّهَ وَرَسُولَهُ وَٱللَّهُ

خَبِيرٌ بِمَا تَعْمَلُونَ ۝١٣

Were you apprehensive of offering
charities before your secret talks?
So, as you did not do it,
and Allah was clement to you,
maintain the prayer and pay the zakat,
and obey Allah and His Apostle.
And Allah is well aware of what you do .

Surat al Bayyinah 98:5

وَمَآ أُمِرُوٓا إِلَّا لِيَعْبُدُوا ٱللَّهَ مُخْلِصِينَ لَهُ ٱلدِّينَ حُنَفَآءَ وَيُقِيمُوا ٱلصَّلَوٰةَ

وَيُؤْتُوا ٱلزَّكَوٰةَ وَذَٰلِكَ دِينُ ٱلْقَيِّمَةِ ۝٥

Yet they were not commanded except to worship Allah,
dedicating their faith to Him
as men of pure faith,
and to maintain the prayer and pay the zakat.
That is the upright religion.

Surat al Baqirah 2:43

وَأَقِيمُوا ٱلصَّلَوٰةَ وَءَاتُوا ٱلزَّكَوٰةَ وَٱرْكَعُوا مَعَ ٱلرَّٰكِعِينَ ۝٤٣

And maintain the prayer, and give the zakat,
and bow along with those who bow [in prayer].

And the General Charity is mentioned in Qu'ran in

Surat al Tawbah 9:60

إِنَّمَا ٱلصَّدَقَٰتُ لِلْفُقَرَآءِ وَٱلْمَسَٰكِينِ وَٱلْعَٰمِلِينَ عَلَيْهَا

وَٱلْمُؤَلَّفَةِ قُلُوبُهُمْ وَفِى ٱلرِّقَابِ وَٱلْغَٰرِمِينَ وَفِى سَبِيلِ ٱللَّهِ

وَٱبْنِ ٱلسَّبِيلِ فَرِيضَةً مِّنَ ٱللَّهِ وَٱللَّهُ عَلِيمٌ حَكِيمٌ ۝

Charities are only for the poor and the needy,
and those employed to collect them,
and those whose hearts are to be reconciled,
and for [the freedom of] the slaves and the debtors,
and in the way of Allah,
and for the traveler.
[This is] an ordinance from Allah,
and Allah is all-knowing, all-wise.

Surat al Tawbah 9:104

أَلَمْ يَعْلَمُوٓا۟ أَنَّ ٱللَّهَ هُوَ يَقْبَلُ ٱلتَّوْبَةَ عَنْ عِبَادِهِ وَيَأْخُذُ ٱلصَّدَقَٰتِ

وَأَنَّ ٱللَّهَ هُوَ ٱلتَّوَّابُ ٱلرَّحِيمُ ۝

Do they not know
that it is Allah who accepts the repentance
of His servants
and receives the charities,
and that it is Allah who is the All-clement,
the All-merciful?

Surat al Baqirah 2:271

إِن تُبْدُوا۟ ٱلصَّدَقَٰتِ فَنِعِمَّا هِىَ وَإِن تُخْفُوهَا وَتُؤْتُوهَا

ٱلْفُقَرَآءَ فَهُوَ خَيْرٌ لَّكُمْ وَيُكَفِّرُ عَنكُم مِّن سَيِّئَاتِكُمْ

وَٱللَّهُ بِمَا تَعْمَلُونَ خَبِيرٌ ۝

If you disclose your charities, that is well,

but if you hide them and give them to the poor,
that is better for you,
and it will atone for some of your misdeeds,
and Allah is well aware of what you do.

Surat al Baqirah 2:276

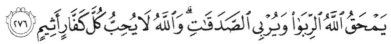

Allah brings usury to naught,
but He makes charities flourish.
Allah does not like any sinful ingrate.

5. *Hajj* (Pilgrimage):

Embarking on the pilgrimage to the Holy city of Makkah at least once in one's lifetime.

Every Muslim who can, must, at least once, make the pilgrimage (hajj) to the holy city of Makkah. This pilgrimage occurs every year during *Dhul Hijjah*, the twelfth month of the Islamic lunar calendar. Those who make the pilgrimage follow in the footsteps of Abraham (peace be upon him), the father of the prophets. Allah (swt) has commanded Muslims to perform Hajj in the following places of the holy Qur'an:

Surat al Baqirah 2:196

وَأَتِمُّواْ ٱلْحَجَّ وَٱلْعُمْرَةَ لِلَّهِ فَإِنْ أُحْصِرْتُمْ فَمَا ٱسْتَيْسَرَ مِنَ ٱلْهَدْيِ وَلَا تَحْلِقُواْ رُءُوسَكُمْ حَتَّىٰ يَبْلُغَ ٱلْهَدْيُ مَحِلَّهُۥ فَمَن كَانَ مِنكُم مَّرِيضًا أَوْ بِهِۦ أَذًى مِّن رَّأْسِهِۦ فَفِدْيَةٌ مِّن صِيَامٍ أَوْ صَدَقَةٍ أَوْ نُسُكٍ فَإِذَآ أَمِنتُمْ فَمَن تَمَتَّعَ بِٱلْعُمْرَةِ إِلَى ٱلْحَجِّ

$$\text{فَمَا ٱسْتَيْسَرَ مِنَ ٱلْهَدْىِ فَمَن لَّمْ يَجِدْ فَصِيَامُ ثَلَٰثَةِ أَيَّامٍ فِى ٱلْحَجِّ وَسَبْعَةٍ}$$

$$\text{إِذَا رَجَعْتُمْ تِلْكَ عَشَرَةٌ كَامِلَةٌ ذَٰلِكَ لِمَن لَّمْ يَكُنْ أَهْلُهُ حَاضِرِى ٱلْمَسْجِدِ}$$

$$\text{ٱلْحَرَامِ وَٱتَّقُوا۟ ٱللَّهَ وَٱعْلَمُوٓا۟ أَنَّ ٱللَّهَ شَدِيدُ ٱلْعِقَابِ ﴿١٩٦﴾}$$

Complete the hajj and the 'umrah for Allah's sake,
and if you are prevented,
then [make] such [sacrificial] offering as is feasible.
And do not shave your heads
until the offering reaches its [assigned] place.
But should any of you be sick,
or have a injury in his head,
let the atonement be by fasting,
or charity, or sacrifice.
And when you have security
for those who enjoy [release from the restrictions]
by virtue of the 'umrah until the hajj—
let the offering be such as is feasible.
As for someone who cannot afford [the offering],
let him fast three days during the hajj
and seven when you return;
that is [a period of] ten complete [days].
That is for someone whose family does not
dwell by the Holy Mosque.
And be wary of Allah,
and know that Allah is severe in retribution.

Surat al Baqirah 2:197

$$\text{ٱلْحَجُّ أَشْهُرٌ مَّعْلُومَٰتٌ فَمَن فَرَضَ فِيهِنَّ ٱلْحَجَّ فَلَا رَفَثَ وَلَا}$$

$$\text{فُسُوقَ وَلَا جِدَالَ فِى ٱلْحَجِّ وَمَا تَفْعَلُوا۟ مِنْ خَيْرٍ يَعْلَمْهُ ٱللَّهُ}$$

وَتَزَوَّدُوا فَإِنَّ خَيْرَ ٱلزَّادِ ٱلتَّقْوَىٰ وَٱتَّقُونِ يَـٰٓأُوْلِي ٱلْأَلْبَـٰبِ ﴿١٩٧﴾

The hajj [season] is in months well-known;
so whoever decides on hajj [pilgrimage] therein,
[should know that] there is to be no sexual contact,
vicious talk, or disputing during the hajj.
And whatever good you do, Allah knows it.
And take provision,
for indeed the best provision is God wariness.
So be wary of Me, O you who possess intellects!

Surat al Baqirah 2:158

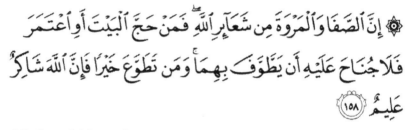

Indeed Safa and Marwah
are among Allah's sacraments.
So whoever makes hajj to the House,
or performs the 'umrah,
there is no sin upon him to circuit between them.
Should anyone do good of his own accord,
then Allah is indeed appreciative, all-knowing.

6. *Jihad* (Striving):

The literal meaning of jihad is **'to strive hard,'** to progress in all aspects of life. Although this word, in English, has taken on purely military connotations, in reality it covers the vast range of human enterprise – family life, work, spiritual development, and, at the end of all this, justified defensive warfare.

The most important jihad is the struggle to purify the soul, and this jihad far outweighs any military jihad. Once, Prophet Muhammad (pbuh) met a group of soldiers returning from a defensive battle and addressed them: *"Welcome to the people who have concluded the minor jihad (struggle)."* Astonished, the soldiers asked, "Was this the minor jihad? Then what is the major jihad?" Prophet Muhammad (pbuh) replied: *"The major jihad is the jihad to purify one's self."*

This Major Jihad is mentioned in Qur'an at several places, some of them are as following places:

Surat al Furqan 25:52

فَلَا تُطِعِ ٱلْكَٰفِرِينَ وَجَٰهِدْهُم بِهِۦ جِهَادًا كَبِيرًا ﴿٥٢﴾

So do not obey the faithless,
but wage against them a great jihad with it.

Surat al Mumtahanah 60:1

يَٰٓأَيُّهَا ٱلَّذِينَ ءَامَنُوا۟ لَا تَتَّخِذُوا۟ عَدُوِّى وَعَدُوَّكُمْ أَوْلِيَآءَ تُلْقُونَ إِلَيْهِم بِٱلْمَوَدَّةِ وَقَدْ كَفَرُوا۟ بِمَا جَآءَكُم مِّنَ ٱلْحَقِّ يُخْرِجُونَ ٱلرَّسُولَ وَإِيَّاكُمْ أَن تُؤْمِنُوا۟ بِٱللَّهِ رَبِّكُمْ إِن كُنتُمْ خَرَجْتُمْ جِهَٰدًا فِى سَبِيلِى وَٱبْتِغَآءَ مَرْضَاتِى تُسِرُّونَ إِلَيْهِم بِٱلْمَوَدَّةِ وَأَنَا۠ أَعْلَمُ بِمَآ أَخْفَيْتُمْ وَمَآ أَعْلَنتُمْ وَمَن يَفْعَلْهُ مِنكُمْ فَقَدْ ضَلَّ سَوَآءَ ٱلسَّبِيلِ ﴿١﴾

O you who have faith!
Do not take My enemy and your enemy for friends,
[secretly] offering them affection
(for they have certainly defied
whatever has come to you of the truth,
expelling the Apostle and you,
because you have faith in Allah, your Lord)
if you have set out for jihad in My way

and to seek My pleasure.
You secretly nourish affection for them,
while I know well whatever you hide
and whatever you disclose,
and whoever among you does that
has certainly strayed from the right way.

Surat Muhammad 47:31

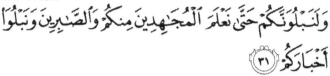

We will surely test you
until We ascertain those of you who wage jihad
and those who are steadfast,
and We shall appraise your record.

Surat al Hujurat 49:15

The faithful are only those who have attained faith
in Allah and His Apostle
and then have never doubted,
and who wage jihad with their possessions
and their persons
in the way of Allah.
It is they who are the truthful

Surat al Saff 61:11

$$\text{تُؤْمِنُونَ بِاللَّهِ وَرَسُولِهِ وَتُجَاهِدُونَ فِي سَبِيلِ اللَّهِ بِأَمْوَالِكُمْ وَأَنْفُسِكُمْ ذَلِكُمْ خَيْرٌ}$$
$$\text{لَكُمْ إِنْ كُنْتُمْ تَعْلَمُونَ ﴿١١﴾}$$

Have faith in Allah and His Apostle,
and wage jihad in the way of Allah
with your possessions and your persons.
That is better for you,
should you know.

Whereas, the Minor Jihad (literally fighting against oppression) is mentioned in the Qur'an at several places, some of them are as following places:

Surat Aly Imran 3:156

$$\text{يَا أَيُّهَا الَّذِينَ ءَامَنُوا لَا تَكُونُوا كَالَّذِينَ كَفَرُوا وَقَالُوا لِإِخْوَانِهِمْ إِذَا}$$
$$\text{ضَرَبُوا فِي الْأَرْضِ أَوْ كَانُوا غُزًّى لَوْ كَانُوا عِنْدَنَا مَا مَاتُوا وَمَا قُتِلُوا}$$
$$\text{لِيَجْعَلَ اللَّهُ ذَلِكَ حَسْرَةً فِي قُلُوبِهِمْ وَاللَّهُ يُحْيِ وَيُمِيتُ وَاللَّهُ بِمَا}$$
$$\text{تَعْمَلُونَ بَصِيرٌ ﴿١٥٦﴾}$$

O you who have faith!
Do not be like the faithless
who say of their brethren,
when they travel in the land or go into battle,
'Had they stayed with us
they would not have died or been killed,'
so that Allah may make it a regret in their hearts.
But Allah gives life and brings death,
and Allah sees best what you do.

Surat al Baqirah 2:217

يَسْـَٔلُونَكَ عَنِ ٱلشَّهْرِ ٱلْحَرَامِ قِتَالٍ فِيهِ قُلْ قِتَالٌ فِيهِ كَبِيرٌ وَصَدٌّ
عَن سَبِيلِ ٱللَّهِ وَكُفْرٌ بِهِۦ وَٱلْمَسْجِدِ ٱلْحَرَامِ وَإِخْرَاجُ أَهْلِهِۦ مِنْهُ
أَكْبَرُ عِندَ ٱللَّهِ وَٱلْفِتْنَةُ أَكْبَرُ مِنَ ٱلْقَتْلِ وَلَا يَزَالُونَ يُقَٰتِلُونَكُمْ
حَتَّىٰ يَرُدُّوكُمْ عَن دِينِكُمْ إِنِ ٱسْتَطَٰعُوا وَمَن يَرْتَدِدْ مِنكُمْ
عَن دِينِهِۦ فَيَمُتْ وَهُوَ كَافِرٌ فَأُولَٰٓئِكَ حَبِطَتْ أَعْمَٰلُهُمْ فِى
ٱلدُّنْيَا وَٱلْءَاخِرَةِ وَأُولَٰٓئِكَ أَصْحَٰبُ ٱلنَّارِ هُمْ فِيهَا
خَٰلِدُونَ ﴿٢١٧﴾

They ask you
concerning warfare in the holy month.
Say, 'It is an outrageous thing to fight in it,
but to keep [people] from Allah's way,
and to be unfaithful to Him,
and [to keep people from] the Holy Mosque,
and to expel its people from it
are more outrageous with Allah.
And faithlessness is graver than killing.
And they will not cease fighting you
until they turn you away from your religion,
if they can.
And whoever of you turns away from his religion
and dies faithless
they are the ones whose works have failed
in this world and the Hereafter.
They shall be the inmates of the Fire,
and they shall remain in it [forever].

Surat al Nisa 4:76

$$\text{اَلَّذِينَ ءَامَنُوا يُقَـٰتِلُونَ فِى سَبِيلِ اللَّهِ ۖ وَالَّذِينَ كَفَرُوا يُقَـٰتِلُونَ فِى سَبِيلِ}$$

$$\text{الطَّـٰغُوتِ فَقَـٰتِلُوٓا أَوْلِيَآءَ الشَّيْطَـٰنِ ۖ إِنَّ كَيْدَ الشَّيْطَـٰنِ كَانَ ضَعِيفًا ﴿٧٦﴾}$$

Those who have faith fight in the way of Allah,
and those who are faithless
fight in the way of the Rebel.
So fight the friends of Satan;
indeed the stratagems of Satan are always flimsy.

7. *Amr bil Maruf* (enjoining the good):

To call people to do good deeds.

8. *Nahi anul Munkar* (Forbidding the evil):

To stop people and call people away from evil deeds.

In order for religion to progress and society to flourish, people must take the initiative and attempt to guide each other towards the right and away from the wrong. This kind of advising is mandatory for those who believe in Allah and the Day of Judgment. Giving sincere advice is not, as some may argue, meddling in someone else's business, but is in fact a valuable favor and one of the best forms of charity.

The command to enjoin the good and forbid the evil is mentioned in Qur'an simultaneously at several places, some of them are as follows:

Surat Aly Imran 3:104

$$\text{وَلْتَكُن مِّنكُمْ أُمَّةٌ يَدْعُونَ إِلَى الْخَيْرِ وَيَأْمُرُونَ بِالْمَعْرُوفِ وَيَنْهَوْنَ عَنِ}$$

$$\text{الْمُنكَرِ ۚ وَأُو۟لَـٰٓئِكَ هُمُ الْمُفْلِحُونَ ﴿١٠٤﴾}$$

There has to be a nation among you
summoning to the good,
bidding what is right,

and forbidding what is wrong.
It is they who are the felicitous.

Surat Aly Imran 3:114

يُؤْمِنُونَ بِاللَّهِ وَالْيَوْمِ الْآخِرِ وَيَأْمُرُونَ بِالْمَعْرُوفِ
وَيَنْهَوْنَ عَنِ الْمُنكَرِ وَيُسَارِعُونَ فِي الْخَيْرَاتِ وَأُوْلَئِكَ مِنَ
الصَّالِحِينَ ۝١١٤

They have faith in Allah and the Last Day,
and bid what is right
and forbid what is wrong,
and are active in [performing] good deeds.
They are among the righteous.

Command to do good deeds

Surat al Baqirah 2:83

وَإِذْ أَخَذْنَا مِيثَاقَ بَنِي إِسْرَءِيلَ لَا تَعْبُدُونَ إِلَّا اللَّهَ وَبِالْوَالِدَيْنِ
إِحْسَانًا وَذِى الْقُرْبَى وَالْيَتَمَى وَالْمَسَاكِينِ وَقُولُوا لِلنَّاسِ
حُسْنًا وَأَقِيمُوا الصَّلَوٰةَ وَءَاتُوا الزَّكَوٰةَ ثُمَّ تَوَلَّيْتُمْ إِلَّا
قَلِيلًا مِّنكُمْ وَأَنتُم مُّعْرِضُونَ ۝٨٣

And when We took a pledge
from the Children of Israel:
Worship no one but Allah,
do good to parents,
relatives, orphans,
and the needy,
and speak kindly to people,
and maintain the prayer, and give the zakat,

you turned away, except a few of you,
and you were disregardful.

Accountability for good and bad deeds

Surat al Zalzalah 99:7-8

$$فَمَن يَعْمَلْ مِثْقَالَ ذَرَّةٍ خَيْرًا يَرَهُ ۝٧$$

7 *So whoever does an atom's weight of good*
will see it,

$$وَمَن يَعْمَلْ مِثْقَالَ ذَرَّةٍ شَرًّا يَرَهُ ۝٨$$

8 *and whoever does an atom's weight of evil*
will see it.

Surat al Nisa 4:40

$$إِنَّ ٱللَّهَ لَا يَظْلِمُ مِثْقَالَ ذَرَّةٍ وَإِن تَكُ حَسَنَةً يُضَاعِفْهَا وَيُؤْتِ$$
$$مِن لَّدُنْهُ أَجْرًا عَظِيمًا ۝٤٠$$

Indeed Allah does not wrong [anyone]
[even to the extent of] an atom's weight,
and if it be a good deed He doubles it[s reward],
and gives from Himself a great reward.

Surat al Nisa 4:85

$$مَّن يَشْفَعْ شَفَاعَةً حَسَنَةً يَكُن لَّهُ نَصِيبٌ مِّنْهَا وَمَن يَشْفَعْ شَفَاعَةً$$
$$سَيِّئَةً يَكُن لَّهُ كِفْلٌ مِّنْهَا وَكَانَ ٱللَّهُ عَلَىٰ كُلِّ شَيْءٍ مُّقِيتًا ۝٨٥$$

Whoever intercedes for a good cause
shall receive a share of it,
and whoever intercedes for an evil cause
shall share its burden,
and Allah is proponent over all things.

Good and bad deeds are not equal !!!

Surat al Maidah 5:100

$$\text{قُل لَّا يَسْتَوِي الْخَبِيثُ وَالطَّيِّبُ وَلَوْ أَعْجَبَكَ كَثْرَةُ الْخَبِيثِ}$$

$$\text{فَاتَّقُوا اللَّهَ يَا أُولِي الْأَلْبَابِ لَعَلَّكُمْ تُفْلِحُونَ ﴿١٠٠﴾}$$

Say, 'The good and the bad are not equal,
though the abundance of the bad should amaze you.'
So be wary of Allah, O you who possess intellect,
so that you may be felicitous!

Surat Fussilat 41:34

$$\text{وَلَا تَسْتَوِي الْحَسَنَةُ وَلَا السَّيِّئَةُ ادْفَعْ بِالَّتِي هِيَ أَحْسَنُ فَإِذَا الَّذِي}$$

$$\text{بَيْنَكَ وَبَيْنَهُ عَدَاوَةٌ كَأَنَّهُ وَلِيٌّ حَمِيمٌ ﴿٣٤﴾}$$

Good and evil [conduct] are not equal.
Repel [evil] with what is best.
[If you do so,] behold, he
between whom and you was enmity,
will be as though he were a sympathetic friend.

9. *Tawalla:*

Loving and supporting those who walk in the path of Allah

The phrase *'tawalli li awliyaa Allah'* means to be a friend and a helper of the righteous, pious people who are on the side of Allah and religion. Specifically, it includes the Prophets and Imams (successors to the prophets) as well as those who work to establish order, justice, and religion on earth.

Surat al Maidah 5:56

$$\text{وَمَن يَتَوَلَّ اللَّهَ وَرَسُولَهُ وَالَّذِينَ آمَنُوا فَإِنَّ حِزْبَ اللَّهِ هُمُ الْغَالِبُونَ ﴿٥٦﴾}$$

Whoever takes for his guardians Allah,
His Apostle and the faithful [should know that]

the confederates of Allah are indeed the victorious.

10. *Tabarrah*

Disassociating or turning away from the enemies of Allah

The phrase *'tabarri min a'daa Allah'* refers to the opposite of *'tawalli li awliyaa Allah,'* meaning those who sincerely believe in Allah (swt), must disassociate themselves from those people who obstruct truth and justice and prevent the light of Allah (swt) from reaching others.

Although *'Tawalla'* and *'Tabarrah'* are NOT equal, meaning a Muslim doesn't necessarily have to discuss the disassociation towards the enemy of the Prophet (pbuh) and his Ahlul Bayt (as) in comparison to showing love towards the Prophet (pbuh) and his Ahlul Bayt (as); it is important to acknowledge the virtues of the Prophet (pbuh) and his Ahlul Bayt (as) in order to identify the characteristics of their enemies, and disassociate oneself from those characteristics.

Surat al Maidah 5:57

يَٰٓأَيُّهَا ٱلَّذِينَ ءَامَنُوا۟ لَا تَتَّخِذُوا۟ ٱلَّذِينَ ٱتَّخَذُوا۟ دِينَكُمْ هُزُوًا وَلَعِبًا مِّنَ ٱلَّذِينَ

أُوتُوا۟ ٱلْكِتَٰبَ مِن قَبْلِكُمْ وَٱلْكُفَّارَ أَوْلِيَآءَ ۚ وَٱتَّقُوا۟ ٱللَّهَ إِن كُنتُم مُّؤْمِنِينَ ﴿٥٧﴾

O you who have faith!
Do not take those who take your religion
in derision and play,
from among those who were given the Book
before you,
and the infidels,
as friends,
and be wary of Allah, should you be faithful.

Surat Aly Imran 3:28

$$\text{لَا يَتَّخِذِ ٱلْمُؤْمِنُونَ ٱلْكَٰفِرِينَ أَوْلِيَآءَ مِن دُونِ ٱلْمُؤْمِنِينَ وَمَن يَفْعَلْ}$$

$$\text{ذَٰلِكَ فَلَيْسَ مِنَ ٱللَّهِ فِى شَىْءٍ إِلَّآ أَن تَتَّقُوا۟ مِنْهُمْ تُقَىٰةً}$$

$$\text{وَيُحَذِّرُكُمُ ٱللَّهُ نَفْسَهُۥ وَإِلَى ٱللَّهِ ٱلْمَصِيرُ ﴿٢٨﴾}$$

The faithful should not take the faithless for allies
instead of the faithful,
and whoever does that
Allah will have nothing to do with him,
except when you are wary of them out of caution.
Allah warns you to beware of [disobeying] Him,
and toward Allah is the return.

Curse of Allah be upon…

Surat al Baqirah 2:159

$$\text{إِنَّ ٱلَّذِينَ يَكْتُمُونَ مَآ أَنزَلْنَا مِنَ ٱلْبَيِّنَٰتِ وَٱلْهُدَىٰ مِنۢ بَعْدِ مَا}$$

$$\text{بَيَّنَّٰهُ لِلنَّاسِ فِى ٱلْكِتَٰبِ أُو۟لَٰٓئِكَ يَلْعَنُهُمُ ٱللَّهُ وَيَلْعَنُهُمُ}$$

$$\text{ٱللَّٰعِنُونَ ﴿١٥٩﴾}$$

Indeed those who conceal what We have sent down
of manifest proofs and guidance,
after We have clarified it in the Book for mankind,
they shall be cursed by Allah
and cursed by the cursers,

Surat al Baqirah 2:161-162

إِنَّ ٱلَّذِينَ كَفَرُوا۟ وَمَاتُوا۟ وَهُمْ كُفَّارٌ أُو۟لَـٰٓئِكَ عَلَيْهِمْ لَعْنَةُ ٱللَّهِ وَٱلْمَلَـٰٓئِكَةِ وَٱلنَّاسِ أَجْمَعِينَ ﴿١٦١﴾

*161 Indeed those who turn faithless
and die while they are faithless,
it is they on whom shall be the curse of Allah,
the angels and all mankind.*

خَـٰلِدِينَ فِيهَا لَا يُخَفَّفُ عَنْهُمُ ٱلْعَذَابُ وَلَا هُمْ يُنظَرُونَ ﴿١٦٢﴾

*162 They will remain in it [forever],
and their punishment shall not be lightened,
nor will they be granted any respite.*

Surat Aly Imran 3:86-89

كَيْفَ يَهْدِى ٱللَّهُ قَوْمًا كَفَرُوا۟ بَعْدَ إِيمَـٰنِهِمْ وَشَهِدُوٓا۟ أَنَّ ٱلرَّسُولَ حَقٌّ وَجَآءَهُمُ ٱلْبَيِّنَـٰتُ وَٱللَّهُ لَا يَهْدِى ٱلْقَوْمَ ٱلظَّـٰلِمِينَ ﴿٨٦﴾

*86 How shall Allah guide a people
who have disbelieved after their faith
and [after] bearing witness that the Apostle is true,
and [after] manifest proofs had come to them?
Allah does not guide the wrongdoing lot.*

أُو۟لَـٰٓئِكَ جَزَآؤُهُمْ أَنَّ عَلَيْهِمْ لَعْنَةَ ٱللَّهِ وَٱلْمَلَـٰٓئِكَةِ وَٱلنَّاسِ أَجْمَعِينَ ﴿٨٧﴾

*87 Their requital is that there shall be upon them
the curse of Allah, the angels,
and all mankind.*

خَـٰلِدِينَ فِيهَا لَا يُخَفَّفُ عَنْهُمُ ٱلْعَذَابُ وَلَا هُمْ يُنظَرُونَ ﴿٨٨﴾

*88 They will remain in it [forever],
and their punishment shall not be lightened,*

nor will they be granted any respite,

$$إِلَّا ٱلَّذِينَ تَابُوا۟ مِنۢ بَعْدِ ذَٰلِكَ وَأَصْلَحُوا۟ فَإِنَّ ٱللَّهَ غَفُورٌ رَّحِيمٌ ﴿٨٩﴾$$

89 except such as repent after that
and make amends,
for Allah is all-forgiving, all-merciful.

Surat Hud 11:59-60

$$وَتِلْكَ عَادٌ جَحَدُوا۟ بِـَٔايَٰتِ رَبِّهِمْ وَعَصَوْا۟ رُسُلَهُۥ وَٱتَّبَعُوٓا۟ أَمْرَ كُلِّ جَبَّارٍ عَنِيدٍ ﴿٥٩﴾$$

59 Such were [the people of] Ad:
they impugned the signs of their Lord
and disobeyed His apostles,
and followed the dictates of every obdurate tyrant.

$$وَأُتْبِعُوا۟ فِى هَٰذِهِ ٱلدُّنْيَا لَعْنَةً وَيَوْمَ ٱلْقِيَٰمَةِ أَلَآ إِنَّ عَادًا كَفَرُوا۟ رَبَّهُمْ أَلَا بُعْدًا لِّعَادٍ قَوْمِ هُودٍ ﴿٦٠﴾$$

60 So they were pursued by a curse in this world
and on the Day of Resurrection.
Look! Indeed defied their Lord.
Look! Away with Aad, the people of Hud!

Surat ar Raad 13:25

$$وَٱلَّذِينَ يَنقُضُونَ عَهْدَ ٱللَّهِ مِنۢ بَعْدِ مِيثَٰقِهِۦ وَيَقْطَعُونَ مَآ أَمَرَ ٱللَّهُ بِهِۦٓ أَن يُوصَلَ وَيُفْسِدُونَ فِى ٱلْأَرْضِ أُو۟لَٰٓئِكَ لَهُمُ ٱللَّعْنَةُ وَلَهُمْ سُوٓءُ ٱلدَّارِ ﴿٢٥﴾$$

But as for those who break Allah's compact
after having pledged it solemnly,
and sever

what Allah has commanded to be joined,
and cause corruption in the earth
it is such on whom the curse will lie,
and for them will be the ills of the [ultimate] abode.

Surat al Ahzab 33:57

إِنَّ ٱلَّذِينَ يُؤْذُونَ ٱللَّهَ وَرَسُولَهُۥ لَعَنَهُمُ ٱللَّهُ فِى ٱلدُّنْيَا وَٱلْأَخِرَةِ وَأَعَدَّ لَهُمْ عَذَابًا مُّهِينًا ﴿٥٧﴾

Indeed those who torment Allah and His Apostle
are cursed by Allah in the world and the Hereafter,
and He has prepared a humiliating punishment for them.

Source: Sayed Mustafa al-Qazwini, (2012). *Invitation to Islam.*
Chapter 4, P. 33-51

Other Shi'a Practices from Qur'an

Shi'a Ablution (*Wudhu*) in Surah Maidah (5:6)

يَٰٓأَيُّهَا ٱلَّذِينَ ءَامَنُوٓا۟ إِذَا قُمْتُمْ إِلَى ٱلصَّلَوٰةِ فَٱغْسِلُوا۟ وُجُوهَكُمْ وَأَيْدِيَكُمْ إِلَى ٱلْمَرَافِقِ وَٱمْسَحُوا۟ بِرُءُوسِكُمْ وَأَرْجُلَكُمْ إِلَى ٱلْكَعْبَيْنِ

O you who have faith!
When you stand up for prayer,
Wash your faces
And your hands up to the elbows,
And wipe a part of your heads and your feet,

Up to the ankles.

The word *'mas'sah'* means to wipe and in this ayat, it is used for wiping the head and 'و' is used as 'and' feet; therefore, there is no need to disregard the Qur'an and wash the feet!

Why Shi'as prostrate on pure earth?

The answer to this question can be explained only 'if' one knows why there are two *Sujood* (prostrations) in each *Rakat* (unit) of *Salat*. The two *Sujood* represent a Muslim's proclamation and a reminder that *"We came from this Earth and it We shall return"!!!* Therefore, the followers of Ahlul Bayt (as) prostrate on pure Earth just like the Holy Prophet (pbuh) did, during his lifetime.

Qur'anic references:

Surat al Sajdah 32:7

ٱلَّذِىٓ أَحۡسَنَ كُلَّ شَىۡءٍ خَلَقَهُۥ وَبَدَأَ خَلۡقَ ٱلۡإِنسَـٰنِ مِن طِينٍ ۝

Who perfected everything that He created,
and commenced man's creation from clay.

Surat al Hijr 15:26

وَلَقَدۡ خَلَقۡنَا ٱلۡإِنسَـٰنَ مِن صَلۡصَـٰلٍ مِّنۡ حَمَإٍ مَّسۡنُونٍ ۝

Certainly We created man
out of a dry clay
[drawn] from an aging mud,

Surat al Baqirah 2:156

ٱلَّذِينَ إِذَآ أَصَـٰبَتۡهُم مُّصِيبَةٌ قَالُوٓاْ إِنَّا لِلَّهِ وَإِنَّآ إِلَيۡهِ رَٰجِعُونَ ۝

Those who, when an affliction visits them,
say, 'Indeed we belong to Allah,

and to Him do we indeed return.'

The Holy Prophet (pbuh) prayed his entire life and always made prostration (*sujood*) on pure Earth or dirt. Even his companions made prostration on Earth.

Also, Imam al-Bukhari narrates that when the Holy Prophet (pbuh) used to do the prayers in his own room, he would pray on *khumra* (a solid piece of dirt or a piece of straw).

Maimuna said, *"Allah's Messenger (pbuh) was praying while I was in my menses, sitting beside him and sometimes his clothes would touch me during his prostration."* Maimuna added, *"He prayed on a Khumra."*

Source: *Sahih Bukhari*, Book 8, Hadith 31
http://sunnah.com/bukhari/8/31

Crying for the Holy Prophet (pbuh), and his beloved members of his household (pbut)

Prophet Yaqoob/Jacob (as) cried for Yousef/Joseph (as) in

Surat Yousuf 12:84-86

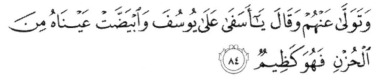

84 And he turned away from them and said,
'Alas for Joseph!'
His eyes had turned white with grief,
and he choked with suppressed agony.

قَالُوا۟ تَٱللَّهِ تَفْتَؤُا۟ تَذْكُرُ يُوسُفَ حَتَّىٰ تَكُونَ حَرَضًا أَوْ تَكُونَ مِنَ ٱلْهَٰلِكِينَ ٨٥

85 They said, 'By Allah!
You will go on remembering Joseph
until you wreck your health
or perish.'

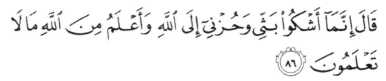

86 He said,
'I complain of my anguish and grief only
to Allah.
I know from Allah what you do not know.'

Holy Prophet cried for Hazrat Hamza (as)

When the Holy Prophet (pbuh) returned from the Battle of Uhud, he heard voices crying for those who had been martyred. The Prophet's (pbuh) eyes filled with tears. Then, he said, *"But Hamzah has no one to cry for him."* When the women of Bani 'Abd al-Ashhal heard this, they started weeping for the uncle of the Holy Prophet (pbuh)."

Source: *Sunan Ibn Majah* Vol. 1, Book 6, Hadith 1591
http://sunnah.com/urn/1289410

The Holy Prophet cried for Imam Hussain (as)

Ayesha recounted, 'Al-Hussain Ibn Ali came into the house while revelation was being given to the Holy Prophet (pbuh). He grabbed the Prophet's waist and climbed up on his back and started playing. The Archangel Jibrael (Gabriel) said to the Holy Prophet (pbuh), 'O Muhammad! Verily, soon it will be that your *ummah* will create sedition and conspiracy after you and kill this child of yours.' Then, Gabriel stretched his fist out and brought out clay, which he gave to the Holy Prophet (pbuh). He said, 'It is in this land where your child will be killed. A land called *'Taff'*.'

When the Archangel Gabriel left, the Prophet of Allah joined his companions. He still had the clay in his hands. Among them were Abu Bakr, Umar, Ali, Hadhayfah, Ammar and Abu Dharr. The Holy Prophet (pbuh) started crying.

They asked, 'Why are you crying, O Prophet of Allah?' He answered, 'Gabriel has told me that my child al-Hussain will surely be killed in a land called *Taff*. He brought clay for me from that land. He also informed me that al-Hussain will be buried in that same place'.

Source: Ahmad Ibn Hanbal, *Al-Musnad*, Vol. 3, P. 342. And

Ismail Ibn Kathir, *Tarikh Ibn Kathir*, Vol. 11, P. 29-30

Visiting the Holy graves and shrines of the Holy Prophet (pbuh), and his beloved members of his household (pbut) and their loved ones, friends and companions.

Ayesha reported Whenever it was her turn to spend with the Messenger of Allah (pbuh), he used to go to the Baqi (graveyard in Al-Madina) at the last part of the night and say, *"May you be safe, O abode of the believing people. What you have been promised has come to you. You are tarried till tomorrow and certainly we shall follow you if Allah wills. O Allah, forgive the inmates of the Baqi'-al-Gharqad."*

Source: Imam A-Nawawee, *Riyad as-Salihin* Book 1, Hadith 581.
http://sunnah.com/riyadussaliheen/1/581

Ibn Majah, *Sunan Ibn Majah*, Book 6, Hadith 1613.
http://sunnah.com/urn/1288960

The Wahabi/ Salafi argument:

Wahabis and Salafis in Saudi Arabic use the following verse of the holy Qur'an *Not in its entirely, but just the first half and out of context,* against the Muslims and try to banish them from visiting the holy graves at *Janatul Baqi* and *Janat ul Mualla* (the Baqi and Mualla cemeteries).

Surat al-Tawbah 9:84

$$وَلَا تُصَلِّ عَلَىٰ أَحَدٍ مِّنْهُم مَّاتَ أَبَدًا وَلَا تَقُمْ عَلَىٰ قَبْرِهِ إِنَّهُمْ كَفَرُوا بِاللَّهِ وَرَسُولِهِ وَمَاتُوا وَهُمْ فَاسِقُونَ ﴿٨٤﴾$$

And never pray over any of them when he dies,
nor stand at his graveside.
They indeed defied Allah and His Apostle
and died as transgressors.

In this verse Allah (swt) states NOT to visit the graves of the transgressors/unbelievers, but doesn't add-in a clause for NOT to visit the graves of the believers as well. Whereas, in Surat al Kahf, 18, verse 21 Allah (swt) allows the believers to build a place of worship (a *Masjid*) over the companions of the cave.

Surat al Kahf 18:21

$$وَكَذَٰلِكَ أَعْثَرْنَا عَلَيْهِمْ لِيَعْلَمُوا أَنَّ وَعْدَ اللَّهِ حَقٌّ وَأَنَّ السَّاعَةَ لَا رَيْبَ فِيهَا إِذْ يَتَنَازَعُونَ بَيْنَهُمْ أَمْرَهُمْ فَقَالُوا ابْنُوا عَلَيْهِم بُنْيَانًا رَّبُّهُمْ أَعْلَمُ بِهِمْ قَالَ الَّذِينَ غَلَبُوا عَلَىٰ أَمْرِهِمْ لَنَتَّخِذَنَّ عَلَيْهِم مَّسْجِدًا ﴿٢١﴾$$

So it was that We let them come upon them,
that they might know that Allah's promise is true,
and that there is no doubt in the Hour.
As they were disputing among themselves
about their matter,
they said, 'Build a building over them.
Their Lord knows them best.'
Those who had the say in their matter said,

'We will set up a place of worship over them.'

Why Shi'as DON'T fast on the day of Aashura (10th of Muharram)?

Imam Jafar al Sadiq (as) said: The Syrian army, on the plains of Karbala, rejoiced on the 9th, after forming and moving forward to surround Imam Hussain (as) and his companions. Ubaydullah Ibn Ziad reinforced his army and proudly looked at the endless rows of his soldiers, which had outnumbered the few companions of Imam Hussain (as). He was convinced no one will come forward to join Imam Hussain's (as) camp and the people of Iraq will consider him (as) weak and will not dare to protect Imam (as) against his huge build-up.

Aashura (10th) was the day when Imam Hussain (as) along with companions were lying on the sands of Karbala, with heads removed from their bodies. Is it appropriate to fast on that day? Surely not! By the Lord of Kabah! It is not a fasting day; it's the day of sadness and moaning. All Believers, on the earth and in the heavens should be grieved on this day. This was a day of joy for the people of Syria, descendants of Marjana and Ibn Ziad (*parents of Ubaydullah Ibn Ziad*). Allah (swt) admonished them on this day; this is the day when all parts of the world cried expect the Syrian segment. Allah (swt) will resurrect him with a dead heart and punish him severely who would fast on this day for the purpose of seeking blessings. Allah (swt) will take back His (swt) blessings and implant disbelief in his heart, to remain there, until the final day, for the one who would indulge in acquiring and piling worldly goods, not only for himself but also for his family and relatives. And Iblis (Satan) will have shared in his deeds and activities.

Source: Sheikh Muhammad Ibn Ya'qub Ibn Ishaq al-Kulayni, *Faroo-e-Kafi*, tradition 7, Vol. 3, P. 321.

Vis-à-vis why do 'they' persist on fasting on the 10th of Muharram?

In Sahih Bukhari, this tradition is narrated by **Ibn Abbas, Ayesha** and **Abu Musa**. In Sahih Muslim, it is narrated by **Ibn Bishr, Muawiya Ibn Abu Sufiyan** and **Abu Huraira**

When the Prophet (pbuh) arrived at Medina, the Jews were observing the fast on 'Ashura' (10th of Muharram) and they said, "This is the day when Moses became victorious over Pharaoh," On that, the Prophet (pbuh) said to his companions, "You (Muslims) have more right to celebrate Moses' victory than they have, so observe the fast on this day."

Source: *Sahih Bukhari*, Book 65, Hadith 4726
http://sunnah.com/urn/43570

Sahih Muslim, Book 13, Hadith 163
http://sunnah.com/muslim/13/163

Issues with this Hadeeth:

1. The Prophet (pbuh) migrated to Medina in the month of Rabiul Awwal and not Muharram.
2. At the time of migration of the Holy Prophet (pbuh) Ibn Abbas was 4 years old, Abu Musa was in Yemen, Abu Huraira wasn't a Muslim, nor was in Medina, Ayesha marriage to the Holy Prophet (pbuh) took place in 2ndyear After Hijra (A.H.), and Muawiya didn't join Islam until 8th A.H.
3. The Prophet (pbuh) wouldn't take a tradition of Jews and order Muslims to follow it.
4. Some Jews fast on the 10th of *Tishri* (in the Hebrew calendar, which differs from Islamic Lunar Calender) The 10th of Tishri NEVER fell on the 10th of Muharram during the Prophet's (pbuh) life.
5. The Prophet (pbuh) wouldn't tell Muslims to do something he sees Jews doing without Allah's (swt) command as stated in **Surat An Najm 53:3**
   Nor does he speak out of [his own] desire

How come shia's don't pray *Tarawih* (congregational prayer) in the holy month of Ramadhan?

The *Tarawih* was innovated by Umar bin Khattab during his reign as the caliph, as evident by his narration in *Sahih Bukhari*; Therefore, the followers of Ahlul Bayt (as) do not pray any *Nawafil* prayer in the congregation; other than the prayer for rain. Narrated by Abdur Rahman bin Abdul Qari:

> *"I went out in the company of Umar bin Al-Khattab one night in Ramadan to the mosque and found the people praying in different groups. A man praying alone or a man praying with a little group behind him. So, Umar said, **In my opinion, I would better collect these (people) under the leadership of one Qari (Reciter) (i.e. Let them pray in congregation!).***

> *So, he made up his mind to congregate them behind Ubai bin Ka'b. Then on another night I went again in his company and the people were praying behind their reciter. On that, Umar remarked, **What an excellent Bid'a** (i.e. Innovation in religion) this is; but the prayer which they do not perform, but sleep at its time is better than the one they are offering.' He meant the prayer in the last part of the night. (In those days) people used to pray in the early part of the night."*

Source: *Sahih Bukhari*, Book 31, Hadith 3
http://sunnah.com/bukhari/31/3

Intercession of the Holy Prophet (pbuh) and his holy household (as)

Surat Maryam 19:87

$$\text{لَا يَمْلِكُونَ ٱلشَّفَٰعَةَ إِلَّا مَنِ ٱتَّخَذَ عِندَ ٱلرَّحْمَٰنِ عَهْدًا ﴿٨٧﴾}$$

No one will have the power to intercede [with Allah],
except *for him who has taken*
a covenant with the All-beneficent.

Surat al Anbiya 21:28

يَعْلَمُ مَا بَيْنَ أَيْدِيهِمْ وَمَا خَلْفَهُمْ وَلَا يَشْفَعُونَ إِلَّا لِمَنِ ٱرْتَضَىٰ وَهُم مِّنْ خَشْيَتِهِ مُشْفِقُونَ ﴿٢٨﴾

He knows that which is before them
and that which is behind them,
and they do not intercede
except *for someone He approves of,*
and they are apprehensive for the fear of Him.

Surat al Zukhruf 43:86

وَلَا يَمْلِكُ ٱلَّذِينَ يَدْعُونَ مِن دُونِهِ ٱلشَّفَٰعَةَ إِلَّا مَن شَهِدَ بِٱلْحَقِّ وَهُمْ يَعْلَمُونَ ﴿٨٦﴾

Those whom they invoke besides Him have no power
of intercession,
except *those who are witness to the truth*
and who know [for whom to intercede].

Surat al Maida 5:35

يَٰأَيُّهَا ٱلَّذِينَ ءَامَنُوا۟ ٱتَّقُوا۟ ٱللَّهَ وَٱبْتَغُوا۟ إِلَيْهِ ٱلْوَسِيلَةَ وَجَٰهِدُوا۟ فِى سَبِيلِهِ لَعَلَّكُمْ تُفْلِحُونَ ﴿٣٥﴾

O you who have faith!
Be wary of Allah,
*and seek the **means of recourse** to Him,*
and wage jihad in His way,
so that you may be felicitous.

End of Chapter notes
Forbidden Acts for a Muslim

Surat al Nisa 4:31

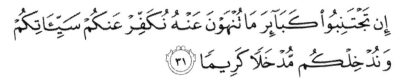

If you avoid the major sins that you are forbidden,
We will absolve you of your misdeeds,
and admit you to a noble abode.

Imam Ali Reza (as) wrote a letter to Mamun prohibiting the following sinful acts, as they were Greater Sins:

1. To kill those whose murder is prohibited by Allah
2. Adultery and rape
3. Stealing
4. Drinking wine
5. To disobey the parents
6. Fleeing the battle field
7. Stealing the property of orphans
8. Eating animals found already dead, animals not slaughtered in the name of Allah, blood, and pigs. (The prohibition stands unless you are compelled)
9. Accepting usury when it is obvious
10. Consuming prohibited wealth
11. Gambling
12. Cheating in business by under weighing

13. To accuse chaste women of adultery

14. Homosexuality and pedophilia

15. To despair of the mercy of Allah

16. Not fearing the divine retribution

17. Not acknowledging the bounties of Allah

18. Cooperating with the oppressors

19. To associate with the oppressors

20. Taking a false oath

21. To obstruct the rights of someone without any valid reason

22. Lying

23. Pride

24. Wasting wealth

25. Spending in ways not permitted by Allah

26. To betray the trust

27. To consider Hajj of the Holy Kabah unimportant

28. To fight the friends of Allah

29. To enjoy vain pre-occupations

30. To persist in sins

Source: Ayatollah Sayed Abd al-Hussain Dastaghay Shirazi, *Greater Sins* Vol. 1, P. 23.

Books on Practicing of the Shi'a faith

A Code of Practice for Muslims in the West by Sayid Muhammad Rizvi

A Concise Guide of Islamic Laws by Ayatollah Basheer Hussain Najafi

A Glance at Historiography in Shiite Culture by al-Shaykh Rasul Ja'fariyan

A General Outlook at Islamic Rituals by Ayatollah Muhammad Baqir al-Sadr

A Guide to Shariah and Islamist Ideology in Western Europe by Dr Irfan Al-Alawi, Stephen Schwartz, et al.

A Study in the Philosophy of Islamic Rites by Ayatollah Muhammad Baqir al-Sadr

Al-Muraja At: A Shi'i-Sunni Dialogue by Sayyid Abdul Hussain Sharafud-Din al-Musawi, English Translation by Yasin T. al-Jibouri

An Inquiry into Intercession by Dr. Asiyah Banu

An Inquiry into Religious Dissimulation by Azizah Adib

An Introduction to Islam by Dr. Liyakat Takim

An Introduction to Islamic Precepts by Ali Akber Talafi

Asl al-Shia wa Usuluh - The Origin of the Shi'ite Islam and its Principles by al-Shaykh Muhammad Hussain aal Kashiful-Ghita

Beneficiation in Islam by Mohammad Sohufi

Discovering Islam by Sayed Moustafa al-Qazwini

Discovering Shi'i Islam by al-Shaykh Mohammad Ali Shomali

Facts about Shias by Ayatollah Sadiq Shirazi

Faith and Reason by al-Shaykh Mahdi Hadavi Tehrani

A General Outlook at Rituals by Martyred Muhammed-Baqir

Greater Sins by Ayatollah Dastaghayb

Jurisprudence And It's Principels by Ayatollah Mutaza Mutahhari

Jurisprudence Made Easy by Ayatollah Sayed Ali al-Hussaini Sistani

Invitation to Islam by Sayed Moustafa al-Qazwini

Islam a code of Social Life by Islamic Seminary Publication

Islamic Laws by Ayatollah Sayed Ali Seestani

Islamic Law by Ayatollah Nasir Makarem Shirazi

Islamic Law by Ayatollah Sayed Muhammad Shirazi

Islamic Law by Ayatollah Sayed Sadiq Hussain Shirazi

Islam and Physical Care by Al-Balagh Foundation

Islam, Fundamental Principals and Teachings by Ayatollah Sayed Muhammad Shirazi

Merits of Turbah [Earth] of Imam Husain's Grave by al-Syed Abdul-Hussain Dastghaib Shirazi

Mystery of the Shia by Mateen J. Charbonneau

Prostration in the Tradition of the Prophet (saws) and the Companions by al-Syed Muhammad Reza Mudarrisi Yazdi

Replies to Inquiries about Practical Laws of Islam by Ayatollah Sayed Ali Hosseini Khamenei

Questions and Answers on Faith and Practice by Muhammad al-Musawi

Shi'ite Authorities in the Age of Major Occultation (Parts 1, 2 & 3) by Ali Naghi Zabihzadeh

Shi'ite Authorities in the Age of Minor Occultation (Parts 1, 2 & 3) by Ali Naghi Zabihzadeh

Shi'ites under attack by Imam Muhammad Jawad Chirri

Spurious Arguments about the Shia by Abu Talib at-Tabrizi

Taqiyah by Ayatollah Saeed Akhtar Rizvi

Tarawih Prayer and Shia Position by Mustafa Fazel

Taqwa (Piety) by Ayatollah Murtadha Mutahhari

Tawassul by al-Syed Abd al-Karim Bi-Azar Shirazi

The Beauty of Charity by Ahmed Ali al-Kuwaity

The practices of Shi'a Islam: From Qur'an and Sunni Books by Abdul Malik Mujahid

The Right Path (Al-Muraje'at) A Shia Sunni dialog by Sayed Sharafuddin Al-Musawi

The Wilayah of Ali in the Shia Adhan by Dr. Liyakat A. Takim

Truth About Shi'ah Ithna 'Ashari Faith by Asad Wahid al-Qasim

Why Prostrate on Karbala's Turba? by Yasin T. al-Jibouri

Why Pray in Arabic? by Ahmed H. Shariff

Why Do the Shi'ah Prostrate on Turbah? – In a Nutshell by Ahlul Bayt Digital Islamic Library Project

We Cry for Hussain, So Did the Prophet of Islam by Yasser al-Madani

Wudhu' in the Holy Qur'an and the Hadith by al-Syed Muhammad Reza Mudarrisi Yazdi

Chapter 12

Qur'an on the wives of the Prophet (pbuh)

The followers of the Ahlul Bayt (as) hold the same view about the wives of the Prophets (pbut) that the holy Qur'an explains. One would clearly contradict the Qur'an, if one is to say "*All wives of the Holy Prophet (pbuh) were pious and virtuous women*" and because they were married to such a holy figure (pbuh) they are guaranteed paradise and must be respected regardless of their actions.

In the holy Qur'an, Allah (swt) has set the wives of two noble Prophets (pbut) as an example; even though those two women were married to the Prophets of Allah (swt), they died as unbelievers (*Kuffar*), and will end up in Hell, as stated in:

Surat al Tahrim 66:10

ضَرَبَ ٱللَّهُ مَثَلًا لِّلَّذِينَ كَفَرُواْ ٱمْرَأَتَ نُوحٍ وَٱمْرَأَتَ لُوطٍ

كَانَتَا تَحْتَ عَبْدَيْنِ مِنْ عِبَادِنَا صَٰلِحَيْنِ فَخَانَتَاهُمَا فَلَمْ يُغْنِيَا

عَنْهُمَا مِنَ ٱللَّهِ شَيْـًٔا وَقِيلَ ٱدْخُلَا ٱلنَّارَ مَعَ ٱلدَّٰخِلِينَ ﴿١٠﴾

Allah draws an example for the faithless:
the wife of Noah and the wife of Lot.
They were under two of our righteous servants,
yet they betrayed them.
So they did not avail them in any way against Allah,
and it was said [to them],
'Enter the Fire, along with those who enter [it].

Therefore, the '**barometer**' for revering or not revering the wives of the Holy Prophet (pbuh) is Qur'an. Now, one has to carefully examine the verses of the noble Qur'an, which relate to the wives of the Holy Prophet (pbuh), and determine what the noble Qur'an says about the wives of the Prophet (pbuh), and whether, the wives of the Holy Prophet (pbuh) followed the commands of Allah (swt), which are mentioned in the holy Qur'an. As, the Qur'an doesn't state any names or mentions the situation; one has to look at the historical context and the actions of the personalities (in discussion) from studying their lives.

Meaning of the 'Mother of the believers'

(*Ummul Momineen*)

Before, any discussion can take place about the wives of the Holy Prophet (pbuh); one must know the meaning of the title "*Umul Momineen*" or Mother of the Believers, which was given to all of the wives of the Holy Prophet (pbuh).

Surat al Ahzab 33:6

ٱلنَّبِىُّ أَوْلَىٰ بِٱلْمُؤْمِنِينَ مِنْ أَنفُسِهِمْ وَأَزْوَٰجُهُۥٓ أَمَّهَٰتُهُمْ وَأُوْلُواْ ٱلْأَرْحَامِ بَعْضُهُمْ أَوْلَىٰ بِبَعْضٍ فِى كِتَٰبِ ٱللَّهِ مِنَ ٱلْمُؤْمِنِينَ وَٱلْمُهَٰجِرِينَ إِلَّآ أَن تَفْعَلُوٓاْ إِلَىٰٓ أَوْلِيَآئِكُم مَّعْرُوفًا كَانَ ذَٰلِكَ فِى ٱلْكِتَٰبِ مَسْطُورًا ﴿٦﴾

The Prophet is closer to the faithful
than their own souls,
and his wives are their mothers.

And

Surat al Ahzab 33:53

يَـٰٓأَيُّهَا ٱلَّذِينَ ءَامَنُوا۟ لَا تَدْخُلُوا۟ بُيُوتَ ٱلنَّبِىِّ إِلَّآ أَن يُؤْذَنَ لَكُمْ
إِلَىٰ طَعَامٍ غَيْرَ نَـٰظِرِينَ إِنَىٰهُ وَلَـٰكِنْ إِذَا دُعِيتُمْ فَٱدْخُلُوا۟ فَإِذَا طَعِمْتُمْ
فَٱنتَشِرُوا۟ وَلَا مُسْتَـْٔنِسِينَ لِحَدِيثٍ إِنَّ ذَٰلِكُمْ كَانَ يُؤْذِى ٱلنَّبِىَّ
فَيَسْتَحْىِۦ مِنكُمْ وَٱللَّهُ لَا يَسْتَحْىِۦ مِنَ ٱلْحَقِّ وَإِذَا سَأَلْتُمُوهُنَّ
مَتَـٰعًا فَسْـَٔلُوهُنَّ مِن وَرَآءِ حِجَابٍ ذَٰلِكُمْ أَطْهَرُ لِقُلُوبِكُمْ
وَقُلُوبِهِنَّ وَمَا كَانَ لَكُمْ أَن تُؤْذُوا۟ رَسُولَ ٱللَّهِ وَلَآ أَن
تَنكِحُوٓا۟ أَزْوَٰجَهُۥ مِنۢ بَعْدِهِۦٓ أَبَدًا إِنَّ ذَٰلِكُمْ كَانَ عِندَ ٱللَّهِ
عَظِيمًا ﴿٥٣﴾

O you who have faith!
Do not enter the Prophet's houses
unless permission is granted you for a meal,
without waiting for it to be readied.
But enter when you are invited,
and disperse when you have taken your meal,
without settling down to chat.
Indeed, such conduct torments the Prophet,
and he is ashamed of [asking] you [to leave];
but Allah is not ashamed of [expressing] the truth.
And when you ask anything of [his] womenfolk,
ask it from them from behind a curtain.
That is more chaste for your hearts and their hearts.
You may not torment the Apostle of Allah,
nor may you ever marry his wives after him.
Indeed, that would be a grave [matter] with Allah.

The above verse (33:6) of the Qur'an, which states: *"His wives are their mothers"* directly refers to the command of Allah (swt) in the verse 53, which states: *"nor may you ever marry his wives after him"*; Because there were several companions who wanted to marry the wives of the Holy Prophet (pbuh) after his demise, therefore, Allah (swt) declared them (the wives) as their mothers, so they absolutely cannot marry any of the wives of the Holy Prophet (pbuh) after his (pbuh) demise.

Therefore, there is no significance in the title of *"Ummul Momineen"* or Mother of the Believers itself, other than the fact that whatever is associated with the Holy Prophet (pbuh) is to be respected and honored even if the thing or person possesses no merits of his/her own.

Source: Ayatollah Agha Mahdi Puya, *Tafsir of Holy Qur'an* Surat 33, verse 6, P. 17-18.
http://www.islamicmobility.com/elibrary_14.htm

Surat al Tahrim (the Forbidding) was revealed in Medina and it is number 99 in the order of revelation. All interpreters of the holy Qur'an agree that this Chapter is discussing the behavior of Ayesha and Hafsa, the two wives of the Holy Prophet (pbuh). In *Sahih Muslim, Sahih Bukhari* and *Sunan Abu Dawood:* It is narrated by Ayesha that Allah's Apostle (pbuh) used to spend time with Zainab daughter of Jahsh and drank honey at her house. Both, Ayesha and Hafsa became resentful, and Ayesha devised a plot. Knowing the Holy Prophet's dislike of unpleasant smells she held her nose when he came to her apartment after drinking a glass of honey-syrup prepared by Zainab, and accused him of having eaten *maghafir* (a nauseating herb). The Holy Prophet said that he had taken only honey. When he visited Hafsa she also acted, just like Ayesha. Displeased with their obnoxious behavior the Holy Prophet (pbuh) vowed not to eat honey any more.

In another narration as reported by Umar bin al-Khatab, On a day the Prophet (pbuh) was assigned to Hafsa, when she was not found in her apartment as she went to her parent's house, the Holy Prophet (pbuh) spent the night with Marya, the Coptic girl, presented to him by the ruler of Egypt, who became the mother of his son, Ibrahim. To calm the quarrelsome bad temper of Hafsa he vowed to cut off conjugal relations with Marya. It is then, after these two incidences, Surat al Tahrim was revealed:

Sources:

Sahih Muslim, Book 18, Hadith 27 *http://sunnah.com/muslim/18/27*

Sahih Bukhari, Vol. 6, Book 60, Hadith 434
   http://sunnah.com/urn/45890

Sunan Abu Dawood, Book 27, Hadith 46
   http://sunnah.com/abuDawood/27/46

Sahih Bukhari, Book 65, Hadith 4962 *http://sunnah.com/urn/45900*

Ismail bin Umar bin Kathir, *Tafsir Ibn Kathir: http://quran.cc/66*

   Jalal ad-Din al-Mahalli, *Tafsir Jalalayn: http://quran.cc/66*

Surat al Tahrim (the Forbidding)

In the Name of Allah,
the All-beneficent, the All-merciful.

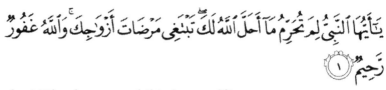

1 O Prophet! Why do you prohibit [yourself]
what Allah has made lawful for you,
seeking to please your wives?
And Allah is all-forgiving, all-merciful.

$$قَدْ فَرَضَ ٱللَّهُ لَكُمْ تَحِلَّةَ أَيْمَـٰنِكُمْ وَٱللَّهُ مَوْلَـٰكُمْ وَهُوَ ٱلْعَلِيمُ ٱلْحَكِيمُ ٢$$

2 Allah has certainly made lawful for you
the dissolution of your oaths,
and Allah is your master
and He is the All-knowing, the All-wise .

$$وَإِذْ أَسَرَّ ٱلنَّبِيُّ إِلَىٰ بَعْضِ أَزْوَٰجِهِ حَدِيثًا فَلَمَّا نَبَّأَتْ بِهِ وَأَظْهَرَهُ ٱللَّهُ$$

$$عَلَيْهِ عَرَّفَ بَعْضَهُ وَأَعْرَضَ عَنۢ بَعْضٍ فَلَمَّا نَبَّأَهَا بِهِ قَالَتْ مَنْ أَنۢبَأَكَ هَـٰذَا$$

$$قَالَ نَبَّأَنِيَ ٱلْعَلِيمُ ٱلْخَبِيرُ ٣$$

3 When the Prophet confided to one of his wives
a matter,
but when she divulged it,
and Allah apprised him about it,
he announced [to her] part of it
and disregarded part of it.
So when he told her about it,
*she said, '**Who informed you about it?**'*
He said,
'The All-knowing and the All-aware, informed me. '

$$إِن تَتُوبَا إِلَى ٱللَّهِ فَقَدْ صَغَتْ قُلُوبُكُمَا وَإِن تَظَٰهَرَا عَلَيْهِ فَإِنَّ ٱللَّهَ هُوَ$$

$$مَوْلَٰهُ وَجِبْرِيلُ وَصَٰلِحُ ٱلْمُؤْمِنِينَ وَٱلْمَلَٰٓئِكَةُ بَعْدَ ذَٰلِكَ$$

$$ظَهِيرٌ ٤$$

4 If the two of you repent to Allah. . .
for your hearts have certainly swerved,
and if you back each other against him,
then [know that] Allah is indeed his guardian,
*and Gabriel, **the righteous one among the faithful**,*
and, thereafter, the angels are his supporters .

عَسَىٰ رَبُّهُۥٓ إِن طَلَّقَكُنَّ أَن يُبْدِلَهُۥٓ أَزْوَٰجًا خَيْرًا مِّنكُنَّ مُسْلِمَٰتٍ مُّؤْمِنَٰتٍ قَٰنِتَٰتٍ تَٰٓئِبَٰتٍ عَٰبِدَٰتٍ سَٰٓئِحَٰتٍ ثَيِّبَٰتٍ وَأَبْكَارًا ٥

5 It may be that if he divorces you
his Lord will give him, in [your] stead, wives
better than you:
[such as are] muslim, faithful, obedient,
penitent, devout and given to fasting,
virgins and non-virgins.

Verses 3 and 5 discusses the behavior of Hafsa as she came to know about a very personal matter concerning the Holy Prophet (pbuh), which he thought should not be made public, therefore he asked her not to publish it. But, right away she went to Ayesha and told her a version, which was in great part un-true. Hafsa who betrayed confidence and Ayesha who encouraged the betrayal were commanded to turn in repentance to Allah (swt). If they were to resist repentance and amends, they would be abetting each other's crime but could not harm the most perfect messenger of Allah whom all the spiritual forces always surrounded to protect from every type of slander and falsehood.

"Salihul mumini" 'the (mostly) righteous one among the faithful' refers to Imam Ali (as).

Verse 5 is a huge attack on Ayesha and Hafsa from Allah (swt) where Allah (swt) clearly stated, if his Prophet (pbuh) divorced the two!!! Then surely Allah (swt) will bless him (pbuh) with the wives "**better than them**" Muslim Wives, Faithful Wives, Obedient Wives, Repenting Wives, Devout and Pious Wives, Virgin Wives, etc.

Question: If Ayesha & Hafsa lacked faith during the Prophet's (pbuh) life, how would they become virtuous and pious after him?

The Prophet (pbuh) had discretionary power to divorce any or all his wives, and if he did so Allah would give him good women as his wives in place of the existing wives, who were, in view of verse 5, ordinary women harboring envy, jealousy, and ill-will against others; particularly Ayesha's hostility towards Imam Ali (as) has been recorded by all the well known historians, as it was evident in the Battle of the Camel (*Jamal*).

Source: Ayatollah Agha Mahdi Puya, *Tafsir of Holy Qur'an* Surat
66, verses 1-5, P. 3-5
http://www.islamicmobility.com/elibrary_14.htm

Another Chapter of the holy Qur'an, which severely criticizes the character and the behavior of the wives of the Holy Prophet (pbuh) is **Surat al Ahzab** (The Confederates) Chapter 33. In this Chapter Allah (swt) once again exposes the character of Ayesha, as she is the wife of the best of mankind Prophet Muhammad (pbuh) was commanded by Allah (swt) to *"stay in her house"*, and the punishment for an act of *gross indecency*, would be double on her because she was married to the Holy Prophet (pbuh). Ayesha's act of leading an Army of 30,000 men in the battle of Camel against the righteous caliph of the Muslim nation, Imam Ali Ibn Abi Talib (as) negates any discussion about Ayesha's reverence in the light of the holy Qur'an.

Surat al Ahzab 33:28-33

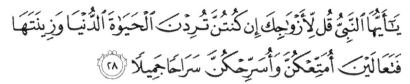

28 O Prophet!
Say to your wives,
'If you desire the life of the world and its glitter,
come,
I will provide for you
and release you in a graceful manner

وَإِن كُنتُنَّ تُرِدْنَ اللَّهَ وَرَسُولَهُ وَالدَّارَ الْآخِرَةَ فَإِنَّ اللَّهَ أَعَدَّ لِلْمُحْسِنَاتِ مِنكُنَّ أَجْرًا عَظِيمًا ﴿٢٩﴾

29 But if you desire Allah and His Apostle
and the abode of the Hereafter,
then Allah has indeed prepared
for the virtuous among you
a great reward.'

يَـٰنِسَآءَ النَّبِيِّ مَن يَأْتِ مِنكُنَّ بِفَاحِشَةٍ مُّبَيِّنَةٍ يُضَاعَفْ لَهَا الْعَذَابُ ضِعْفَيْنِ وَكَانَ ذَٰلِكَ عَلَى اللَّهِ يَسِيرًا ﴿٣٠﴾

30 O wives of the Prophet!
Whoever of you commits a gross indecency,
her punishment shall be doubled,
and that is easy for Allah.

۞ وَمَن يَقْنُتْ مِنكُنَّ لِلَّهِ وَرَسُولِهِ وَتَعْمَلْ صَـٰلِحًا نُّؤْتِهَا أَجْرَهَا مَرَّتَيْنِ وَأَعْتَدْنَا لَهَا رِزْقًا كَرِيمًا ﴿٣١﴾

31 But whoever of you is obedient to Allah and His Apostle
and acts righteously,
We shall give her a twofold reward,
and We hold a noble provision in store for her.

يَـٰنِسَآءَ النَّبِيِّ لَسْتُنَّ كَأَحَدٍ مِّنَ النِّسَآءِ إِنِ اتَّقَيْتُنَّ فَلَا تَخْضَعْنَ بِالْقَوْلِ فَيَطْمَعَ الَّذِي فِي قَلْبِهِ مَرَضٌ وَقُلْنَ قَوْلًا مَّعْرُوفًا ﴿٣٢﴾

32 O wives of the Prophet!
You are not like any other women:
if you are wary [of Allah],
then do not be complaisant in your speech,
lest he in whose heart is a sickness should aspire,
and **speak honorable words**.

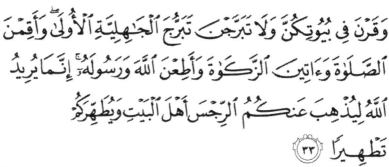

33 ***Stay in your houses***
and ***do not display your finery***
with the display of the former [days of] ignorance.
Maintain the prayer and pay the zakat,
and obey Allah and His Apostle.
Indeed Allah desires to repel all impurity from you,
O People of the Household,
and purify you with a thorough purification.

Battle of the Camel (*Jamal*):

The Prophet (pbuh) stood up and delivered a sermon, and pointing to `Aisha's house (i.e. Eastwards), he said thrice, *"Affliction (will appear from) here,"* and, *"from where the side of the Satan's head comes out (i.e. From the East)."*

Source: *Sahih Bukhari*, Book 57, Hadith 13
   http://sunnah.com/bukhari/57/13

In this battle, Ayesha along with Talha Ibn Ubaydullah and Zubayr Ibn al-Awwam, Marwan bin Hakam (*who was exiled by Prophet Muhammad pbuh from Medina during his lifetime*), and many other of Uthman's governors who were fired from their positions by Imam Ali (as) upon taking caliphate, took up the arms and raised an army of 30,000 men to fight against the newly elected caliph Imam Ali Ibn Abi Talib (as). Alongside Imam Ali (as), his commanders of the Army included Imam Hassan (as), Imam Hussain (as), Malik al-Ashtar, Ammar bin Yassir, Muhammad bin Abi Bakr, Muslim bin Aqeel, Jabir Ibn Abduallah al-Ansari, Abu Ayub Ansari, Muhammad Ibn al-Hanafiyyah with an army of 20,000 soldiers.

The battle took place on the account, to find and kill the killers of Uthman. As proclaimed by Ayesha *"Uthman has been killed unjustly! And, by Allah, I will seek vengeance for his blood!"*(al-Tabari). Ayesha, along with her forefront supporters gathered outside of Basra, where she instigated further deception and gained further support.

Imam Ali's (as) forces arrived outside of Basra, where upon hearing the accusations and deceptive lies, addressed Talha and Zubayr and reminded them that it was their own actions which caused Uthman's murder; whereupon, Talha and Zubayr's main goal was to gain political power or the caliphate for themselves; and to Ayesha, Imam Ali (as) told her that *"...during Uthman's life she despised him and used to call him a long bearded Jew, whereas, now, you want to avenge his murder from me?... I have nothing to do with it!!!"* upon this, Ayesha had nothing else to say, but to insist on fighting Imam Ali (as).

Imam Ali (as) said about the army of Ayesha, Talha and Zubayr:
 "Beware! Satan has collected his group and assembled his horsemen and foot soldiers. Surely, with me is my sagacity. I have neither deceived myself nor ever been deceived. By Allah, I shall fill to the brim for them a cistern from which I alone would draw water. They can neither turn away from it, nor return to it."(Nahjul Balagha, Sermon 10)

The war already began when Ayesha's army killed over 600 Basrans who opposed her or refused to join her army, but the battle of the camel began when Ayesha's army killed the messenger-boy sent by Imam Ali (as) with a Qur'an.

Imam Ali (as) warriors made a quick work of the oppositions, but as long as the camel of Ayesha was in its place surrounded by her men, the battle was to be continued. Imam Ali (as) decided to send Imam Hassan (as) and Malik al Ashtar to cut the legs of the camel on which Ayesha was on.... The camel landed and her howdah fell to the ground, Muhammad bin Abi Bakr (Ayesha's brother) pulled her out of her howdah and told her:

"Ali is with the truth and the truth is with Ali! You roused the people, and they became excited. You stirred up discord among them such that some killed others..."

Ayesha was still resentful towards Imam Ali (as) and was humiliated by the defeat, but her request of an honorable pardon was fulfilled by the man full of justice, Imam Ali (as), as she was returned to Medina, escorted by her own brother.

In the midst of mayhem of the battle, Talha was killed by Marwan Ibn Hakam, whereas, Zubayr tried to flee the battle and was later killed by Umar Ibn Jernuz.

In conclusion, about 20,000 lives of the Muslims (from both sides combined) were lost due to the wicked actions of Ayesha, Talha and Zubayr. Upon her return, Ayesha was asked: *"What do you say about a mother who kills her child?"* Ayesha replied: *"This lady goes straight to Hell."* Ayesha was asked again, *"What do you say about a mother who killed all of her children, twenty thousand of them in one day?"* What a tragedy that a woman honored as a "Mother of the Believers" in the Qur'an was involved in such travesty in the Islamic History.

Sunni Sources:

Muhammad Ibn Jarir al-Tabari, *The History of al-Tabari* Vol. 16.

The Community Divided: The Caliphate of Ali A. D. 656-657/A.H. 35-36. Translated by Adrian Brockett, ISBN10: 0-7914-2391-3. SUNY Press Publishers, NY.

Ismail bin Umar bin Kathir, *Biographies of the Rightly-Guided Caliphs, Chapter: The Battle of Al-Jamal (Camel), P. 356 – 360* *http://www.kalamullah.com/Books/Biographies%20of%20the%20Rightly-Guided%20Caliphs.pdf*

Dr. Ali M. Sallabi, *Ali Ibn abi Talib,* Vol. 2, Chapter 6, P. 19-133 *http://www.kalamullah.com/ali-Ibn-abi-talib.html*

Non-Muslim Historians' Sources:

Wilferd Madelung (1997), *The Succession to Muhammad: A Study of the Early Caliphate.* P. 78 – 311. ISBN-0521646960. Publisher: Cambridge University Press

William Montgomery Watt (1998), *The Formative Period of Islamic Thought.* ISBN-1851681523. Publisher: One world Publications

Shi'a Sources:

Shaykh al-Mufid, *The Battle of the Camel* (An Annotated Edition) Translated by IKA Howard and JA Hamidi. ISBN-10: 1908031026. Publisher: Muhammadi Trust of Great Britain and Northern Island; 1st edition (2014)

Sayed Ali Asgher Razwy, *A Restatement of the History of Islam and Muslims,The Battle of Basra (the battle of Camel).* *http://www.al-islam.org/restatement-history-islam-and-muslims-sayyid-ali-ashgar-razwy/battle-basra-battle-camel*

Dr. A. Asadi (2012) *Shi'ah Islam.* Chapters 69, 79, 80.ISBN-10: 1879402424. Publisher: Tahrike Tarsile Qur'an

End of Chapter notes:

Reason behind Prophet's (pbuh) marriages

Lady Khadijah The only youthful marriage of the Holy Prophet was his first marriage to Khadija, mother of Fatimah, the noblest of women and the best of wives. He married her fifteen years before he made known his Prophethood; their marriage life lasted for twenty five years, and their love and harmony was ideal. During her life he had no other wife. When she died the Holy Prophet observed "the year of grief". He would probably never have married again, as he was most abstemious in his physical life, but for two considerations which governed his later marriages

1. Compassion and clemency;
2. Help in his duties of Prophethood by establishing ties with the tribes of his wives and to eradicate pagan cultural norms.

After lady Khadijah passed away, Prophet Muhammad (pbuh) married **Sawdah Bint Zam'ah** whose husband had passed away during the second migration to Abyssinia. Sawdah was a believing lady who had migrated on account of her faith. Her father and brother were among the bitterest enemies of Islam. If she were left to return to them, they would have tortured her, as they were doing with other believing men and women, oppressing and killing them forcing them to renounce their faith.

At the same time, the Prophet (pbuh) married **Ayesha binte Abu Bakr Abi Quhafa** to strengthen the ties with Banu Taym (Abu Bakr's tribe) and to strengthen the relationship with Abu Bakr.

Prophet (pbuh) married **Zainab bint Khuzaymah** whose husband Abdullah Ibn Jahsh was killed during the Battle of Uhud. She was a very virtuous woman even during the time of *jahiliyya* (ignorance). She used to be called '*ummul-masakin*,' mother of the destitute, due to her generosity to the indigent and the poor. Seeing that by losing her husband, she had none to provide for her, the Prophet married her in order to safeguard her dignity.

When the Prophet (pbuh) migrated to Medina, he began to change the norms and culture of the society by leading by example. He married women who were all either widows or divorcees, old or middle-aged. The Prophet married **Umm Salamah**, Hind, who was the wife of 'Abdullah Abu Salamah (father of Salamah), son of the Prophet's aunt as well as his foster brother. She and her husband were among the first to migrate to Ethiopia, an ascetic and virtuous lady, a very pious one. She had renounced worldly pleasures and was highly distinguished for her wisdom. Her husband died, leaving her an old widow with many orphans for whom she could not provide; so, the Prophet married her in order to maintain her prestige and look after her orphans who were, of course, his own relatives.

The Prophet (pbuh) married **Umm Habibah** or **Ramla binte Abu Sufyan**, who was previously married to Ubaydullah and had migrated to Abyssinia in the second migration. While there, Ubaydullah converted to Christianity, but she remained steadfast on Islam and separated from him. Her father, Abu Sufyan, was in those days raising one army after another in order to annihilate the Muslims. The Prophet (pbuh) married her and afforded protection to her despite the hope of any change in Abu Sufyan's attitude did not materialize.

Hafsah binte Umar Ibn al-Khattab was married to him after her husband Khunays Ibn Huthayfah was martyred during the battle of Badr. Umar himself requested Prophet Muhammad (pbuh) to marry his daughter.

By marrying **Zainab binte Jahsh**, the Prophet (pbuh) wanted to show that it was permitted to marry the ex-wife of an adopted son, as adoption is Islam, unlike in pagan Arabia, does not confer blood rights. As stated in **Surat al Ahzab 33:37**

The Prophet (pbuh) married **Safiyya binte Huyayy Ibn al-Akhtab**, as her husband was killed during the Battle of Khaybar. Her brother was also killed in the same battle. She was a lady of high status and prestige, and when the Prophet saw that she was about to be sold as a slave, he proposed to her, as a way to save her from the degradation of slavery, and she accepted his marriage proposal.

The marriage to **Juwayriyya** or **Barra binte al-Harith** was similar to that of Safiyya, as Juwayriyya was one of the captives of the Banu Mustaliq. The Prophet (pbuh) agreed to pay for her freedom and marry her. Ayesha narrates: "I know of no woman who brought as much good for her people as Jawayriyya."

Mariyah the Coptic was offered as a gift along with her sister Sirin by the Coptic archbishop of Egypt. Since they were sisters, the Prophet (pbuh) married only one of them, honoring her as his wife.

Maymuna or **Barra bint al-Harith al-Hilaliyyah** became attracted to Islam during the peace of Hudaybiyyah. When her second husband died in 7 A.H./628 A.D., she came to the Prophet and "gifted' herself to him if he would accept her. She only desired the honor of being called the wife of the Prophet.

Sources:

Dr. A. Asadi (2012) *Shi'ah Islam*. P. 303-304. ISBN-10: 1879402424. Publisher: Tahrike Tarsile Qur'an

Yasin T. Al-Jibouri, *Muhammad, Marriages of the Prophet.* *http://www.al-islam.org/muhammad-yasin-jibouri/marriages-prophet*

Did the Prophet (pbuh) have a favorite wife?

This question can be answered by asking yourself what are the qualities that you desire in your wife or daughter in law? If an ordinary Muslim desires a faithful, pleasant, virtuous, pious, gentle, caring, obedient, devout, loving-natured wife, than why wouldn't the Prophet of Allah (pbuh) desire similar for himself? Would the Prophet (pbuh) has had a different set of values than an ordinary human being? Why would the Prophet (pbuh) desire a wife who'd argue with him (pbuh)? Insult him (pbuh)? Be disrespectful towards him (pbuh)? Show envy and disregard the command of Allah (swt)? And instigate *Fitna* (mass afflictions and atrocities) after his demise.

Amongst his (pbuh) wives, there's a notion that Ayesha was his favorite wife and the Prophet (pbuh) preferred her to others, even though, Allah (swt) criticizes Ayesha in Qur'an for her ill treatment, and being disrespectful towards the Holy Prophet (pbuh).

How can Ayesha be his (pbuh) favorite wife? As the Holy Prophet (pbuh) was married to Khadija (sa) for 25 years, during his youth. He, not once, took upon another wife while Khadija was alive. Khadija (sa) gave birth to the Prophet's (pbuh) children and gave away all of her wealth for the sake of Islam. After her demise, the Prophet (pbuh) would constantly remember her, praise her and talk about her.

How can the Prophet (pbuh) show favoritism towards Ayesha? While Allah (swt) commands ordinary Muslims to treat their wives fairly and with justice, and the most just man of the entire mankind would do such injustice by favoring only one of his wives while being married to others? As stated in the holy Qur'an:

Surat al Nisa 4:3

وَإِنْ خِفْتُمْ أَلَّا تُقْسِطُوا فِي ٱلْيَتَـٰمَىٰ فَٱنكِحُوا مَا طَابَ لَكُم مِّنَ ٱلنِّسَآءِ مَثْنَىٰ

وَثُلَـٰثَ وَرُبَـٰعَ فَإِنْ خِفْتُمْ أَلَّا تَعْدِلُوا فَوَٰحِدَةً أَوْ مَا مَلَكَتْ أَيْمَـٰنُكُمْ ذَٰلِكَ أَدْنَىٰ

أَلَّا تَعُولُوا ٣

If you fear that you may not deal justly
with the orphans,
then marry [other] women that you like,
two, three, or four.
But if you fear that you may not treat them fairly,
then [marry only] one,
or [marry from among] your slave-women.
That makes it likelier that you will not be unfair.

Ayesha according to *Ayesha*

Ayesha's Jealousy towards Khadija (sa)

Ayesha narrates:

> *I did not feel jealous of any of the wives of the Prophet (pbuh) as much as I did of Khadija (although) she died before he married me, for I often heard him mentioning her, and Allah had told him to give her the good tidings that she would have a palace of Qasab (i.e. Pipes of precious stones and pearls in Paradise), and whenever he slaughtered a sheep, he would send her women-friends a good share of it.*

Sources:

Sahih Bukhari, Book 63, Hadith 42,
 http://sunnah.com/bukhari/63/42

Sahih Bukhari, Book 63, Hadith 44 *http://sunnah.com/bukhari/63/44*

Sahih Muslim, Book 44, Hadith 110
 http://sunnah.com/muslim/44/110

Ayesha's insults towards Khadija (SA)

Ayesha narrates:

> *Once Hala bint Khuwailid, Khadija's sister, asked the permission of the Prophet (pbuh) to enter. On that, the Prophet (pbuh) remembered the way Khadija used to ask permission, and that upset him. He said, "O Allah! Hala!" So I became jealous and said, "What makes you remember an old woman amongst the old women of Quraish an old woman (with a toothless mouth) of red gums who died long ago, and in whose place Allah has given you somebody better than her?"*

Sources:

Sahih Bukhari, Book 63, Hadith 47
 http://sunnah.com/bukhari/63/47

Sahih Muslim, Book 44, Hadith 112

http://sunnah.com/muslim/44/112

Ayesha's further jealousy and mockery of the holy Qur'an

Ayesha narrates:

I felt jealous of the women who offered themselves to Allah's Messenger (pbuh) and said: Then when Allah, the Exalted and Glorious, revealed this: "You may defer any one of them you wish, and take to yourself any you wish; and if you desire any you have set aside (no sin is chargeable to you)" (33:51), I (Ayesha.) said: It seems to me that your Lord hastens to satisfy your desire!

Sources:

Sahih Muslim, Book 17, Hadith 64, *http://sunnah.com/muslim/17/64*

Sahih Muslim, Book 17, Hadith 65, *http://sunnah.com/muslim/17/65*

Ayesha's further jealousy and mocking the Prophet (pbuh)

Ayesha narrates:

Allah's Messenger (pbuh) was fond of honey and sweet edible things and (it was his habit) that after finishing the Asr prayer he would visit his wives and stay with one of them at that time. Once he went to Hafsa, the daughter of Umar and stayed with her more than usual. I got jealous and asked the reason for that. I was told that a lady of her folk had given her a skin filled with honey as a present, and that she made a syrup from it and gave it to the Prophet (pbuh) to drink (and that was the reason for the delay). I said, "By Allah, we will play a trick on him (to prevent him from doing so)." So I said to Sa'da bint Zam'a "The Prophet (pbuh) will approach you, and when he comes near you, say: 'Have you taken Maghafir (a bad-smelling gum)?' He will say, 'No.' Then say to him: 'Then what is this bad smell which I smell from you?' He will say to you, 'Hafsa made me drink honey syrup.' Then say: Perhaps the best of that honey had sucked the juice of the tree of Al-Urfut. I shall also say the same. O you, Safiyya, says the same. "Later Sa'da said, "By Allah, as soon as he (the Prophet (pbuh)) stood at the door, I was about to say to

*him what you had ordered me to say because I was afraid of you."
So when the Prophet (pbuh) came near Sa'da, she said to him, "O
Allah's Messenger (pbuh)! Have you taken Maghafir?" He said,
"No." She said. "Then what is this bad smell which I detect on you"'
He said, "Hafsa made me drink honey syrup." She said, "Perhaps
its bees had sucked the juice of Al-Urfut tree." When he came to me,
I also said the same, and when he went to Safiyya, she also said the
same. And when the Prophet (pbuh) again went to Hafsa, she said,
'O Allah's Messenger (pbuh)! Shall I give you more of that drink?"
He said, "I am not in need of it." Sa'da said, "By Allah, we deprived
him (of it)." I said to her, "Keep quiet!"*

Source:

Sahih Bukhari, Book 68, Hadith 18,
http://sunnah.com/bukhari/68/18

Ayesha's insults towards Prophet Muhammad (pbuh)

Ayesha narrates:

*I used to stretch my legs towards the Qibla of the Prophet (pbuh)
while he was praying; whenever he prostrated, he touched me,
and I would withdraw my legs, and whenever he stood up, I
would restrict my legs.*

Source:

Sahih Bukhari, Vol. 2, Book 22, *http://sunnah.com/bukhari/21/13*

Ayesha's further insults towards Prophet Muhammad (pbuh)

Ayesha narrates:

*Magic was worked on Allah's Messenger (pbuh) so that he used to
think that he had sexual relations with his wives while he actually
had not (Sufyan said: That is the hardest kind of magic as it has
such an effect). Then one day he said, "O Ayesha do you know
that Allah has instructed me concerning the matter I asked Him
about? Two men came to me and one of them sat near my head
and the other sat near my feet.*

The one near my head asked the other. What is wrong with this man? The latter replied he is under the effect of magic. The first one asked, Who has worked magic on him? The other replied Labid bin Al-Asam, a man from Bani Zuraiq who was an ally of the Jews and was a hypocrite. The first one asked, What material did he use)? The other replied, a comb and the hair stuck to it. The first one asked, Where (is that)? The other replied, In a skin of pollen of a male date palm tree kept under a stone in the well of Dharwan. So the Prophet (pbuh) went to that well and took out those things and said "That was the well which was shown to me (in a dream) its water looked like the infusion of Henna leaves and its date-palm trees looked like the heads of devils."

The Prophet (pbuh) added, "Then that thing was taken out," I said (to the Prophet (pbuh)) "Why do you not treat yourself with Nashra?" He said, "Allah has cured me; I dislike to let evil spread among my people."

Sources:

Sahih Bukhari, Book 76, Hadith 79,
  http://sunnah.com/bukhari/76/79

Sahih Bukhari, Book 80, Hadith 86,*http://sunnah.com/bukhari/80/86*

Ayesha disobeying the Prophet (pbuh)

Ayesha narrates:

We poured medicine into the mouth of Allah's Messenger (pbuh) during his illness, and he pointed out to us intending to say, "Don't pour medicine into my mouth." We thought that his refusal was out of the aversion a patient usually has for medicine.

When he improved and felt a bit better, he said (to us.) "Didn't I forbid you to pour medicine into my mouth?" We said, "We thought (you did so) because of the aversion, one usually have for medicine." Allah's Messenger (pbuh) said, "There is none of you but will be forced to drink medicine, and I will watch you, except Al-Abbas, for he did not witness this act of yours."

Sources:

Sahih Bukhari, Book 87, Hadith 36 *http://sunnah.com/bukhari/87/36*

Sahih Bukhari, Book 76, Hadith 29 *http://sunnah.com/bukhari/76/29*

Ayesha's mistrust towards the Holy Prophet (pbuh)

Muhammad bin Qais bin Makhramah narrates from Ayesha:

> *Shall I not tell you about me and about the Prophet? We said: 'Yes.' Ayesha said: 'When it was my night when he was with me' meaning the Prophet (pbuh) He came back (from Isha prayer), put his sandals by his feet and spread the edge of his Izar on his bed. He stayed until he thought that I had gone to sleep, then he put his sandals on slowly, picked up his cloak slowly, then opened the door slowly and went out slowly. I covered my head, put on my veil and tightened my waist wrapper, then I followed his steps until he came to Al-Baqi. He raised his hands three times, and stood there for a long time, then he left and I left. He hastened and I also hastened; he ran and I also ran. He came (to the house) and I also came, but I got there first and entered, and as I lay down he came in. He said: "Tell me, or the Subtle, the All-Aware will tell me." I said: 'O Messenger of Allah, may my father and mother be ransomed for you,' and I told him (the whole story). He said: So you were the black shape that I saw in front of me? I said, 'Yes.' He gave me a nudge on the chest, which I felt, then he said: 'Did you think that Allah and His Messenger would deal unjustly with you?' I said: 'Whatever the people conceal, Allah knows it.' He said: Jibraeel came to me when I saw you, but he did not enter upon me because you were not fully dressed. He called me, but he concealed that from you, and I answered him, but I concealed that from you too. I thought that you had gone to sleep and I did not want to wake you up, and I was afraid that you would be frightened. He told me to go to Al-Baqi and pray for forgiveness for them.' I said: 'What should I say, O Messenger of Allah?' He said: 'Say, Peace be upon the inhabitants of this place among the believers and Muslims. May Allah have mercy upon those who have gone ahead of us and those who come later on, and we will*

join you, if Allah wills."

Sources:

Sunan an-Nasai, Book 21, Hadith, 221,
  http://sunnah.com/nasai/21/221

Sahih Muslim, Book 11, Hadith 132,
  http://sunnah.com/muslim/11/132

Books on this subject

Exemplary Women: Lady Um Salamah by Fahimeh Fahiminejad

Khadija tul Kubra by Sayed Ali Asghar Razwy

Khadija Daughter of Khuwaylid by Yasin T. Al-Jibouri

Role of Ayesha in the History of Islam Vol 1, 2 & 3 by Allama Sayid Murtaza Askari

Shi'ah Women Transmitters of Hadith, Collection of Biographies of the women who have transmitted traditions by Dr. Nahleh Gharavi Naeeni

The Philosophy of Marriages of Prophet Muhammad saws by Ahmed Hussain Sheriff

Chapter 13

Shi'a view of the companions of the Holy Prophet (pbuh) with the Qur'an

According to the vast majority of the Muslims, anyone who was around the Holy Prophet (pbuh) and called himself a believer is considered to be his companion. The notion when Muslims say that ALL Companions of the Holy Prophet (pbuh) were "good" and may Allah be pleased with them, is not only absurd but completely opposes the concept put forward by the holy Qur'an about the companions of the Holy Prophet (pbuh).

The Qur'an places the companions into three categories:

1. Virtuous and pious, who sacrificed everything for the sake of Islam, who showed unconditional obedience to the Prophet (pbuh)

2. Weak in faith, did not make any sacrifices, ran away from the battlefields, argued with the Prophet (pbuh), and argued with one another.

3. Hypocrites, who wore an outer garb of Islam, but inside were the enemies of Islam, they kept close ties with the enemies of Islam.

The **first category of** the companions (who were devout, faithful believers with whom Allah (swt) is pleased with, *Radhi Allah Unho*) is discussed in several places in the holy Qur'an:

Surat al Fath 48:29

مُّحَمَّدٌ رَّسُولُ اللَّهِ وَالَّذِينَ مَعَهُ أَشِدَّاءُ عَلَى الْكُفَّارِ رُحَمَاءُ بَيْنَهُمْ تَرَىٰهُمْ

رُكَّعًا سُجَّدًا يَبْتَغُونَ فَضْلًا مِّنَ اللَّهِ وَرِضْوَانًا سِيمَاهُمْ فِي وُجُوهِهِم

مِّنْ أَثَرِ السُّجُودِ ذَٰلِكَ مَثَلُهُمْ فِي التَّوْرَاةِ وَمَثَلُهُمْ فِي الْإِنجِيلِ كَزَرْعٍ

أَخْرَجَ شَطْأَهُ فَآزَرَهُ فَاسْتَغْلَظَ فَاسْتَوَىٰ عَلَىٰ سُوقِهِ يُعْجِبُ الزُّرَّاعَ

لِيَغِيظَ بِهِمُ الْكُفَّارَ وَعَدَ اللَّهُ الَّذِينَ آمَنُوا وَعَمِلُوا الصَّالِحَاتِ مِنْهُم

مَّغْفِرَةً وَأَجْرًا عَظِيمًا ﴿٢٩﴾

Muhammad, the Apostle of Allah,
and those who are with him
are hard against the faithless
and merciful amongst themselves.
You see them bowing and prostrating [in worship],
seeking Allah's grace and [His] pleasure.
Their mark is [visible] on their faces,
from the effect of prostration.
Such is their description in the Torah
and their description in the Evangel.
Like a tillage
that sends out its shoots and builds them up,
and they grow stout
and settle on their stalks,
impressing the sowers,
so that He may enrage the faithless by them.
Allah has promised those
of them who have faith and do righteous deeds
forgiveness and a great reward.

Surat al Mujadilah 58:22

لَّا تَجِدُ قَوْمًا يُؤْمِنُونَ بِٱللَّهِ وَٱلْيَوْمِ ٱلْءَاخِرِ يُوَآدُّونَ مَنْ حَآدَّ

ٱللَّهَ وَرَسُولَهُۥ وَلَوْ كَانُوٓا۟ ءَابَآءَهُمْ أَوْ أَبْنَآءَهُمْ أَوْ إِخْوَٰنَهُمْ

أَوْ عَشِيرَتَهُمْ أُو۟لَٰٓئِكَ كَتَبَ فِى قُلُوبِهِمُ ٱلْإِيمَٰنَ وَأَيَّدَهُم

بِرُوحٍ مِّنْهُ وَيُدْخِلُهُمْ جَنَّٰتٍ تَجْرِى مِن تَحْتِهَا ٱلْأَنْهَٰرُ خَٰلِدِينَ

فِيهَا رَضِىَ ٱللَّهُ عَنْهُمْ وَرَضُوا۟ عَنْهُ أُو۟لَٰٓئِكَ حِزْبُ ٱللَّهِ أَلَآ إِنَّ حِزْبَ

ٱللَّهِ هُمُ ٱلْمُفْلِحُونَ ﴿٢٢﴾

You will not find a people believing in Allah
and the Last Day
endearing those who oppose Allah and His Apostle
even though they were their own parents,
or children,
or brothers, or kinsfolk.
[For] such, He has written faith into their hearts
and strengthened them with a spirit from Him.
He will admit them into gardens
with streams running in them,
to remain in them [forever],
Allah is pleased with them,
and they are pleased with Him.
They are Allah's confederates.
Look!
The confederates of Allah are indeed felicitous!

Surat al Tawbah 9:100

وَٱلسَّٰبِقُونَ ٱلْأَوَّلُونَ مِنَ ٱلْمُهَٰجِرِينَ وَٱلْأَنصَارِ وَٱلَّذِينَ
ٱتَّبَعُوهُم بِإِحْسَٰنٍ رَّضِىَ ٱللَّهُ عَنْهُمْ وَرَضُوا۟ عَنْهُ وَأَعَدَّ لَهُمْ
جَنَّٰتٍ تَجْرِى تَحْتَهَا ٱلْأَنْهَٰرُ خَٰلِدِينَ فِيهَآ أَبَدًا ذَٰلِكَ ٱلْفَوْزُ
ٱلْعَظِيمُ ﴿١٠٠﴾

The early vanguard
of the Emigrants and the Helpers
and those who followed them in virtue,
Allah is pleased with them
and they are pleased with Him,
and He has prepared for them gardens
with streams running in them,
to remain in them forever.
That is the great success.

Ayatollah Agha Mahdi Puya wrote regarding this verse: This verse clearly proclaims the equality of *the muhajirs* (the emigrants) and *Ansar* (the helpers) in a general sense. The preference given to one individual over another by Allah (swt) or the Holy Prophet (pbuh) was due to the degree of submission to Allah (swt) and *Taqwa* (piety). So the argument put forward by Umar bin Khattab at the time of deciding the issue of taking hold of the reins of power in the conference hall of Saqifa bani Sa'ada by reciting this verse without *'WA'* after ansar to establish the superiority of *muhajirs* over *ansar* (if *WA* is dropped it means the *ansar* should obey or follow the *muhajirs*) was un-islamic or contrary to the teachings of the Qur'an.

This verse and other verses like it in praise of the companions of the Holy Prophet (pbuh), whether *muhajirs* or *ansar*, are applicable only to those who were **sincere in faith**. The hypocrites, who were also 'companions' (sahabah) as per its definition laid down by the Muslim scholars, cannot be accepted as those praised by the Qur'an. So to say that all the companions, even the deserters, we're true believers is illogical and contrary to historical facts.

All the commentators unanimously agree that "the first of the foremost" among women was Khadijah (SA), wife of the Holy Prophet (pbuh), and among men was Ali Ibn Abi Talib (as).

Hakim Nayshapuri, in his *Mustadrak Alal Sahihayn*, writes on page 22 of *kitab al Ma'rafat*:

"There is no difference of opinion among the historians that Ali Ibn Abi Talib was the first Muslim."

Ibn Abd al Bar, Qartabi, Suyuti, Tabarani, Bayhaqi and others also have confirmed it.

Among others refer to *Tarikh Tabari* vol. 2, page 63, for the authenticity of the tradition, according to which Ali was the first Muslim, and his faith was not only accepted by the Holy Prophet (pbuh) but also he was declared by him, whose words were always a revelation revealed (Qur'an 53:4), **to be his brother, a lieutenant and successor** and on that day obedience to him was made obligatory by the Holy Prophet (pbuh) for all the believers. Whosoever raises the issue of his age either does not know that whomsoever Allah (swt) wills He makes him His representative even if he is a baby in the cradle (Aly Imran 3:46 Jesus (as) was a messenger of Allah in the cradle just as he was a messenger of Allah in maturity), or with ulterior motives, wants to introduce someone else as the first Muslim.

The Holy Prophet (pbuh) said:

"Ali prayed with me seven years before the other Muslims. He is the Siddiq al Akbar (the greatest truthful) and the Faruq al Azam (the greatest distinguisher of truth from falsehood). Whoso claims either of these titles is a liar."

Source: Ayatollah Agha Mahdi Puya, *Tafsir of Holy Qur'an, Surah* 9, verse 100, P. 143-144.
http://www.islamicmobility.com/elibrary_14.htm

The **second category** of companions (those who were weak in faith, did not make any sacrifices, preferred to stay home during battles, left the Prophet (pbuh) defenseless in the battlefields, left the Prophet (pbuh) during Jumah prayers for a trade caravan, etc.) are discussed in several places in the holy Qur'an:

Surat al Tawbah 9:38-39

يَٰٓأَيُّهَا ٱلَّذِينَ ءَامَنُواْ مَا لَكُمْ إِذَا قِيلَ لَكُمُ ٱنفِرُواْ فِى

سَبِيلِ ٱللَّهِ ٱثَّاقَلْتُمْ إِلَى ٱلْأَرْضِ أَرَضِيتُم بِٱلْحَيَوٰةِ ٱلدُّنْيَا

مِنَ ٱلْأَخِرَةِ فَمَا مَتَٰعُ ٱلْحَيَوٰةِ ٱلدُّنْيَا فِى ٱلْأَخِرَةِ إِلَّا

قَلِيلٌ ﴿٣٨﴾

38 O you who have faith!
What is the matter with you
that when you are told:
'Go forth in the way of Allah,'
you sink heavily to the ground?
Are you pleased with the life of this world
instead of the Hereafter?
But the wares of the life of this world
compared with the Hereafter
are but insignificant.

إِلَّا نَنفِرُواْ يُعَذِّبْكُمْ عَذَابًا أَلِيمًا وَيَسْتَبْدِلْ قَوْمًا

غَيْرَكُمْ وَلَا تَضُرُّوهُ شَيْئًا وَٱللَّهُ عَلَىٰ كُلِّ شَىْءٍ

قَدِيرٌ ﴿٣٩﴾

39 If you do not go forth,
He will punish you with a painful punishment,
and replace you with another people,
and you will not hurt Him in the least,
and Allah has power over all things

Surat Aly Imran 3:153

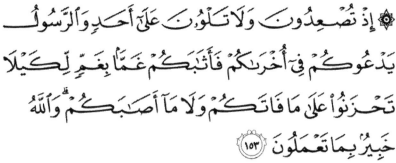

When you were fleeing
without paying any attention to anyone,
while the Apostle was calling you from your rear,
He requited you with grief upon grief,
so that you may not grieve for what you lose
nor for what befalls you,
and Allah is well aware of what you do.

(1) **Narrated by Uthman bin Abduallah bin Muhib:**

An Egyptian who came and performed the Hajj to the Ka'ba saw some people sitting. He inquired, "Who are these people?" Somebody said, "They are the tribe of Quraish." He said, "Who is the old man sitting amongst them?" The people replied, "He is Abdullah bin Umar." He said, *"O Ibn Umar! I want to ask you about something; please tell me about it. Do you know that Uthman fled away on the day (of the battle) of Uhud?"* Ibn Umar said, *"Yes."* The (Egyptian) man said, *"Do you know that Uthman was absent on the day (of the battle) of Badr and did not join it?"* Ibn Umar said, *"Yes."* The man said, *"Do you know that he failed to attend the Ar Ridwan pledge and did not witness it (i.e. Hudaibiya pledge of allegiance)?"* Ibn Umar said, *"Yes"* The man said, 'Allahu Akbar!' Ibn Umar said, "Let me explain to you (all these three things). As for his flight on the day of Uhud, I testify that Allah has excused him and forgiven him; and as for his absence from the battle of Badr, it was due to the fact that the daughter of Allah's Messenger (pbuh) was his wife and she was sick then. Allah's Messenger (pbuh) said to him, "You will receive the same reward and share (of the booty) as anyone of those who participated in the battle of Badr (if you stay with her). As for his absence from the Ar-Ridwan pledge of allegiance, had there been any person in Mecca more respectable than Uthman (to be sent as a representative). Allah's Messenger (pbuh) would have sent him instead of him. No doubt, Allah's Messenger (pbuh) had sent him, and the incident of the Ar-Ridwan pledge of Allegiance happened after 'Uthman had gone to Mecca. Allah's Messenger (pbuh) held out his right hand, saying, 'This is Uthman's hand.' He stroked his (other) hand with it, saying, this (pledge of allegiance) is on the behalf of Uthman. Then Ibn Umar said to the man, bear (these) excuses in mind with you (1).

Note: Indeed Allah (swt) excused the ones who ran away in the battle of Uhud, but historically there is no proof whatsoever that Uthman Ibn Affan actually fought and killed any enemies of Islam and that is why Prophet Muhammad (pbuh) sent him as an ambassador to Makkah (Quraish) during *Hudaibiya* pledge of allegiance, as he (pbuh) couldn't send someone who has actually killed any Quraish in the past battles, as an ambassador to them for a peace treaty. In the battle of Hunayn, Uthman Ibn Affan fled the battlefield once again (besides Khaybar) along with Umar bin Khattab.

(2) Narrated by Abu Qatada

We set out in the company of Allah's Messenger (pbuh) on the day (of the battle) of Hunain. When we faced the enemy, the Muslims retreated and I saw a pagan throwing himself over a Muslim. I turned around and came upon him from behind and hit him on the shoulder with the sword he (i.e. the pagan) came towards me and seized me so violently that I felt as if it were death itself, but death overtook him and he released me. I followed Umar bin Al Khattab and asked (him), "What is wrong with the people (fleeing)?" He replied, *"This is the Will of Allah,"*…

Note: Umar bin Khattab's reply '*This is the Will of Allah*' is clearly a lie against Allah (swt) as the Qur'an clearly states in:

Surat An Afal 8:15-16

يَـٰٓأَيُّهَا ٱلَّذِينَ ءَامَنُوٓاْ إِذَا لَقِيتُمُ ٱلَّذِينَ كَفَرُواْ زَحْفًا فَلَا تُوَلُّوهُمُ ٱلْأَدْبَارَ ﴿١٥﴾

15 O you who have faith!
When you encounter
the faithless advancing [for battle],
do not turn your backs [to flee] from them.

وَمَن يُوَلِّهِمْ يَوْمَئِذٍ دُبُرَهُۥٓ إِلَّا مُتَحَرِّفًا لِّقِتَالٍ أَوْ مُتَحَيِّزًا إِلَىٰ فِئَةٍ فَقَدْ بَآءَ بِغَضَبٍ مِّنَ ٱللَّهِ وَمَأْوَىٰهُ جَهَنَّمُ وَبِئْسَ ٱلْمَصِيرُ ﴿١٦﴾

16 Whoever turns his back [to flee] from them that day
unless [he is] diverting to fight
or retiring towards another troop—
shall certainly earn Allah's wrath,
and his refuge shall be hell, an evil destination.

Sources of hadith:

(1) *Sahih Bukhari*, Book 62, Hadith 49 *http://sunnah.com/urn/34507*

Sahih Bukhari, Book 64, Hadith 111
   http://sunnah.com/bukhari/64/111

Sunan Jami at Tirmidhi, Book 49, Hadith 4071
   http://sunnah.com/urn/635850

(2) *Sahih Bukhari*, Book 57, Hadith 50
   http://sunnah.com/bukhari/57/50

Muwatta Malik, Book 21, Hadith 18 *http://sunnah.com/urn/410000*

Sahih Bukhari, Book 64, Hadith 352
   http://sunnah.com/bukhari/64/352

Sahih Muslim, Book 32, Hadith 49 *http://sunnah.com/muslim/32/49*

Sunan Abu Dawood, Book 15, Hadith 241
   http://sunnah.com/abuDawood/15/241

Other verses about the second category:

Surat Muhammad 47:38

هَٰأَنتُمۡ هَٰٓؤُلَآءِ تُدۡعَوۡنَ لِتُنفِقُواْ فِى سَبِيلِ ٱللَّهِ فَمِنكُم مَّن
يَبۡخَلُ وَمَن يَبۡخَلۡ فَإِنَّمَا يَبۡخَلُ عَن نَّفۡسِهِۦ وَٱللَّهُ ٱلۡغَنِيُّ وَأَنتُمُ
ٱلۡفُقَرَآءُ وَإِن تَتَوَلَّوۡاْ يَسۡتَبۡدِلۡ قَوۡمًا غَيۡرَكُمۡ ثُمَّ لَا يَكُونُوٓاْ
أَمۡثَٰلَكُم ﴿٣٨﴾

Ah! There you are,
being invited to spend in the way of Allah;
yet among you there are those who are stingy;
and whoever is stingy is stingy only to himself.
Allah is the All-sufficient, and you are all-needy,
and if you turn away
He will replace you with another people,
and they will not be like you.

Surat al Jumuah 62:11

وَإِذَا رَأَوْا تِجَـٰرَةً أَوْ لَهْوًا ٱنفَضُّوٓا۟ إِلَيْهَا وَتَرَكُوكَ قَآئِمًا قُلْ مَا عِندَ ٱللَّهِ خَيْرٌ

مِّنَ ٱللَّهْوِ وَمِنَ ٱلتِّجَـٰرَةِ وَٱللَّهُ خَيْرُ ٱلرَّٰزِقِينَ ﴿١١﴾

When they sight a deal or a diversion,
they scatter off towards it
and leave you standing!
Say, 'What is with Allah
is better than diversion and dealing,
and Allah is the best of providers.'

Ayatollah Agha Mahdi Puya wrote regarding this verse: The believers are admonished not to get distracted by involvement in amusement and worldly gain at the cost of their duty to Allah (swt). Once when the Holy Prophet (pbuh) was offering the Friday prayers, a caravan entered the town singing, beating drums and playing musical instruments. According to Jabir, save twelve persons, including Jabir Ibn Abdullah, everyone who was in the congregation standing behind the Holy Prophet (pbuh) left the masjid and ran to witness the merry-making caravan and transact business with them. Thrice did the people behave like this, then this verse was revealed. According to Jabir, whenever the caravans came, all used to leave masjid save a very few.

Source: Ayatollah Agha Mahdi Puya, *Tafsir of Holy Qur'an, Surah* 62, verse 11, P. 143-144.
http://www.islamicmobility.com/elibrary_14.htm

The **third category** of companions is composed of the hypocrites, who implicitly wanted to destroy the religion of Islam from within, for such people Allah (swt) revealed a whole chapter in the Qur'an of **Surat al Munafiqoon** (the Hypocrites), which is at number 96 in the order of revelation, was revealed in Medina in the last years of the life of the Holy Prophet (pbuh). The Hypocrites are discussed in the holy Qur'an at several places:

Surat al Nisa 4:142

إِنَّ ٱلْمُنَٰفِقِينَ يُخَٰدِعُونَ ٱللَّهَ وَهُوَ خَٰدِعُهُمْ وَإِذَا قَامُوٓاْ إِلَى ٱلصَّلَوٰةِ

قَامُواْ كُسَالَىٰ يُرَآءُونَ ٱلنَّاسَ وَلَا يَذْكُرُونَ ٱللَّهَ إِلَّا قَلِيلًا ﴿١٤٢﴾

The hypocrites indeed seek to deceive Allah,
but it is He who outwits them.
When they stand up for prayer,
they stand up lazily, showing off to the people
and not remembering Allah except a little,

Surat al Tawbah 9:101

وَمِمَّنْ حَوْلَكُم مِّنَ ٱلْأَعْرَابِ مُنَٰفِقُونَ وَمِنْ أَهْلِ ٱلْمَدِينَةِ

مَرَدُواْ عَلَى ٱلنِّفَاقِ لَا تَعْلَمُهُمْ نَحْنُ نَعْلَمُهُمْ سَنُعَذِّبُهُم مَّرَّتَيْنِ ثُمَّ

يُرَدُّونَ إِلَىٰ عَذَابٍ عَظِيمٍ ﴿١٠١﴾

*101 **There are hypocrites among the Bedouins around you***
and among the townspeople of Madina,
steeped in hypocrisy.
You do not know them;
We know them,
and We will punish them twice,
then they shall be consigned to a great punishment.
Surat Aly Imran 3:144

وَمَا مُحَمَّدٌ إِلَّا رَسُولٌ قَدْ خَلَتْ مِن قَبْلِهِ ٱلرُّسُلُ أَفَإِيْن مَّاتَ أَوْ

قُتِلَ ٱنقَلَبْتُمْ عَلَىٰٓ أَعْقَٰبِكُمْ وَمَن يَنقَلِبْ عَلَىٰ عَقِبَيْهِ فَلَن يَضُرَّ

ٱللَّهَ شَيْئًا وَسَيَجْزِى ٱللَّهُ ٱلشَّٰكِرِينَ ﴿١٤٤﴾

Muhammad is but an apostle;
[other] apostles have passed before him.
If he dies or is slain,
will you turn back on your heels?
Anyone who turns back on his heels
will not harm Allah in the least,
and soon Allah will reward the grateful.

Surat al Tawbah 9:66-68

$$\text{لَا تَعْتَذِرُوا قَدْ كَفَرْتُم بَعْدَ إِيمَٰنِكُمْ إِن نَّعْفُ عَن طَآئِفَةٍ مِّنكُمْ}$$
$$\text{نُعَذِّبْ طَآئِفَةً بِأَنَّهُمْ كَانُوا مُجْرِمِينَ ﴿٦٦﴾}$$

66 *Do not make excuses.*
You have disbelieved after your faith.'
If We forgive a group among you,
We will punish another group,
for they have been guilty.

$$\text{ٱلْمُنَٰفِقُونَ وَٱلْمُنَٰفِقَٰتُ بَعْضُهُم مِّنۢ بَعْضٍ يَأْمُرُونَ}$$
$$\text{بِٱلْمُنكَرِ وَيَنْهَوْنَ عَنِ ٱلْمَعْرُوفِ وَيَقْبِضُونَ أَيْدِيَهُمْ}$$
$$\text{نَسُوا ٱللَّهَ فَنَسِيَهُمْ إِنَّ ٱلْمُنَٰفِقِينَ هُمُ}$$
$$\text{ٱلْفَٰسِقُونَ ﴿٦٧﴾}$$

67 *The hypocrites, men and women,*
are all alike:
they bid what is wrong
and forbid what is right;
and are tight-fisted.1
They have forgotten Allah,
so He has forgotten them.
The hypocrites are indeed the transgressors.

وَعَدَاللّهُ ٱلْمُنَافِقِينَ وَٱلْمُنَافِقَتِ وَٱلْكُفَّارَ نَارَ جَهَنَّمَ
خَالِدِينَ فِيهَا هِيَ حَسْبُهُمْ وَلَعَنَهُمُ ٱللّهُ وَلَهُمْ عَذَابٌ
مُّقِيمٌ ٦٨

68 Allah has promised the hypocrites, men and women,
and the faithless,
the Fire of hell,
to remain in it [forever].
That suffices them.
Allah has cursed them,
and there is a lasting punishment for them.

Surat al Tawbah 9:83

فَإِن رَّجَعَكَ ٱللّهُ إِلَىٰ طَآئِفَةٍ مِّنْهُمْ فَٱسْتَٔذَنُوكَ لِلْخُرُوجِ فَقُل لَّن
تَخْرُجُواْ مَعِيَ أَبَدًا وَلَن تُقَٰتِلُواْ مَعِيَ عَدُوًّا إِنَّكُمْ رَضِيتُم بِٱلْقُعُودِ أَوَّلَ
مَرَّةٍ فَٱقْعُدُواْ مَعَ ٱلْخَٰلِفِينَ ٨٣

If Allah brings you back [from the battlefront]
to a group of them
and they seek your permission to go forth,
say, 'You shall never go forth with me,
and you shall not fight with me against any enemy.
You were indeed pleased to sit back the first time,
so sit back with those who stay behind.'

Surat al Tawbah 9:74

يَحۡلِفُونَ بِٱللَّهِ مَا قَالُوا۟ وَلَقَدۡ قَالُوا۟ كَلِمَةَ ٱلۡكُفۡرِ وَكَفَرُوا۟

بَعۡدَ إِسۡلَٰمِهِمۡ وَهَمُّوا۟ بِمَا لَمۡ يَنَالُوا۟ وَمَا نَقَمُوٓا۟ إِلَّآ أَنۡ أَغۡنَىٰهُمُ ٱللَّهُ

وَرَسُولُهُۥ مِن فَضۡلِهِۦ فَإِن يَتُوبُوا۟ يَكُ خَيۡرًا لَّهُمۡ وَإِن يَتَوَلَّوۡا۟ يُعَذِّبۡهُمُ

ٱللَّهُ عَذَابًا أَلِيمًا فِى ٱلدُّنۡيَا وَٱلۡءَاخِرَةِ وَمَا لَهُمۡ فِى ٱلۡأَرۡضِ مِن وَلِىٍّ

وَلَا نَصِيرٍ ﴿٧٤﴾

They swear by Allah that they did not say it.
But they certainly did utter the word of unfaith
and renounced faith after their islam.
They contemplated what they could not achieve,
and they were vindictive only
because Allah and His Apostle had enriched them
out of His grace.
Yet if they repent, it will be better for them;
but if they turn away,
Allah shall punish them with a painful punishment
in this world and the Hereafter,
and they shall not find on the earth
any guardian or helper.

In the *Tafseer* (exegesis) of this verse (9:74) Ismail Ibn Kathir (*an author of classical Tafseer of the Qur'an from Ahle Sunnah*) wrote: "*It was reported that some hypocrites plotted to kill the Prophet (pbuh), while he was at the battle of Tabuk, riding one night. They were a group of more than ten men.*" Ad-Dahhak said, "*This Ayah was revealed about them.*" Ammar bin Yasir narrated in a Hadith collected by Muslim that Hudhayfah said to him that the Prophet said:

"Among my Companions are twelve hypocrites who will never enter Paradise or find its scent, until the camel enters the thread of the needle. Eight of them will be struck by the Dubaylah, which is a missile made of fire that appears between their shoulders and pierces their chest."

This is why Hudhayfah was called the holder of the secret, for he knew who these hypocrites were, since the Messenger of Allah gave their names to him and none else.(1)

Ibn Hajar in his book *Matalib Al-A'lia wrote:* Hudhaifah is one of the 14 noble companions of the Messenger of Allah (pbuh). The Messenger of Allah (pbuh) revealed to him the names of *the Munafiqeen* (the hypocrites), and protected him from the difficulties of the Hour, and Umar bin Khattab was swearing him by Allah (swt): *"Am I among these Munafiqeen?"* to which, Hudhaifah replied, *"By Allah (swt), no! I will never tell anyone after you."*(2)

Abu Tufail reported that there was a dispute between Hudhaifa and one of the people of Aqaba as it happens amongst people. He said:

> *"I adjure you by Allah to tell me as to how many people from Aqaba were. The people said to him (Hudhaifa) to inform him as he had asked. We have been informed that they were fourteen and if you are to be counted amongst them, then they would be fifteen and I state by Allah that twelve amongst them were the enemies of Allah and of His Messenger (pbuh) in this world."*(3)

Sunni Sources:

(1) Ismail Ibn Kathir, *Tafsir Ibn Kathir*, P. 2123, *http://www.kalamullah.com/Books/Tafsir%20Ibn%20Kathir%20 all%2010%20volumes.pdf*

(2) Ahmad bin Ali bin Hajar al Asqalani, *Matalib Al-A'lia.* Vol. 14, P. 702.

(3) *Sahih Muslim,* Book 51, Hadith 14, *http://sunnah.com/muslim/51/14*

Ten Granted Paradise

Sunni hadith literature famously names a list of "ten promised paradise" in *Jami al Tirmidhi, Sunan Ibn Majah* and *Musnad Ahmad Ibn Hanbal.*

Narrated Abdur-Rahman bin Awf:

The Messenger of Allah (pbuh) said: *"Abu Bakr is in Paradise, Umar is in Paradise, Uthman is in Paradise, Ali is in Paradise, Talhah is in Paradise, Az-Zubayr is in Paradise, Abdur-Rahman bin 'Awf is in Paradise, Sa'd bin Abi Waqqas is in Paradise, and Abu Ubaidah bin Al-Jarrah is in Paradise."*

Firstly, this hadith is considered a 'solitary report,' which, some theologians did not consider to be valid in establishing theological tenets. Secondly, the narrators (Abdur-Rahman bin Awf and Saeed bin Zaid bin Amr bin Nufail) have placed themselves in the list. In the light of the Qur'anic prohibition in **Surat al Najm 53:32**

So do not flaunt your piety

Since, attesting to one's own character has not been considered authoritative in legal disputes; this hadith is rejected since other trustworthy witnesses besides the claimants themselves have not collaborated it. There are several other issues, such as chain of narrators, putting Imam Ali's (as) famous rivals Talha and Zubayr in the list who were killed during fighting against Imam Ali (as) in the battle of Jamal.

Sources for the hadith:

Jami al Tirmidhi, Vol. 1, Book 46, Hadith 3747,
   http://sunnah.com/urn/636260

SunanIbn Majah, Book 1, Hadith 138,
   http://sunnah.com/urn/1251330

Musnad Ahmad Ibn Hanbal hadith 1631, P. 116
   *https://ia601702.us.archive.org/21/items/MusnadAhmadBinHan
   balArabicEnglishTranslation/Musnad%20Ahmad%20Bin%20Ha
   nbal%2C%20Arabic%20-English%20Translation-
   Volume%202_text.pdf*

Therefore, it is extremely important to look at the behavior, personalities, and characteristics, how the companions acted during the lifetime of the Holy Prophet (pbuh) and how they acted after his (pbuh) demise. Now, I'll discuss some of the most revered companions from the books of Ahle Sunnah to see how they acted during Prophet Muhammad's (pbuh) lifetime and after his (pbuh) demise. As recorded by al-Bukhari:

The Prophet (pbuh) said:

"I am your predecessor at the Lake-Fount, and some of you will be brought in front of me till I will see them and then they will be taken away from me and I will say, O Lord, my companions!" It will be said, **You do not know what they did after you had left.**

Sources:

Sahih Bukhari, Book 81, Hadith 164
   http://sunnah.com/bukhari/81/164

Sahih Bukhari, Book 92, Hadith 2 *http://sunnah.com/bukhari/92/2*

Sahih Bukhari, Book 81, Hadith 172
   http://sunnah.com/bukhari/81/172

Sahih Bukhari, Book 81, Hadith 181
   http://sunnah.com/bukhari/81/181

With slight variation in *Sahih Muslim*

".....My Lord, they are my followers and belong to my Umma, and it would be said to me: **Do you know what they did after you? By Allah, they did not do good after you, and they turned back upon their heels...***"*

Sources:

Sahih Muslim, Book 43, Hadith 33 *http://sunnah.com/muslim/43/33*

Sahih Muslim, Book 43, Hadith 34 *http://sunnah.com/muslim/43/34*

Sahih Muslim, Book 43, Hadith 31 *http://sunnah.com/muslim/43/31*

Taking companions as role models

Any educated follower of Ahlul Bayt (as) would acknowledge the merits of the companions of the Holy Prophet (pbuh). The virtuous and pious companions such as Abu Dhar al Ghaffari, Miqdad al Aswad, Salman al Muhammadi, Jabir bin Abdullah al Ansari, Jafar Ibn Abu Talib, **Hujr Ibn Adi al Kindi, Uwais al-Qarani, Ammar bin Yasir** (*whose Shrines were bombed, destroyed and graves were exhumed in Syria recently by the Wahabi/Salafi/al-Nusra/ISIS terrorists*), and many other prominent companions are venerated and taken as role models by the followers of Ahlul Bayt (as).

An educated follower of Ahlul Bayt (as) would also not deny the facts that under the caliphate of Abu Bakr and Umar the religion of Islam flourished throughout the Arabian Peninsula. Abu Bakr and Umar as caliphs lived simple lives, they conquered many areas, they struck fear in the hearts and minds of the enemies of Islam, and they have left an everlasting legacy in the Islamic history. But, Islam is not the religion to be spread far and wide by conquering lands, rather conquering hearts with the best of morals, kindness towards other, knowledge and by living a holistic way of lifestyle.

A true follower of Prophet Muhammad (pbuh) and his holy household (as) cannot put a blindfold on the way certain companions acted and treated the Prophet's (pbuh) family after his (pbuh) demise. Any companion regardless of what they may have contributed to the religion of Islam, if they insulted, disrespected or hurt Prophet Muhammad (pbuh), then they do not deserve any reverence what so ever.

Following are some of the examples from the six most authentic books of *Ahle Sunnah Wal Jam'a* and the history of Ibn Kathir and Tabari a well-known historian according to *Ahle Sunnah Wal Jam'a* about the well-known companions who insulted, disrespected the Prophet (pbuh) and his family, murdered, instigated affliction, usurped the rights, fought against other companions and committed mass atrocities in the name of Islam. Firstly;

Umar bin Khattab: during Prophet Muhammad's (pbuh) life.

It is very well-acknowledged by the historians, biographers, and the experts in the field of exegesis of the holy Qur'an that Umar bin Khattab used to raise his voice to Prophet Muhammad (pbuh) and around him. There are numerous incidences of such rudeness recorded in history, and criticized by Allah (swt) in the holy Qur'an

Surat Hujurat, 49:2

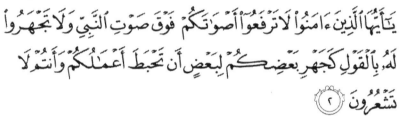

O you who have faith!
Do not raise your voices
above the voice of the Prophet,
and do not speak aloud to him
as you shout to one another,
lest your works should fail
without your being aware.

Muhammad Ibn Isa at-Tirmidhi has recorded that the warning in the aforementioned verse of the holy Qur'an was revealed when Abu Bakr and Umar started quarreling in front of the Holy Prophet (pbuh).

Source: *Jami at Tirmidhi* Book 47, Hadith 3576
  http://sunnah.com/urn/643020

Such quarreling and insults towards Prophet Muhammad (pbuh) is recorded, even in the last days of the Holy Prophet (pbuh). *Hadith e Qirtas* is very famous in *Sahih Bukhari* and *Sahih Muslim* that the Holy Prophet (pbuh) was on his deathbed and asked for pen and paper to write something for his companions, so **they won't go astray from the right path.** Umar bin Khattab along with a group of companions refused to fulfill Prophet's (pbuh) request, they quarreled in front of the Prophet (pbuh) so much that Prophet Muhammad (pbuh) asked all of them to go away.

Narrated by Ubaidullah bin Abdullah:

> Ibn Abbas said, *"When the ailment of the Prophet (pbuh) became worse, he said, bring for me (writing) paper and I will write for you a statement after which you will not go astray, but Umar said,* **The Prophet is seriously ill,** *and we have got Allah's Book with us and that is sufficient for us. The companions of the Prophet (pbuh) differed about this and there was a hue and cry. On that the Prophet (pbuh) said to them, Go away (and leave me alone). It is not right that you should* **quarrel** *in front of me."* Ibn Abbas came out saying, "It was most unfortunate (a great disaster) that Allah's Messenger (pbuh) was prevented from writing that statement for them because of their **disagreement and noise.**"

Sources:

Sahih Bukhari, Book 3, Hadith 56, *http://sunnah.com/bukhari/3/56*

Sahih Muslim, Book 25, Hadith 29 *http://sunnah.com/muslim/25/29*

Sahih Muslim, Book 25, Hadith 30 *http://sunnah.com/muslim/25/30*

In another translation to preserve the dignity of Umar bin Khattab, the publishers have taken his name out of this narration.

Narrated by Ibn Abbas

Thursday! And how great that was Thursday! The ailment of Allah's Messenger (pbuh) became worse (on Thursday) and he said, fetch me something so that I may write to you something after which you will never go astray. The people (present there) differed in this matter, and it was not right to differ before a prophet. Some said, "What is wrong with him? **He is delirious (seriously ill)** *Ask him (to understand his state)."* So they went to the Prophet (pbuh) and asked him again. The Prophet (pbuh) said, *"Leave me, for my present state is better than what you call me for."*

Source:

Sahih Bukhari, Book 64, Hadith 453
http://sunnah.com/bukhari/64/453

Also in *Sahih Bukhari,* Book 54, Hadith 19, under the chapter of *the conditions of Jihad and peace treaties,* Narrated Al-Miswar bin Makhrama and Marwan that after reporting the episode of the treaty of al-Hudaybiyya and Umar bin Khattab's opposition to what the Prophet of Allah (pbuh) had agreed to, he doubted him, saying to him openly: ***"Aren't you truly the Apostle of Allah?"*** to the end of the story... Al-Bukhari wrote: When they finished the matter of writing down the terms [of the treaty], the Prophet of Allah (pbuh) said to his companions: *"Get up and' slaughter your sacrifices and get your head shaved."* Umar said: ***"By Allah none of them got up, and the Prophet repeated his order thrice..."***

Source:

Sahih Bukhari, Book 54, Hadith 19 *http://sunnah.com/bukhari/54/19*

After Prophet Muhammad's (pbuh) demise

The day after the Saqifah, Umar Ibn al Khattab, along with a group of individuals came to the house of the daughter of the Holy Prophet (pbuh). In the house, there was Ali Ibn Abi Talib (as), Fatima (as), and their two sons, Hassan (as) and Hussain (as), who were still in a state of deep sorrow over the death of the Prophet (pbuh)

Fatima (as) opened the door and asked Umar, "Did you come here to burn our house?" 'Umar retorted, "Yes, unless you enter into what the nation entered in [meaning allegiance to Abu Bakr]." 'Umar then slammed open the door against Fatima (as) at which point she found herself being squeezed between the door and the wall of her house, causing one of her ribs to break. At that time, she was pregnant with the third grandson of the Holy Prophet (pbuh); however, the force that Umar applied on the door caused her to have a miscarriage, and the baby who had been named Muhsin by the Prophet (pbuh), was stillborn only a few days after the death of his grandfather.

Source:

Sayed Mustafa al-Qazwini (2009), *When Power and Piety Collide. Chapter 5: Backlash.* P. 35. ISBN: 978-0-9711538-0-6. Publisher Islamic Publishing House.

Other Sources:

Muhammad Ibn Jarir al-Tabari, *The History of al-Tabari* Vol. 9 *The Last Years of the Prophet: The Formation of the State A.D. 630-632/A.H. 8-11.* Translated by Ismail K. Poonawala, ISBN 10: 0-88706-691-7. SUNY Press Publishers, NY.

Wilferd Madelung (1997), *The Succession to Muhammad: A Study of the Early Caliphate.* P. 43-44, 78-311. ISBN-0521646960. Publisher: Cambridge University Press

Edward Gibbon (1788), *Decline and Fall of the Roman Empire* Vol. 5. *http://www.sacredtexts.com/cla/gibbon/05/daf05013.htm*

Denise L Soufi (1997), The image of Fatima in classical Muslim thought. P. 206.Published by: Princeton University, NJ

Lesley Hazleton (2009), *After the Prophet: The Epic Story of the Shia-Sunni Split in Islam,* P. 71-73. ISBN: 0385523939, Publisher: Doubleday

Fatima (sa) vs. Abu Bakr

No one (who knows Islamic history and literature) can deny the fact that **lady Fatima (SA) died angry with Abu Bakr and Umar**. After the demise of Prophet Muhammad (pbuh), Abu Bakr usurped Lady Fatima's (sa) property (Fadak) and the rights of Ahlul Bayt (as). Abu Bakr concocted a lie against Prophet Muhammad (pbuh) by saying "Prophets do not leave behind inheritance" even though Lady Fatima (as) proved him wrong from the holy Qur'an that *Solomon inherited from David* (27:16) And *John inherited Zechariah* (19:6); yet Abu Bakr did not return lady Fatima's (as) property to her and she died angry with Abu Bakr and Umar and did not allow them to come to her funeral (*Bukhari,* and *Muslim*); and the biggest proof for the travesties conducted by Abu Bakr is that "no one until today knows, where exactly is Lady Fatima (sa) buried?"

Sources:

Sahih Bukhari, Book 85, Hadith 3, *http://sunnah.com/bukhari/85/3*

Sahih Bukhari, Book 57, Hadith 2, *http://sunnah.com/bukhari/57/2*

Sahih Bukhari, Book 62, Hadith 62,
  http://sunnah.com/bukhari/62/62

Sahih Muslim, Book 32, Hadith 61 *http://sunnah.com/muslim/32/61*

Sahih Muslim, Book 32, Hadith 63, *http://sunnah.com/muslim/32/63*

Sunan Jami at Tirmidhi, Book 21, Hadith 72
  http://sunnah.com/tirmidhi/21/72

Sunan Jami at Tirmidhi, Book 21, Hadith 71
  http://sunnah.com/tirmidhi/21/71

Sunan an Nasai, Book 36, Hadith 6, *http://sunnah.com/nasai/36/6*

Question:

Who is Lady Fatima's Imam after the demise of Holy Prophet (pbuh)?

If one says Abu Bakr was her Imam! than how is it *"the woman, who was declared as one of the four women of the Paradise"* and *"leader of all women of the paradise"* could die angry with her Imam (Abu Bakr)?

If one is to say, it was Imam Ali (as), as she went to Abu Bakr to defend her Imam's rights, which he rejected, then why shouldn't one follow the daughter of the Holy Prophet (pbuh) as an example?

Source of the Hadith:

Sahih Bukhari, Book 79, Hadith 58 *http://sunnah.com/bukhari/79/58*

Sahih Muslim, Book 44, Hadith 144
   http://sunnah.com/muslim/44/144

Extracts of Lady Fatima's (SA) Speech to Abu Bakr (known as Fadak sermon)

Sayyidah Fatima Az-Zahra (as) began her speech by Praising and Eulogizing for the Lord and Witness of the Unity of Allah and the Prophethood of Muhammad; she (as) continued her speech with reminding Muslims of their duties, about the decisiveness of the Prophethood of Prophet Muhammad (pbuh) and the role of Imam Ali (as) in defending Islam from day one, and criticized the treacherous behavior of Abu Bakr, Umar and those who usurped her rights by saying:

   ...Now you presume that we do not have any inheritance from the Prophet - do you follow the customs of the (age of) ignorance? Is it the judgement of (the days of) ignorance (the Pagan era) that they desire? Who (else) can be better than Allah to judge for the people of assuring faith? (5:50) Indeed, it is as bright as the sun that I am the daughter of the Prophet of Allah.

   O Muslims! Is it befitting that I am deprived of my inheritance? O son of Abu Quhafah (Abu Bakr)! Is it contained in the Glorious Qur'an that one should inherit from their father; while in your opinion, I should not inherit from my father? Indeed, you have come with an unusual thing (19:27) (attributed) upon Allah and

His Prophet. Did you then intentionally forsake the Book of Allah and leave it behind your backs? Allah says: And Sulayman inherited Dawood (27:16); in regards to the life of Zakariyyah, He says: (So grant me from Yourself an heir who shall inherit from me and inherit from the family of Ya'qub (19:5-6); 'Allah also says: (And the blood relations are nearer to each other in the Book of Allah (8:75); Allah says: (Allah enjoins upon you about your children - the male shall have the equal of the shares of two females (4:11); and He also says, (If he (the believer) leaves behind any goods that he makes a bequest for parents and (the nearest) kinsmen in goodness (this is) a duty upon the pious ones (2:180).

You assume that I do not have a share and an allowance (in the inheritance) and that I should not inherit from my father and that there is no relation between us? Has Allah in His verses (of the Qur'an) not taken into consideration, everyone in general and are not all (of the) classes of men included in these verses? Is my father discharged from the applicability of this verse, or do you say that two people of the same community do not inherit from one another? Are my father and I not a part and parcel of one community?

Then, are you more cognizant of understanding the general and particular verses of the Qur'an than my father and my cousin (Imam Ali)? Then take it (Fadak) until we meet you on the Day of Judgement - where Allah will be the Best Judge, and Muhammad will be the claimant on that day, and our destined time of meeting will be the Resurrection and on that promised day, the fallacious ones will be engulfed in deep loss and their regret (on that day) will be of no use to them! For every prophecy, there is a (prefixed) time (6:67) and you will soon realize upon whom a torment (of tribulations) will descend which will disgrace him, and on who falls this lasting punishment..."

Lady Fatima (sa) finished her speech with the following:

...Be aware! I have said what I wanted to say, even though I know

that you will not assist me as this slackness of yours to assist us has become a part of your heart (your practice). But all of this complaint is the result of the grief of the heart and the internal rage (that I feel) and (I know that) it is of no use, but I have said this to manifest my internal sorrow and to complete my proof upon you.

Thus usurp it (Fadak) and fasten it firmly, for it is weak and feeble, while its a shame and disgrace will always remain over you. The sign of the rage of the Supreme Allah has been cast upon it, and it will be an everlasting disgrace upon you, and it will lead you to the fire of Allah, which will engulf the heart. Thus Allah sees whatever you do,

'And soon shall those who deal unjustly know what an (evil) turning they will be turned into.' (26:227)

I am the daughter of that Prophet (pbuh) who was sent to warn you against the severe wrath of Allah,

(Act (you) whatever you can, and verily we (too) act, and wait, indeed we too are waiting." (10:121-122)

Source: The Historic Fadak Sermon of Fatima *http://www.al-islam.org/fatimiyyah-ashura-lutfullah-safi-al-gulpaygani/historic-fadak-sermon-fatima*

Imam Ali (as) vs. Talha and Zubair

As mentioned in the previous Chapter, Ayesha binte Abu Bakr along with Talha Ibn Ubaydullah and Zubayr Ibn al-Awwam led an Army to fight Imam Ali Ibn Abi Talib (as) in the Battle of the Camel. Imam Ali (as) reminded them of his merits and virtues and warned them about the consequences of fighting against him; yet they persisted in fighting him.

Prophet Muhammad (pbuh) has said:

Ali is with the Truth and the Truth is with Ali (1)

Ali is with the truth and the truth is with Ali. They will not separate from each other, even as they reach the spring in Heaven. (2)

O Ali, very soon you will be put to fight with a group of tyrants, but you will be on the right. On that day, whoever forsakes you shall not be reckoned among my people. (3)

Then how could it be that those who fought against Imam Ali (as) could also be deemed as virtuous and pious and after death end up in the Paradise, whereas in this world wanted to kill him?

Source:

1. Matbaah al-Islamiyah, *Ihqaq al-Haqq*, Vol. 5, P 637
2. Shaykh Abd al-Latif Ibn abu Jami al-Amili, *Jami al-Akhbar*, P 51
3. Matbaah al-Islamiyah, *Ihqaq al-Haqq*, Vol. 5, P 635

Abu Dhar (ra) vs. Uthman Ibn Affan

Prophet Muhammad (pbuh) said, praising Abu Dhar al-Ghaffari (ra):
Heaven has not shaded, nor has the earth carried a person more straightforward than Abu Dhar. He walks on earth with the immaterialistic attitude of Jesus, the son of Mary.

Source:

Sahih al-Tirmidhi, v5, p334, Tradition #3889

Musnad Ahmad Hanbal, #6519, #6630, #7078

When Abu Dhar noticed the extreme nepotism, corruption, and usurpation of Muslims's rights under the caliphate of Uthman Ibn Affan, he didn't stay quiet. Abu Dhar al-Ghaffari (Ra) spoke out against Uthman Ibn Affan for his favoritism towards the most corrupt, mischief-makers of the time of Prophet Muhammad (pbuh) such as Marwan bin Hakam whom the Prophet (pbuh) exiled from Medina was brought back into Medina by Uthman and was given 100,000 Dirham as a gift. Uthman made Ibn Abi Sarh (an apostate) the governor of Egypt, and Walid Ibn Uqba, whom Allah (swt) called *Fasiq* (a wicked person) in the Quran 49:6 was made the governor of Kufa. Upon such atrocities, Abu Dhar al-Ghaffari (Ra) protested, rallied the people and spoke out against all of the corrupt actions of Uthman Ibn Affan upon, which he was beaten, exiled and banished to Rabdha where he died of starvation.

Source: Dr. A. Asadi (2012) *Shi'ah Islam.*Chapters 62-67, ISBN-10: 1879402424. Publisher: Tahrike Tarsile Qur'an

Malik Ibn Nuwayrah vs. Khalid bin Waleed

Khalid bin Waleed accepted Islam in the 17th year of the Prophetic mission. Prior to joining Islam, Khalid fought against Prophet Muhammad (pbuh) to eradicate the message of Islam. After Khalid joined Islam, he was made a commander to fight in several battles for the sake of Islam. In the battle of Mutah and Hunayn, just like others Khalid too showed cowardice and ran away from the battlefield. After Abu Bakr became the caliph, he made Khalid, the general of his army.

Malik Ibn Nuwayrah was a chief of Banu Yarbu. During the lifetime of Prophet Muhammad, he was the tax-collector for his tribe. Ibn Khalikan, the historian, says that Malik Ibn Nuwayrah was a man of high rank in Arabia. He was a famous cavalier, a knight, a distinguished poet and a friend of Muhammad Mustafa (pbuh).

Ibn Hajar Asqalani says in his biography of the companions that when Malik accepted Islam, the Apostle of God (pbuh) appointed him a Revenue Officer for the tribe of Banu Yerbo. He collected taxes from his tribe, and sent them to Medina, but when he heard the news of the death of the Apostle (pbuh), he stopped collecting taxes, and said to his tribesmen that before making any remittances to Medina, he wanted to know how the new government in the City of the Prophet had taken shape.

Malik did not pay taxes to the new government in Medina, and Abu Bakr sent a punitive force under the command of Khalid bin al-Walid to assert his authority, and to collect the defaulted taxes.

Khalid had a brief meeting with Malik, and the latter knew that he was going to be killed. Some historians say that Khalid was in love with Malik's wife, and he ordered his execution. Malik turned to his wife, and said: "You are the one to bring death upon me."

Khalid denied this and said: "No. You have become an apostate, and your apostasy is responsible for your death." Though Malik protested that he was a Muslim, Khalid did not listen, and the former was executed.

Abu Qatada Ansari was a companion of the Prophet. He came with Khalid from Medina. He was so shocked at Malik's murder by Khalid that he immediately returned to Medina, and told Abu Bakr that he would not serve under a commander who had killed a Muslim.

After killing Malik Ibn Nuwayrah, Khalid raped his widow. In Medina, Umar was so scandalized that he demanded, from Abu Bakr, the immediate dismissal of Khalid. He said that Khalid had to be put on trial for the twin crimes of murder and adultery. According to Islamic law, Khalid had to be stoned to death. But Abu Bakr defended Khalid, and said that he had simply made "an error of judgment."

The tribesmen of Banu Yerbo had withheld taxes (zakat) but apart from that they were Muslims in every sense of the term. Abu Qatada himself testified that he heard the Adhan (the call to prayer) in the village of Malik, and saw his tribesmen offering congregational prayers. Even so, Khalid ordered his troops to massacre them.

Tabari writes in his *History* that when Khalid and his troops entered the Banu Yerbo territory, they said to the tribesmen: "We are Muslims." They said: "We are also Muslims." Khalid's men asked: "If you are Muslims, why are you bearing arms? There is no war between us. Lay down your weapons so that we may all offer our prayers."

The tribesmen put down their weapons. But no sooner had they done so, then Khalid's warriors seized them, bound them, and let them to shiver in the cold night. On the following morning, they were all put to death. Khalid then plundered their houses, captured their women and children, and brought them as prisoners of war to Medina.

Source: Sayed Ali Asgher Razwy, *A Restatement of the History of Islam and Muslims.* P. 261. *http://www.al-ijtihad.com/library/history%20of%20islam/History%20Of%20Islam_book.pdf*

This incident is mentioned in the <u>History of Tabari</u> (English, Vol 10, Translated by Fred M. Donner), <u>Tareekh Ibn Kathir</u> (Arabic only) and <u>Musnad by Ahmad Ibn Hanbal</u> (Arabic only): All three are books of Ahle Sunnah Wal Jam'a.

Some unanswered questions

- On what basis did Abu Bakr allow a murder of a human yet alone a Muslim, for not paying the taxes to be ok?
- Why did Abu Qatada Ansari leave the ranks of Khalid, if Khalid did not do anything wrong by killing an apostate?
- Why would a newly-widowed Layla bint al Minhal "marry" the killer of her husband immediately after her husband was murdered?
- Why did Umar bin Khattab wanted to dismiss Khalid from the ranks of the army and punish him for his crimes?

End of Chapter notes:

10 virtues of Imam Ali (as) <u>no other companion</u> of the Holy Prophet (pbuh) can match

1. **Birth inside the Kaaba:** Imam Ali (as) is the only person who was born inside the walls of the Kaaba. Imam Ali (as) was born on Friday, 13th of Rajab, 12 years before the proclamation of the Messengership.

2. **First to Proclaim Islam:** Prophet Muhammad (pbuh) said: *'Ali is the first to declare his faith'* and *'If everything on Earth and in the Skies is kept on one side of the scale and Ali's faith is kept on the other side, the balance would surely tilt towards Ali's faith'*

3. **Night of Migration:** on the night when Ali (as) replaced the Prophet (pbuh) and spent that night in his bed, God said Gabriel and Michael, 'Today, I have established brotherhood between you two and I have extended your lives, one longer than the other. Of the two of you which one will sacrifice his life for the sake of the other?' Both of them said that they loved their life and refused to part with their life for the sake of another. Then God said, 'Won't you be like Ali, whom I made Muhammad's brother and he preferred the Prophet's life to his own and slept on the Prophet's bed exposing himself to the risk of being mistaken to be the Prophet and thus slain?
Go down to Earth and protect him from the mischief of his enemies.' Gabriel stood at the head and Michael stood at the foot of the bed, even as Imam Ali (as) slept on the Prophet's (pbuh) bed. They said, 'Congratulations, Ali! God joins His angels in praising you.' At that time, this verse was revealed.

Surat al Baqirah 2:207

And among the people is he who sells his soul
seeking the pleasure of Allah,
and Allah is most kind to [His] servants.

4. **Pact of Brotherhood:** When Prophet Muhammad (pbuh) migrated to Medina, he established the infamous 'pact of brotherhood' between *al-muhajiroon* (the emigrants) and *al-ansaar* (the helpers); but for Imam Ali (as) he declared him as his brother in this world and in the hereafter. Prophet Muhammad (pbuh) said: *'God has ordered me to choose you as my brother and my legatee. You are my nominee and successor during my life and after I die. Whoever obeys you, is deemed to have obeyed me and whoever disobeys you is deemed to have disobeyed me; whoever refutes you has in fact refuted me; whoever oppresses you is deemed to have oppressed me. O Ali, you are from me and I am from you...'*

5. **Bravery in the battles:** No one comes near the bravery, valor and chivalry of Imam Ali (as) in all of the battles Imam Ali (as) participated in.

   Prophet Muhammad (pbuh) said: *'A single blow of Ali with his sword upon Amr Ibn Abd-Wudd on the day of the Battle of the Ditch (AKA Trench, Khandaq, Confederates, Ahzab) is more precious than all the good deeds of my community until doomsday.'*

6. **Marriage to Lady Fatima (as):** Imam al-Sadiq (as) said: *'Had God, not created Ali (as), there would have been no ideal pair of Fatima (SA) right from Adam (as) until death.'*

7. **Prophet's (pbuh) *Nafs* at *Mubahilah*:** As explained in Chapter 3 of this book, when the Holy Prophet (pbuh) was commanded by Allah (swt) to enter into *Mubahilah* (Malediction, asking Allah (swt) to remove His mercy from the opposite party) with the Christians of Najran in the verses:

Surat Aly Imran 3:61

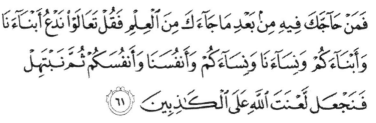

Should anyone argue with you concerning him,
after the knowledge that has come to you,
say, 'Come! Let us call our sons and your sons,
our women and your women,
our souls and your souls,
then let us pray earnestly
and call down Allah's curse upon the liars.

Prophet Muhammad (pbuh) took Imam Ali (as) as his Nafs (self or soul) to the event; which is a clear proof for the believers that only the *Nafs* of the Prophet (pbuh) can take his place after his demise.

8. **Ali on the shoulders of the Holy Prophet (pbuh):** On the day of the conquest of Mecca, the Prophet (pbuh) lifted Imam Ali (as) onto his shoulders to bring down an idol sitting on a high pillar outside of the Holy Kaaba, at that moment Imam Ali (as) said: *'God has blessed me through you that if I wanted I could touch the farthest skies.'*

9. **Imam Ali's Spirituality:** When it comes to the Spirituality, no companion can come near the merits of spirituality with Imam Ali (as). None of the companions of the Holy Prophet (pbuh) have left any *Duas* for his Ummah other than Imam Ali (as). The *Duas* (supplication, invocations, prayers and praises for Allah (swt)) Imam Ali (as) have left behind for the believers not only touch the heart of believer, but also give guidance and show a path towards forgiveness for a believer. Some of those supplications are: *Dua Kumayl, Dua Sabah, Dua Mashlool, Munajat of Masjid-e-Kufa, etc.*

These supplications can be found in a published book titled: *Sahifa Alawiya* by Amirul Mo-mineen Ali Ibne Abi Talib (a.s.). PDF link:
http://www.duas.org/pdfs/SahifaAlawiya.pdf

Links for other duas:

http://www.duas.org/alaviya/

http://www.duas.org/ramazan/munajaat_e_amir.htm

http://www.haydarya.com/maktaba_moktasah/09/book_06/ Sahifa_e_Alawiya%20ar%20eng.pdf

10. **Eloquence:** Imam Ali (as) is the peak of eloquence. He (as) has given the most magnificent sermons not only in just his time when in the entire history of mankind. There are over 200 sermons and close to 80 letters written by Imam Ali (as) recorded in the book *Nahjul Balagha,* which no companion of the Holy Prophet (pbuh) can come close to. Out of those hundreds of magnificent sermons of Imam Ali (as) here are two examples:

A sermon without any dots: there are 28 alphabets in the Arabic language out of those 15 contains dots. Imam Ali (as) gave this sermon without any preparation, rehearsal or thought:

الخطبة العارية عن النقطة للإمام علي (عليه السلام)

الحمد لله الملك المحمود والمالك الودود مصور كل مولود مآل كل مطرود ساطح المهاد وموطد الأوطاد ومرسل الأمطار ومسهل الأوطار عالم الأسرار ومدركها ومدمر الأملاك ومهلكها ومكور الدهور ومكررها ومورد الأمور ومصدرها عم سماحه وكمل ركابه وهمل وطاوع السؤال والأمل أوسع الرمل وأرسل أحمده حمدا ممدودا وأوحده كما وحد الأواه و هو الله لا إله للأمم سواه ولا صادع لما عد له وسواه أرسل محمدا علما للاسلام وإماما للحكام ومسددا للرعاء ومعطل أحكام ود وسواع أعلم وعلم وحكم وأحكم أصل الأصول ومهد وأكد الموعود وأوعد أوصل الله له الأكرام وأودع روحه السلام ورحم آله وأهله الكرام

ما لمع رائل وملع دال وطلع هلال وسمح اهلال.

اعملوا رعاكم الله اصلح الأعمال واسلكوا مسالك الحلال واطرحوا الحرام ودعوه واسمعوا أمر الله وعوه وصلوا الأرحام وراعوها وعاصوا الأهواء واردعوها وصاهروا أهل الصلاح والورع وصارموا رهط المهر والطمع ومصاهركم أطهر الأحرار مولدا وأسراهم سؤددا وأحلاهم موردا وها هو أمكم وحل حرمكم مملكا عروسكم المكرمه وماهر لها كما مهر رسول الله أم سلمه وهو أكرم صهر أودع الأولاد وملك ما أراد وماسها مملكه ولا وهم ولا وكس ملاحمه ولا وصم اسأل الله لكم احماد وصاله ودوام اسعاده وألهم كلا اصلاح حاله والاعداد لمآله ومعاده وله الحمد السرمد والمدح لرسوله أحمد (ص).

Translation:

All praise be to Allah: the praised King, the affectionate Owner, the Fashioner of all who are born, the Recourse for every downtrodden, the Outstretched of lands, the Establisher of firm mountains, the Sender of rain, the Alleviator of difficulties, the Knower and Perceiver of secrets, the Destroyer of kingdoms and Perisher of possessions, the Renewal of eras and their Repeater, the Source of all things and their Destination. Widespread is His generosity and sufficient are the layered clouds and the supply of rain. He responds to the one who asks or hopes, giving wide and with abundance.

I praise Him endlessly. I consider Him one as He is considered one by those who turn to Him. Lo! He is Allah, there is no god for the nations except Him. No one can distort what He set upright and established. He sent Muhammad as the standard-bearer of submission (*Islam*), the leader for the rulers and preventer of their oppression, the crippler of the authorities of *Wudd* and *Sawa`* (two idols). He informed and educated, appointed and perfected. He founded the fundamentals and eased them in. He emphasized the appointed promise (Day of Judgment) and forewarned. Allah has linked him with honor and granted his soul the peace, and may Allah have mercy on his progeny and his venerated family; as long as the guiding stars shine, the crescent continues to rise, and the chant of the oneness (*La ilaha illa Allah*) is made to be heard around.

May God protect you! Work towards the best of deeds. So tread the path seeking the lawful, and give up the forbidden and abandon it. Listen to the command of Allah and be aware of it. Maintain the ties with relations and nurture them. Disobey desires and repel them. Bond as kins with the righteous and pious, and discontinue the company of amusement and greed.

Your groom is the most impeccable of free men by birth, most generous and honorable with glories, and of the sweetest of descent. Here he came to you, took your kin with permission, in marriage, the gracious bride. Offered a dowry, just as the Messenger of Allah did to Umm Salamah. Certainly, he [s] was the most gracious son-in-law. Kind to his progeny. He gave them in marriage to whom he wanted. He was neither confused in his choice of wife nor had an oversight.

I ask Allah, on your behalf, for the lasting graciousness of His connection. And the continuation of His pleasures, and that He may inspire all: the reform of their own condition, and the preparation for their individual destiny and the hereafter. Gratitude is for Him forever and the praise for His Messenger Ahmad (pbuh).

Source:

http://www.al-islam.org/nutshell/files/nodots.pdf

A sermon without the letter *Alif*:

حمدت من عظمت منته، و سبغت نعمته، و سبقت غضبه رحمته، و تمت
كلمته، و نفذت مشيته، و بلغت حجته (قضيته)، و عدلت قضيته. حمدته حمد
مقر بربوبيته، متخضع لعبوديته، متنصل من خطيئته، معترف بتوحيده، مستعيذ من
وعيده، مؤمل من ربه رحمة (مغفرة) تنجيه، يوم يشغل كل عن فصيلته و بنيه، و
نستعينه و نسترشده و نستهديه، و نؤمن به و نتوكل عليه. و شهدت له تشهد
عبد مخلص موقن، و فردته تفريد مؤمن متق و وحدته توحيد عبد مذعن، ليس له
شريك في ملكه و لم يكن له ولي في صنعه؛ جل عن مشير و وزير، و تنزه عن
مثل وعون و معين و نظير، علم فستر و بطن فخبر، و نظر فجبر، و ملك
فقهر؛ و عصي فغفر، و عبد فشكر، و حكم فعدل، و تكرم و تفضل،. لن يزول
و لم يزل، ليس كمثله شيء، و هو قبل كل شيء و بعد كل شيء رب متفرد
بعزته، متمكن بقوته، متقدس بعلوه، متكبر بسموه، ليس يدركه بصر و لم يحط
به نظر، قوي منيع، بصير سميع، حليم حكيم، رؤوف رحيم، عجز عن وصفه من
وصفه، و ظل نعته من نعته، وصل به من نعمته من يعرفه، قرب فبعد، و بعد
فقرب، يجيب دعوة من يدعوه، و يرزق عبده و يحبوه، ذو لطف خفي، و بطش
قوي، و رحمة موسعة، و عقوبة موجعة، و رحمته جنة عريضة مونقة، و عقوبته
جحيم موصدة موبقة (موثقة).

I praise the One Whose benefits are great, whose blessings overwhelms, whose mercy is faster than His anger, the One whose word is perfect, whose will is affected, whose argument (issue) is wise, whose case is just. I praise Him like one recognizing His Godhead, submissive while adoring Him, dissociating himself from his sin, recognizing His Unity, seeking refuge with Him against His warning, hopeful for the mercy (forgiveness) of his Lord that saves him [from the Fire] on a Day when everyone will be distracted even from his offspring and tribe. We seek His help, guidance and directions. We believe in Him and depend on Him. I have testified to Him as a sincere and convinced servant/slave; I recognize His Uniqueness as a pious believer, and I have recognized His Unity like a submissive servant/slave.

He has no partner in His domain; He relies on none in doing whatever He does. He is exalted above having an adviser or a vizier. He is above using a model or an assistant or a helper or a peer. He knows, so He covers; He is acquainted with the innermost, so He is most familiar [with our intentions]. He cast a look, so He assisted; He owns everything, so He subdues. He is disobeyed, yet He forgives; He is adored, so He thanks. He rules, so He affects justice, and He is generous and grants favors.

He shall never come to an end, and He has always been as He is; there is nothing like Him. He, first and foremost, is a unique Lord in His exaltation, able through His might, holy through His sublimity, proud of His Majesty; no (mental) vision can realize Him, nor can anyone ever see Him. He is strong, invincible, seeing, hearing, clement, wise, affectionate and kind. One who attempts to describe Him can never do so; one who attempts to describe His attributes can never do so [either]. His blessing reaches those who get to know Him: He is near, so He is far [above mental or physical vision]; He is far yet He is near [closer to us than anything else].

He responds to the call of those who call on Him; He sustains His servant and surrounds him with His love; His niceties are hidden [from our comprehension]; His power is mighty; His mercy is wide; His penalty is painful; His mercy is a broad and a Garden of grandeur (Paradise); His punishment is Hell filled with horrors and chains.

و شهدت بعث محمد (ص) عبده و رسوله، و نبيه و صفيه و حبيبه و خليله،
صلة تحظيه، و تزلفه و تعليه، و تقربه و تدنيه، بعثه في خير عصر و حين فترة
كفر، رحمة لعبيده و منة لمزيده، ختم به نبوته، و قوى (وضح) به حجته، فوعظ
و نصح و بلغ و كدح، رؤوف بكل مؤمن رحيم، رضي ولي سخي زكي، عليه
رحمة و تسليم و بركة و تكريم، من رب غفور رؤوف رحيم، قريب مجيب
حكيم.

I have testified that He sent Muhammed (pbuh) as His servant and messenger, prophet, chosen one, loved one, friend, a link [with the Almighty] that grants him [Muhammed] fortune, bringing him closer to Him, elevating him, granting him nearness and closeness [to the

Almighty]. He sent him during a good (opportune) period of time, when there was disbelief, as a mercy for His servants and a boon for more.

Through him He sealed His prophetic messages, strengthened (explained) His argument. So he admonished, advised, conveyed the message and worked hard [for people. He was, affectionate towards every believer, merciful, easy to please, the friend of anyone who is generous and pure: mercy, salutation, blessing and honor be with him from a forgiving, affectionate, kind, near, responsive and wise Lord.

وصيتكم معشر من حضرني بتقوى (بوصية) ربكم، و ذكرتكم بسنة نبيكم،

فعليكم برهبة تسكن قلوبكم، و خشية تذرف دموعكم، و تقية تنجيكم يوم

يذهلكم و يليكم، يوم يفوز فيه من ثقل وزن حسنته، و خف وزن سيئته. لتكن

مسألتكم مسألة (سؤل) ذل و خضوع و شكر و خشوع، و توبة و نزوع، و ندم

و رجوع، و ليغتنم كل مغتنم منكم صحته قبل سقمه، و شبيبته قبل هرمه فكبره

و مرضه، و سعته قبل فقره و خلوته (فرغته) قبل شغله، و ثروته قبل فقره، و

حضره قبل سفره، و حيته قبل موته، ثم يكبر و يهن و يهرم و يمرض و يسقم و

يمل طبيبه و يعرض عنه حبيبه، و ينقطع عمره و يتغير لونه، و يقل عقله، ثم

قيل: هو موعوك و جسمه منهوك، قد جد في نزع شديد، و حضره قريب و

بعيد، فشخص ببصره و طمح بنظره و رشح جبينه و خطف عرنينه و سكن حنينه

و جنبت نفسه و بكته عرسه و حفر رمسه و يتم منه ولده و تفرق عنه عدده

(عدوه و صديقه)، و قسم جمعه و ذهب بصره و سمعه، و لقن و مدد، و وجه

و جرد، و غسل و عري و نشف و سجي، و بسط له و هيئ،

I have admonished you, O folks who are present here with me, to be pious (as your Lord has admonished) towards your Lord, and I have reminded you of the teachings of your Prophet; so, take in awe that calms your hearts, fear that draws your tears, piety that saves you on a Day which will puzzle your minds and put you to the test, a day in which one shall win if the weight of his good deeds is heavy while that of his sin is light. Let your plea be in humility and surrender, appreciation and submission, repentance and dissociation [from sin], regret and return [to righteousness].

Let everyone of you seize the opportunity when he is healthy before the time when he is sick, when he is young, before he is aged, old and sick, [the opportunity] of his ease before he is poor, of having free time before he is busy, of being wealthy before being impoverished, of being present at home before he is away traveling, of being alive before his death. He shall grow old, become weak, aged, sick, ailing, so much so that even his doctor is fed-up with him, even those who love him turn away from him. His lifespan will have come to an end. His color of complexion is changed. His mental power is decreased, so it is said that he is ailing and his body is failing. He is having a hard time as he finds himself suffering from the throes of death: He is attended by those who are close and who are distant.

He gazes his looks, yearns as he turns his eyes, his forehead sweating, his [physical] senses being snatched away from him [one by one]. His sighs are now silent, his soul has departed, so he is mourned by his wife. His grave is dug, his children are now orphans, those who were around him (his friends or foes) are now dispersed from around him. What he had accumulated (legacy) has now been divided [among heirs]. Gone now are his faculty of seeing and hearing; so he receives Talqeen; he is stretched [on the ground] and directed [towards the Qibla]. He is stripped of his clothes, bathed, in the nude, dried then directed [towards the Qibla].

و نشر عليه كفنه، و شدد منه ذقنه، و قبض و ودع ، و قمص و عمم و لف و
سلم و حمل فوق سرير و صلي عليه بتكبير بغير سجود و تعفير و نقل من دور
مزخرفة و قصور مشيدة و حجر منضدة، فجعل في ضريح ملحود، ضيق
مرصود، بلبن منضود، مسقف بجلمود، و هيل عليه عفره و حثي عليه مدره،
فتحقق حذره، و تخفق صدره، و نسي خبره، و رجع عنه وليه و صفيه و نديمه
و نسيبه و حميمه، و تبدل به قرينه و حبيبه، فهو حشو قبر و رهين قفر، يسعى
في جسمه دود قبره، و يسيل صديده في منخره على صدره و نحره، تسحق
تربته لحمه و ينشف دمه و يرق عظمه و يقم في قبره حتى يوم حشره و نشره،
فينشر من قبره و ينفخ في صوره و يدعى لحشره و نشوره، فثم بعثرت قبور و
حصلت سريرة في صدور و جئ بكل نبي و صديق و شهيد و نطيق، و وقف
لفصل حكمه عند رب قدير بعبيده خبير بصير، فكم من زفرة تضفيه و حسرة
تنضيه (تقصيه)، في موقف مهول و مشهد جليل، بين يدي ملك عظيم،

Something has been spread on the floor for him as his shrouds are being prepared. His chin has been tied, his soul has already departed from his body and he has been bidden farewell by all. He is now shrouded, his head wrapped, so is his body, and he has been handed over [for burial]. He is carried in a wooden box (coffin); his funeral prayers have been performed with Takbir but without prostration or the rubbing of the forehead. He is taken away from a decorated abode [this life], from well-built mansions and chambers topping each other, so he is now in an enclosure of a grave which is very narrow and separated from others; it is built with baked clay on top of each other and is sealed with a rock.

Dust has been settled on him, so he now is sure about that of which he was warned; his chest is now heavy; he is now a thing of the past. His friends, chosen ones, companions, in-laws and close friends have all left him behind. His company and loved ones are now changed, for he is now nothing but the filling of a grave and the pawn of a waste: Worms crawl all over his body, his pus drips from his nostrils on his neck and chest. Soil crushes his flesh as his blood dries and bone decays. He remains in his grave till the Day when he is herded with others and is given a new life; so, he is taken out of his grave. His trumpet is blown, he is called on to gather with others and stand trial. Graves are scattered around, the innermost in the hearts are recorded and calculated.

Every prophet, Siddiq, martyr, anyone who speaks is brought and made to stand in the final judgment of an Able God Who is fully knowledgeable of His servants, seeing [all what they do]. Countless exhalations engulf him, sighs fade him (distance him), in a horrific position and an awesome scene before a Great King.

بكل صغيرة و كبيرة عليم، يلجمه عرقه و يجفوه قلقه، فعبرته غير مرحومة و صرخته (حجته) غير مقبولة، و برزت صحيفته و تبينت جريرته، و نطق كل عضو منه بسوء عمله، فشهدت عينه بنظره و يده ببطشه و رجله بخطوه و جلده بلمسه و فرجه بمسه، و يهدده منكر و نكير، و كشف له حيث يسير، فسلسل جيده و غلت يده و سيق يسحب وحده، فورد جهنم بكرب و شده، فظل يعذب في جحيم، و يسقى من حميم، يشوي وجهه و يسلخ جلده، يضربه زبانيته بمقمع من حديد، و يعود جلده بعد نضجه كجلد جديد، يستغيث فتعرض عنه خزنة جهنم، و يستصرخ فيلبث حقبة بندم، فلم يجده ندمه، و لم ينفعه حينئذ ندمه. نعوذ برب قدير من شر كل مصير،

Who knows about everything small and big. He is reined by his sweat, his worry crushing him, yet his tear has none to feel sorry for, his scream (defense) is not accepted. His record of deeds is brought, his innermost becomes visible, and every part of his body now speaks of his wrongdoings:

His eyes testify about what he had seen, his hands about whom he beat, his legs about where he had gone, his skin about what he had contacted, his private parts about with whom he had intercourse. He is threatened by Munkir and Nakir; and it is unveiled for him where he is heading; so his neck is now tied with chains and his hands are cuffed. He is taken alone, dragged and brought to Hell as he is in a great distress and hardship. He remains in the torment of hell given to drink of very hot pus that grills his face and separates his skin from his body. He is beaten by the torture angels of hell with iron clubs. His skin returns again and again anew after having been baked. He cries for help, yet even the angels in Hell turn away from him. He pleads for mercy, so he stays for a while regretful, yet he finds none to care about his regret. His regret will then be in vain.

We seek refuge with an Able Lord from the evil of any final end such as this,

و نطلب منه عفو من رضى عنه، و مغفرة من قبل منه، فهو ولي سؤلي و منجح طلبتي، فمن زحزح عن تعذيب ربه سكن في جنته بقربه و خلد في قصور مشيده، و ملك حور عين و حفدة، و طيف عليه بكؤوس و سكن حضير فردوس، و تقلب في نعيم، و سقي من تسنيم و شرب من عين سلسبيل ممزوجة بزنجبيل، مختومة بمسك و عبير، مستديم للسرور و مستشعر للحبور، يشرب من خمور، في روضة مغدق ليس يصدع من شربه و ليس ينزف، هذا منقلب من خشى ربه و حذر ذنبه و نفسه، و تلك عقوبة من عصى منشئه و سولت له نفسه معصية مبدئه، ذلك قول فصل، و حكمة حكم عدل، قص قصص، و وعظ نص، تنزيل من حكيم حميد، نزل به روح قدس مبين (متين) من عند رب كريم على نبي مهتد مهدي رشيد رحمة للمؤمنين، مبين من عند رب كريم، و سيد حلت عليه سفرة، مكرمون بررة.

and we plead for forgiveness similar to that of one with whom He is pleased and for an overlooking similar to that of one whose good deeds He has accepted; for He is my Master, ultimate pursuit and the one Who grants success to what I seek. Surely one who is pushed away from the torment of his Lord shall reside in Paradise near to Him and remain forever in well-built mansions, having huris with large lovely eyes and servants. He is given to drink of fresh, cool water mixed with ginger and sealed with musk and fragrance that perpetuates happiness and provides the sense of pleasure. He drinks of wines in an orchard filled with all types of pleasures, a wine that does not cause any headache to one who drinks it, and it never runs out; such is the ultimate end of one who fears his Lord, who is on guard about his sin, about the insinuations of his nafs (self), and that was the penalty of one who opposes the [sinless] way [in which] he was created, the one whose evil self-decorates for him to do what is against his nature. Such is the final judgment and the ruling of One Who is just: He narrated parables, admonished through texts, revealed revelations from a Praiseworthy Wise One, revelations which He descended with a clear (able) Holy Spirit [arch-angel Gabriel] from a Glorious Lord unto a Prophet who is rightly guided and who guides others, one who shows others the right way, a mercy to the believers, clearly from a Great Lord, a master frequented by messengers (angels) who are honored and obedient [of their Lord].

عذت برب عليم حكيم، قدير رحيم، من شر عدو و لعين رجيم، فليتضرع متضرعكم، و يبتهل مبتهلكم، و يستغفر رب كل مربوب لي و لكم.

I have sought refuge with a Lord Who is knowing, wise, able, merciful, from the evil of an enemy who is cursed and stoned; so, let everyone who pleads plead, and let everyone who seeks [favors of his Lord] seek and ask forgiveness of the Lord of lords for myself and for you all.

Having finished his miraculous sermon, the Imam (as) recited this following verse of the Holy Qur'an:

"We shall grant that (eternal) abode of the hereafter to those who intend neither high-handedness nor mischief on earth, and such end is (the best reward) for the righteous" (Qur'an, 28:83).

Source: *http://www.al-islam.org/articles/sermon-imam-ali-without-letter-alif-imam-ali-Ibn-abu-talib*

Source for virtues 1 - 8:

Ali Reza Sabiri Yazdi (2010), *1000 Virtues & Merits of Amir al Muminin Ali Ibn Abi Talib,* Publisher: Ansariyan Publications.

Imam al Baqir (as) exposed the truth

In his book by Sulaym Ibn Qays Al-Hilali, which is the oldest Shia book, written during the time of Imam Ali (as) through Imam al Baqir (as), for this book, Imam al Sadiq (as) have said:

> *"If anyone from our Shia and devotees does not have the book of Sulaym Ibn Qays al Hilali, then he does not have any of our things, and he does not know any of our matters. This is the first book of Shia and is one of the secrets of Ale-Muhammad (as)."*

Narrates a tradition from Imam al Baqir (as):

The oppression that the Quraysh have subjected us to and the way they have over powered us and killed us and the tyranny that our Shia tolerated and the oppression that our lovers have tolerated from people! No doubt, the day that the Holy Prophet (pbuh) passed away, he informed of our rights and ordered to obey us, and made our Wilayat and Muwaddah compulsory and informed everyone that we have more authority over them than they themselves and he ordered those present to inform those that were not present. But people over powering Ali (as) and Ali (as) told them everything that the Holy Prophet (pbuh) had told him and what people had heard about him. People said "You say the truth that the Holy Prophet (pbuh) had said that, but he withdrew them and said that we Ahlulbayt are those for whom Allah has given high esteem and has chosen us, and did not prefer *duniya* for us and Allah will not gather *Nubuwah* and *Imamah* for us." Four people bore witness to this – Umar, Abu Ubeydah, Ma'az Ibn Jabal and Salim Mawla Abi Huzayfah, thus creating doubts in people's minds, so people confirmed what they said, and they reversed (from Deen). They took away Caliphate from the mines where Allah had kept it.

They talk about our rights and used them as an argument to keep the Ansar quiet and then gave the Caliphate to Abu Bakr. Then Abu Bakr gave it to Umar to pay him back. Then Umar declared a Shura (committee) among six people, and everyone gave it to Abdul Rahman. Then Ibn Awf gave it to Uthman on the condition that he returned it to him. Uthman cheated, so Ibn Awf said he (Uthman) was a kafir and ignorant and taunted him in his lifetime. The children of Abdul Rahman believed that Uthman poisoned him and he died. Then Talha and Zubayr stood up and both willingly paid allegiance to Ali (a.s) and then broke the allegiance and they cheated. They took 'Aishah to Basra with them and demanded blood (revenge) of Uthman.

Then Muawiyah called the evil people of Shaam to take revenge of Uthman's blood and brought war upon us. Then *Ahle Harura* (Kharjites) opposed Ali (as) saying that Ali (as) should make a decision according to the Book of Allah and the Tradition of the Holy Prophet (pbuh). If the two had made a decision according to the condition above, then according to the Book of Allah and the Tradition of His Prophet, Ali (as) should have been Amirul Mumineen. Ahle Nehrwan opposed this and fought with him.

Then people paid allegiance to Hassan Ibn Ali (as) after his father and agreed to support him and then cheated and tried to hand him over to Muawiyah and attacked him until they poked a knife in his thigh, looted his army and the *khalkhal* (an ornament worn in ankle) of the mothers of his children.

After that when he had no helpers, he signed a peace treaty with Muawiyah, saved his blood and the blood of his Ahlulbayt and his Shi'a, who were very few.

The 18,000 people of Kufa paid allegiance to Hussain (as). They cheated him and opposed him and fought with him until he was martyred. Since the death of the Holy Prophet (pbuh) we Ahlulbayt have been humiliated, made distant and have been deprived and killed and made to leave our home town and we felt frightened for our blood and the blood of our followers. The cheaters, through their lies, got nearer to the leaders, judges and governors in every city and our enemies told false and invalid traditions relating to their past leaders and quoted riwayah (narrations) that we had never told. They only wanted to humiliate us and wanted to accuse us of falsehood, and wanted to get nearer to their leaders through lies.

After the passing away of Hassan (as) this became very common during the time of Muawiyah. At that time, in every city, Shias were killed, their hands and feet were cut off and they were hanged on accusations of their being near to us and talking above their love for us. Then after that adversities increased in numbers and strength, from the martyrdom of Hussain (as) until the time of Ibn Ziyad. Then came Hajjaj and he killed them (Shi'a of Ali) for every doubt and accusation until it was said that this person (Shia) was zindiq and majusi and Hajjaj liked it better that these words be used rather than say that they were Shi'a of Hussain (as).

Sometimes you find a person talks about another person as being good. It is possible that he may be God fearing, and is also honest. He mentions such a big tradition which is surprising and in which he mentions the virtues of previous rulers, whereas Allah has not even created any such thing. And he thinks that this is true because he has heard it from people about whom he did not think were dishonest or less God fearing. And they narrate such bad things from Ali (as) and Hassan (as) and Hussain (as) that only Allah knows that they (narrators) have attributed lies, invalid and wrong things."

Imam (as) was asked to give examples to which he (as) said:

"Some people have narrated that the two leaders of the old people in Heaven are Abu Bakr and Umar. Umar is he, whom Angels speak to and talk to him and contentment talks on his tongue, and Angels feel embarrassed with Uthman. There is a representative of those of skies and a representative of those of the earth and follow those two leaders who are going to come after me and stay firm and, except Nabi, Siddique and Shahid do not listen to anybody, (until Imam Baqir (as) counted more than 100 narrations) and people think that this is true." By God, this is all lies and wrong.

The narrator said: "May God keep you good, is not there anything correct?"

Imam (as) said: "Some of these are fabricated and some have been turned and twisted. Surely when it is said that it is compulsory for you to listen to Nabi, Siddique and Shahid, it means ALI (as). So he accepted this and it is like this: 'how can it not be congratulations for you when higher than you is Nabi, Siddique, Shahid?" Here it is meant Ali (as), and all narrations like this are wrong, invalid and lies.

O Allah (swt) let my talk be the talk of the Holy Prophet (pbuh) and the saying of Ali (as) until the Ummah of Muhammad (pbuh), after him, continues opposing until Allah presents Mahdi (atf).

Source:

Sulaym Ibn Qays, *The book of Sulaym Ibn Qays*, Hadith 10, P. 46 – 49

Books about the Companions

1000 Virtues & Merits of Amir al Muminin Ali Ibn Abi Talib by Ali Reza Sabiri Yazdi

A Restatement of the History of Islam and Muslims by Sayed Ali Asgher Razwy

Ali, the Best of the Sahabah by Toyib Olawuyi

Al-Miqdad bin al-Aswad by Kamal al-Syyed

Ammar Bin Yasir by Kamal al-Syyed

Ammar b. Yasir by al-Syed Sadruddin Sharafuddin

And Once Again Abu-Dhar by Dr. Ali Shariati

Ask Those Who Know by Sayed Mohamed Tijani Smaoui

Bilal of Africa by Islamic Seminary Publication

Certainty Uncovered (Kashf al Yaqin) Virtues of Imam Ali by Jamal al-Din Ibn Yusuf Allamah Hilli

Companions by Q. Fatima

Essence of Life (Ain al-Hayat) by Allama Baqir al-Majlisi

Exemplary Youths during the Early Days of Islam by Muhammad Ali Chanarani

Fadak in History by Sayed Muhammad Baqir As Sadr

Habib Bin Mudhahir by Kamal al-Syyed

Hamza Ibn Abdul Muttalib by Kamal al-Syyed

Hazrat Bilal (ra) by World Organization for Islamic Services

Heros of Islam by islamicmobility

History of the Caliphs by Rasul Jafarian

Hujr Ibn Adi: A Victim of Terror by Dr. Sayed Ammar Nakshawani

Justice of the Companions by Allama Sayid Murtaza Askari

Jafar al-Tayyar by Kamal al-Syyed

Kumayl Bin Ziyad by Kamal al-Syyed

Maytahm al Tammar by Kamal al-Syyed

Musab al Khair by Kamal al-Syyed

Polarization around the Character of Ali Ibn Abi Talib by Ayatollah Murtaza Mutahhari

Reflections of Hazrat Ali (as) by Dr. Azmat Hayaat

Salman al-Muhammadi by Kamal al-Syyed

Salman El-Farsi: Friend of Prophet Muhammad (pbuh) by Sayed Ali Asghar Razwy

Sayings and Preachings of Hazrat Ali (as) by Anwar Hussain Zaidi

Ten Granted Paradise by Dr. Sayed Ammar Nakshawani

The Christian Lovers of Ali Ibn Abi Talib (as) by Jarrar Hussain Rizvi

The Emergence of Shi'ism & the Shi'ites by Sayed Muhammad Baqir As Sadr

The Prophet's last prayer by Allama Sayyid Murtada Askari

When Power and Piety Collide by Sayed Mustafa al-Qazwini

Chapter 14

Imam Mahdi (atf) from Qur'an

Imam Mahdi (aft) is mentioned numerous times in various verses of the Holy Qur'an. According to a great Sunnite scholar al-Balkhi al-Qunduzi, who died in 1294 AH/ 1877 CE, has allocated one section in his book *Yanabi Al Mawaddah* (volume 3, Section 71) to this topic and has recorded **57 verses** of the Holy Quran about Imam Mahdi (atf).

In this chapter, I only intend to mention a few of these verses from the Holy Qur'an to inform the readers about the basic Shi'a concept of Imam Mahdi (atf).

Mahdi in Arabic means "The Rightly Guided One", it is the name given to the restorer of religion and justice who, according to a widely held Muslim belief, will rule before the end of the world. According to Shi'a Islam, the title of "*Mahdi*" exclusively refers to our 12th Imam, Imam Muhammad Ibn Hassan (atf), hence, fulfilling many prophecies of the Holy Prophet (pbuh):

First is Muhammad, middle is Muhammad and last is Muhammad, All are Muhammad pbut (referring to himself and his 12 successors)

Source: Muhammad Baqir Allama Majlisi, *Bihar ul Anwar*, Vol. 26, P. 6-7, and *Bihar ul Anwar*, Vol. 25, P. 363, and *Mashariq UL Anwar* (Urdu) P. 203.

"The world will not pass away before the Arabs are ruled by a man of my family _whose name will be the same as mine_."

Source: *Sunan Abu Dawood*, Book 38, Hadith 4
http://sunnah.com/abuDawood/38/4

Before I mention the Qur'anic verses about Imam Mahdi (aft), here are the ahadith of the Holy Prophet (pbuh) about Imam Mahdi (aft) from each of the *Sahih Sitta* books "The Six Authentic Books" of the *Ahl Sunnah Wal Jammah*, also known as Sunni Muslims.

1. In *Sahih Bukhari*, Chapter 49 titled: Isa Ibn Maryam, Vol. 4, p. 143
   by Muhammad Ibn Ismail al-Bukhari

The Prophet (pbuh) said: *"How will you react when the son of Mary
(Jesus) descends among you while your Imam will be from among
yourselves?"*

2. In *Sahih Muslim*, book Kitab Al-Iman, (Arabic) Vol. 2, P. 193 by
   Muslim Ibn al-Hajjaj

Reported by Jabir bin Abdullah Al-Ansari: I heard the Messenger of
Allah (pbuh) saying: *"A group of my Ummah will fight for the truth
until near the day of judgment when Jesus, the son of Mary, will
descend, and the leader of them will ask him to lead the prayer, but
Jesus declines, saying: "No, Verily, among you Allah has made
leaders for others and He has bestowed his bounty upon them."*

These two hadiths from *Sahih Bukhari* and *Sahih Muslim* prove one
thing that Jesus the messenger of God, upon his return, will have his
own Imam, a Leader or an Amir.

3. In Sunan Abu Dawood by Abu Dawood Sulayman Ibn al-Ash'ath:
   book no. 38 *The Promised Deliverer (Kitab Al-Mahdi)* there is a
   total of 13 Ahadith about the Mahdi (atf), here are few:

"Al-Mahdi will be of my family, of the descendants of Fatima"

*"If only one day of this time (world) remained, Allah would raise up
a man from my family who would fill this earth with justice as it has
been filled with oppression."*

*"The Mahdi will be of my stock, and will have a broad forehead and
a prominent nose. He will fill the earth with equity and justice as it
was filled with oppression and tyranny, and he will rule for seven
years."*

4. In *Jami al-Tirmidhi* Vol. 4, Book 7, Hadith 2232 by Muhammad
   Ibn Isa at-Tirmidhi:

Zaid bin al-Ammi said: I heard Abu as-Siddiq an-Naji narrate a Hadith
from Abu Sa'eed Al-Khudri who said: 'We feared events to occur
after our Prophet, so we asked Allah's Prophet (pbuh), and he said:

"Indeed, there will be a Mahdi, who comes in my Ummah (ruling) living for five, seven, or nine." We said: *"What is that?"* He (pbuh) said: *"Years"..."A man will come to him and say: O Mahdi! Give to me, give to me! So he will fill in his garment whatever he is able to carry."*

5. In *Sunan Ibn Majah*, Vol. 1, Book 36, Hadith 4085, by Abu Abdulllah Muhammad Ibn Yazid Ibn Majah:

"Mahdi is one of us, the people of the Household. Allah rectifying him in a single night."

6. In *Sunan al-Sughra* by Ahmad Ibn Shuayb al-Nasai there are no hadiths on the topic of Mahdi (atf), but is mentioned in the glossary of the book (English version):

Imam Mahdi: He will make his appearance when the Muslims will be at their weakest position. With his advent, the greater signs of Qiyamah (Resurrection) will commence. He will be the leader of the Muslims, and after his death, Prophet Isa (Jesus) will take over the leadership.

Source: *Sunan al-Sughra*, Glossary Of Islamic Terms 383 http://archive.org/stream/SunanAn-nasai/Sunan-an-Nasa-i-Vol-6-English_djvu.txt

Note: Please see Chapter Notes about al-Nasai's work at the end of this Chapter.

Qur'anic verses about the Imam Mahdi ATF
Surat Baqirah 2:1-3

الٓمّ ١

Alif, Lam, Mem.

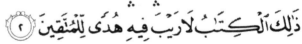

This is the Book, there is no doubt in it, a guidance to the Godwary,

$$\text{ٱلَّذِينَ يُؤْمِنُونَ بِٱلْغَيْبِ وَيُقِيمُونَ ٱلصَّلَوٰةَ وَمِمَّا رَزَقْنَٰهُمْ يُنفِقُونَ ﴿٣﴾}$$

*who **believe in the Unseen**, and maintain the prayer, and spendout of what We have provided for them*

Imam al Sadiq (as): "The pious are the Shia of Ali (as). As for the unseen: it is the *Hujjah* (proof, refers to Imam Mahdi atf) gone into occultation. The evidence of that is the saying of Allah swt (in **Surat Yunus 10:20**)

$$\text{فَقُلْ إِنَّمَا ٱلْغَيْبُ لِلَّهِ فَٱنتَظِرُوٓاْ}$$
$$\text{إِنِّى مَعَكُم مِّنَ ٱلْمُنتَظِرِينَ ﴿٢٠﴾}$$

*Say, '[The knowledge of] the **Unseen belongs only to Allah**.*
So wait.
I too am waiting along with you

Source: Shaykh Sudooq, *Kamaluddin* Vol. 2, P. 340 and Muhammad Baqir Allama Majlisi, *Bihar ul Anwar* (English Translation), Vol 51, Chp 5, P. 85

Surat Hud 11:86

$$\text{بَقِيَّتُ ٱللَّهِ خَيْرٌ لَّكُمْ إِن كُنتُم مُّؤْمِنِينَ وَمَآ أَنَا۠ عَلَيْكُم}$$
$$\text{بِحَفِيظٍ ﴿٨٦﴾}$$

*What remains of **Allah's provision is** better for you,*
should you be faithful,
and I am not a keeper over you.

Imam Muhammad al Baqir (as) described the events of the days of the reappearance of Imam Mahdi (aft) as such: "When al-Mahdi (aft) reappears his back will rest on the wall of the Holy Kaaba. The scene would be such that he would be completely surrounded by 313 of his most obedient and loyal supporters. The first words that he shall utter would be the Qur'anic verse: *"What remains of Allah's provision (Baqiyatullah) is better for you, Should you be faithful* (11:86). After this he will declare, *"I am the Baqiyatullah, the divine vicegerent and His proof upon you."* Then, the people (surrounding him) will approach him, will salute him and say, *'As Salamo Alaika Ya Baqiyatallahe Fil Arz'* (Salutations upon you, O Allah's provision upon the Earth)."

Source: Syed Momin Shablanjee Shafaee (172 AH) *Nurul Absar*

Surat Hud 11:8

$$
\text{وَلَئِنْ أَخَّرْنَا عَنْهُمُ ٱلْعَذَابَ إِلَىٰٓ أُمَّةٍ مَّعْدُودَةٍ لَّيَقُولُنَّ مَا يَحْبِسُهُ}
$$

$$
\text{أَلَا يَوْمَ يَأْتِيهِمْ لَيْسَ مَصْرُوفًا عَنْهُمْ وَحَاقَ بِهِم مَّا كَانُوا بِهِ}
$$

$$
\text{يَسْتَهْزِءُونَ ﴿٨﴾}
$$

And if We defer their punishment
*until a **certain time**,*
they will surely say, 'What holds it back?'
Look! On the day it overtakes them
it shall not be turned away from them,
and they will be besieged
by what they used to deride.

Imam Ali (as) explained: '*Ummatun Madooda*' (certain time) implies to the time of the companions of Qaim of Aale Muhammad (atf), who will be 313 in number.

And in *Tafsir Ayyashi*

Imam Jafar al Sadiq (as): *The Almighty Allah in a moment will gather the companions of our Qaim like the dispersed clouds of autumn*

Source: Muhammad Baqir Allama Majlisi,*Bihar ul Anwar* (English Translation), Vol. 51, Chp 5, P. 71

Imam al Baqir (as) said: *I swear by God! It is as if I am right now seeing the al-Qa'im who is leaning against the Hajar (al-Hajar al-Aswad or the black stone) and is inviting people in the name of God to maintain his right, and then he is saying: O people, whoever talks with me about God, I know the best about Him. O people, whoever wants to talk to me about Adam, I know the best about him and I am the closest to him. O people, whoever wants to talk to me about Nuh (Noah), I know more than anyone, the best about him. O people, whoever wants to talk to me about Ibrahim (Abraham), I am closer to Ibrahim than anyone else is. O people, whoever wants to talk to me about Musa (Moses), I know the best about him. O people, whoever wants to talk to me about Isa (Jesus), I am closer to Isa than anyone else is. O people, whoever wants to talk to me about Muhammad (pbuh), I am closer to Muhammad (pbuh) than anyone else is and I know him the best. O people, whoever wants to talk to me about the Book of God, I am closer to the Book of God than anyone else.* At that moment, he will get closer to the Maqam Ibrahim (sanctuary of Abraham) and will perform two-rak'a prayers and will swear by God as to his truthfulness.

Imam al Baqir (as) then said: *"By God, he is the one in distress in the Qur'an."*(1)

Surat Al-Naml 27:62

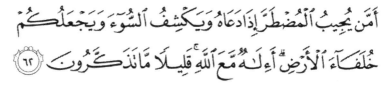

Is He who answers the call of the distressed [person]
when he invokes Him
and removes his distress,
and makes you the earth's successors. . . ?
What! Is there a god besides Allah?
Little is the admonition that you take.

Imam Jafar al Sadiq (as):*"This verse has been revealed about the Qaim (aft). He is, by Allah, the constraint. When he prays two rakats at Maqam and supplicates to Allah, He will answer him and will remove the evil and will appoint him the heir on the earth."*(2)

(1) Source: Allama Tabatabai, *Tafsir al-Mizan*, Vol.16, P. 592

(2) Source: Muhammad Baqir Allama Majlisi,*Bihar ul Anwar* (English Translation), Vol 51, Chp 5, P. 77

Surat Ibrahim 14:5

$$وَلَقَدْ أَرْسَلْنَا مُوسَىٰ بِآيَاتِنَا أَنْ أَخْرِجْ قَوْمَكَ مِنَ الظُّلُمَاتِ إِلَى النُّورِ وَذَكِّرْهُم بِأَيَّامِ اللَّهِ إِنَّ فِي ذَٰلِكَ لَآيَاتٍ لِّكُلِّ صَبَّارٍ شَكُورٍ ﴿٥﴾$$

Certainly We sent Moses with Our signs:
Bring your people out from darkness
into light
*and remind them of **Allah's days.***
There are indeed signs in that
for every patient and grateful [servant].

Imam al Baqir (as):*"The Days of Allah are three: The Day of the reappearance of the Qaim, the day of Rajat and Judgment Day.*

Source: Muhammad Baqir Allama Majlisi, *Bihar ul Anwar* (English Translation), Vol 51, Chp 5, P. 72

Surat Shoara 26:4

$$إِن نَّشَأْ نُنَزِّلْ عَلَيْهِم مِّنَ السَّمَاءِ آيَةً فَظَلَّتْ أَعْنَاقُهُمْ لَهَا خَاضِعِينَ ﴿٤﴾$$

If We wish We will send down to them
a sign from the sky
before which their heads will remain bowed in humility.

Imam Jafar al Sadiq (as): *"Their heads will bow, and the sign will be the call from the heavens on the name of the Qaim of Aale Muhammad."*

Source: Muhammad Baqir Allama Majlisi, *Bihar ul Anwar* (English Translation), Vol 51, Chp 5, P. 77

Surat Mulk 67:30

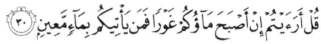

Say, 'Tell me,
should your water sink down [into the ground],
who will bring you running water?'

Imam Muhammad al Baqir (as): *"This verse is revealed about the Qaim (aft). It implies that if your Imam goes into hiding from you, while you don't know where he is, who will bring you an apparent Imam who can bring you the news of the heavens and the earth and the orders and prohibitions of Allah, the Exalted."* Then the Imam (as) said: *"This verse has not been actualized as yet and it will be actualized in the future."*

Source: Muhammad Baqir Allama Majlisi, *Bihar ul Anwar* (English Translation), Vol 51, Chp 5, P. 84-85

Surat Al-Tawbah 9:33

هُوَ ٱلَّذِىٓ أَرْسَلَ رَسُولَهُۥ بِٱلْهُدَىٰ وَدِينِ ٱلْحَقِّ لِيُظْهِرَهُۥ عَلَى ٱلدِّينِ كُلِّهِۦ وَلَوْ كَرِهَ ٱلْمُشْرِكُونَ ﴿٣٣﴾

It is He who has sent His Apostle with the guidance
and the religion of truth,
that He may make it prevail over all religions,
though the polytheists should be averse.

Imam al Baqir (as): *This event will occur during the time of the reappearance of the Mahdi from the progeny of the Prophet when there will be no one left on the earth who did not accept the message of the Prophet Muhammad (pbuh).*

Source: Shaykh Tabarsi, *Tafsir Majma' al-Bayan*, Vol 11, P. 73

Surat Anbiya 21:105

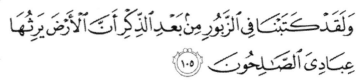

Certainly We wrote in the Psalms,
after the Torah:
*'Indeed My **righteous servants** shall inherit the earth.'*

Imam al Baqir (as): *"The righteous servants in the last age shall be the companions of Mahdi (atf)."*

Source: Sayed Sharif ud Din Ali, *Taweel al-Ayaat* under interpretation of 21:105

End of Chapter Notes:

Imam Ahmad Ibn Shuayb al-Nasai is an author of many books such as *Sunan as Sughra AKA Sunan al Nasai* (one of the six most authentic ahadith books in Ahle Sunnah), *Amul Yawmi Wallaylah, Kitaby Dufai wal Matrookeen, Al-Jurhu wa Ta'adeel*, and few other books. When he reached Damascus in 303 A.H, he saw that, because of the Bani Umayya, the residents of that place openly abused the name of Amir-ul-Muminin Ali Bin Abi Talib (as) after every ritual prayer, particularly in the address of congregational prayers. He was much grieved to see this and he decided to collect all the hadith of the Holy Prophet (pbuh) in praise of Amir-ul-Muminin with the chain of their sources, all of which he remembered. Accordingly, he wrote a book, *Khasa'isu'l-Alawi* (The virtues Imam Ali as), in support of the exalted position and virtues of Imam Ali (as). He used to read to the people from the pulpit the hadith from his book the praises of the Holy Imam (as).

One day when he was narrating the high merits of Ali (as), amongst the listeners asked Imam Nasai to tell them something about Muawiya bin Abu Sufiyan, Imam Nasai replied: *there is nothing about the virtues of Mu'awiya*, one narration says that Imam Nasai also said there is one hadith about Muawiya that the Holy Prophet (pbuh) have said about Muawiya: *"May Allah not fill his belly"*, a rowdy group of fanatics (amongst the listeners) dragged him from the pulpit and beat him. They punched his testicles and, catching hold of his penis, dragged him out of the mosque and threw him into the street. As a result of these injuries he died after a few days. His body was taken to Mecca where he was laid to rest. These events are the consequence of enmity towards Imam Ali (as) and ignorance towards the teachings of the Holy Qur'an and Prophet Muhammad (pbuh).

Sources:

Sultanul Waizin Shirazi, *Peshawar Nights*, Nasai's Murder. P. 236

Also in

Shah Abdul Aziz Mohaddas Dehlvi, *Bustan al Mohaddiseen*, P.189-190

Books on this topic:

40 Ahadith Series - The Awaited Savior of Humanity by World Federation of Khoja Shia Ithna-Asheri Muslim Communities

A Reply to Belief in the Shia Mahdi by al-Shaykh Lutfollah Saafi Golpayegani

Al Imam Al Mahdi (atf) by Ayatollah Ibrahim Amini

An Inquiry concerning Al-Mahdi by Ayatu'llah as-Sayyid Muhammad Baqir as-Sadr

Bihar UL Anwar Volumes 51, 52 and 53 about *the Promised Mahdi* by Mulla Muhammad Baqir *AKA* Allama Majlisi

Candle of Hope by Ayatollah Sayed Muhammad Reza Shirazi

Imam Mahdi - According to Sunni Muslims by Fayaz Ahmad. Published on http://www.shianews.com/hi/articles/islam/0000290.php

In Memory of the Last Ruler of God by Ayatollah Wahid Khorasani

Mahdi in Quran by N. Vasram & A. Toussi

Mahdi according to four Sunni Schools by Haroon Yahya group available at: http://www.mahdiaccordingtofoursunnischools.com/kutubasitta.php

Mikyalul Makarim: Fee Fawaaid ad-Duaa Lil Qaaim (Perfection of morals among the benefits of praying for al-Qaim) by Ayatullah Sayyid Muhammad Taqi Musawi Isfahani

Prophecies About Imam Al Mahdi (A.S) by Ayatollah Sayyid Saeed Akhtar Rizvi

Sunan Abu Dawood by Abu Dawood Sulayman Ibn al-Ash'ath: book no. 38 *The Promised Deliverer (Kitab Al-Mahdi)*

The Awaited Saviour by Islamic Seminary Publications

The Life of Imam Al-Mahdi ATF by Allama Baqir Sharif Qarashi

The Special Deputies of Imam Mahdi (as) by Zahra Ra'isi

Conclusive Remarks

I thank Allah (swt) for giving me an ability to compile this book, and I hope this book can serve as a good source of reference for those who seek to enhance their knowledge. I hope that I have not made many mistakes in this book, but if you did find a mistake I want to apologize from the bottom of my heart, and would like to ask you to please bring it to my attention, or If you have any questions, comments, suggestions, complaints, please feel free to contact me via email at:

sjzaidi313@gmail.com

or write to

Yasin Publication

ATTN: SFQ

P.O. Box 338
8253-A Backlick Rd.
Newington, VA 22122

Web: http://www.yasinpublications.org/

Dua e Faraj

بِسْمِ ٱللّٰهِ ٱلرَّحْمٰنِ ٱلرَّحِيمِ

اَللّٰهُمَّ صَلِّ عَلَىٰ مُحَمَّدٍ وَآلِ مُحَمَّدٍ

اَللّٰهُمَّ كُنْ لِوَلِيَّكَ الْحُجَّةِ بْنِ الْحَسَنِ صَلَوَاتُكَ

عَلَيْهِ وَ عَلَى آبَائِهِ فِىْ هٰذِهِ السَّاعَةِ وَ فِىْ كُلِّ سَاعَةٍ

وَلِيًّا وَّ حَافِظًا وَّ قَائِدًا وَّ نَاصِرًا وَّ دَلِيْلاً وَّ عَيْنًا حَتّىٰ

تُسْكِنَهُ اَرْضَكَ طَوْعًا وَ تُمَتِّعَهُ فِيْهَا طَوِيْلاً ـ

In the name of Allah, the most Beneficent, the most Merciful.

O Allah, (please do) send blessings to Muhammad and the Household of Muhammad,

O Allah, be, for Your representative, the Hujjat (proof), son of Al-Hassan AS, Your blessings be on him and his forefathers, in this hour and in every hour, a guardian, a protector, a leader, a helper, a proof, and an eye; until You settle him on the earth, in obedience (to You), and cause him to live in it for a long time.

Made in the USA
Columbia, SC
10 November 2024